The Russian Arn

Japanese War,

Volume. 1

Being Historical and Critical Comments on the

Military Policy and Power of Russia and on the

Campaign in the Far East

A. N. Kuropatkin

Editor: E. D. Swinton

Translator: A. B. Lindsay

Alpha Editions

This edition published in 2023

ISBN : 9789357930215

Design and Setting By
Alpha Editions
www.alphaedis.com
Email - info@alphaedis.com

Contents

TRANSLATOR'S PREFACE

"The General stands higher than any other Russian officer, not only in Russian opinion, but in that of professional soldiers all the world over, and if any human agency can change the deplorable situation to Russia's advantage, Kuropatkin may be the man to do it."[1] This sentence, written by the military correspondent of the *Times* in February, 1904, well expresses the sentiment that predominated when General Kuropatkin's appointment to command the Russian army in Manchuria was announced.

"It may be that a military genius would have overcome the moral and physical difficulties we had to encounter. Possibly; but an Alexeieff, a Kuropatkin, a Linievitch, a Grippenberg, a Kaulbars, and a Bilderling were unable to do so,"[2] were the words used by the General himself two years later when reporting to his Sovereign.

Though these two quotations epitomize the *raison d'être* and tendency of this book, they by no means afford a complete description of its scope. Were it nothing but an *apologia*, not even the former reputation and position of its author would save it from the neglect which invariably awaits the excuses of the man who has failed. But it is no mere *apologia*. For, apart from its tone of disappointment, apart from the dominant note of failure which is current throughout, and the explanations and reasons repeated on almost every page, the work is one long-continued protest. It is a protest from first to last that the war was not—as far as Russia was concerned—fought to anything like a finish; that it was brought to a premature conclusion; that peace was declared at the moment when victory lay within Russia's grasp, when her strength was at its greatest, and that of her enemy had begun to ebb. Whether true or otherwise, this view should not be rejected without consideration as the natural cry of an unsuccessful party. These pages give food for thought; they, moreover, contain much that has hitherto rested in obscurity with regard to the attitude of the Russian War Ministry, its efforts to prevent the war, its general policy, and other matters.

The author endeavours to drive home his protest by marshalling an array of facts, and by analogy from the military history of his country for more than two centuries. Whether he proves his case is for the reader to judge.
Be that as it may, his book must claim attention as being the absolute opinion of the one man on the Russian side best qualified to throw light upon the causes and course of the greatest world-disturbing international struggle that has taken place for more than a third of a century. It has also a sentimental interest in that it is the utterance of one who, after a long and meritorious career in his country's service, and after holding the highest appointments

his profession offered, has failed and retired discredited into the depths of the country. Whether he will reappear in public life or not is unknown; but when his distinguished services for Russia are called to mind, and a few of the stupendous difficulties with which he had to contend in this last campaign are realized, it is impossible to withhold sympathy.

The son of a Russian provincial official, Alexei Nicolaevitch Kuropatkin was born on March 17, 1845. After being educated in the cadet corps and the Pavlovsk War School, he was, at the age of eighteen, posted as a Lieutenant to the 1st Turkestan Rifle Battalion, with which he saw active service in Central Asia. Having passed with success through the Staff College, and being graded as Staff Captain, he in 1874 accompanied a French expedition into the Sahara. In 1876 he took part in the Central Asian Campaign of that year, being on Skobeleff's staff, winning many laurels, and being wounded. During the Turkish War of 1877–78 he was Chief of the Staff, and was again wounded. In the Akhal Tekhe Expedition of 1880–81 he once more distinguished himself, commanding the Turkestan Rifle Brigade, and being twice wounded at the storming of Geok-Tepe. From 1883–90 he was General in Charge of strategical questions on the great General Staff. In 1890 he reached the rank of Lieutenant-General, and from that year till 1898 did valuable service as Commander-in-Chief of the Trans-Caspian Military District. In 1898 he received his portfolio as Minister of War, which position he filled until February 20, 1904, when he was appointed Commander-in-Chief of the Manchurian Army of Operations (having been promoted to General of Infantry in 1900). On March 27, 1904, he reached Liao-yang to take up his duties, and after several battles, in which the Russians were almost invariably defeated, he was, in March, 1905, superseded in the chief command by General Linievitch. Henceforward he continued to serve on in a subordinate position in command of the 1st Army until the end of the war. After peace was concluded, he remained in Manchuria superintending the demobilization of the Russian forces, proceeding, on the completion of this duty, to his country seat in Russia, where he has since remained in retirement. It was during his stay in Manchuria, after hostilities had ceased, and later at his home, that he wrote this book, with the assistance acknowledged by him in the introduction. Its publication in Russia was suppressed almost as soon as the book appeared, and it is believed that the subject-matter of this translation was never printed in Russia. Of the four volumes of the original work, the fourth has alone been translated, and is now presented to the British public in these pages.[3]

Among the many facts presented to us by the author there are some which call for special reference. The first point to claim our attention is the fact that though General Kuropatkin was Commander-in-Chief of an army engaged in active operations in the field, he was for a long time not supreme. Indeed, from the day he arrived at Liao-yang until October 25, 1904, he was subordinate to an officer not actually at the front, being appointed as *assistant* (the italics are ours) to the Viceroy—Admiral Alexeieff—whose headquarters were at Harbin. Curiously enough, General Kuropatkin says very little upon this subject. He merely points out that he was really in supreme command only for four and a half months of the war—between Admiral Alexeieff's departure and his own supersession by General Linievitch—and incidentally mentions various actions and orders of the Viceroy which forced him to act against his own judgment. How detrimental such control must have been to the conduct of operations needs no emphasis. It is not within the scope of this preface to attempt criticism or justification of the Russian strategy or conduct of the war—be it that of General Kuropatkin or another—but such a vicious system of command may account for much that has hitherto appeared inexplicable. Other points which stand out are: the absolute unreadiness of Russia, the causes which led her into hostilities in spite of this unreadiness, the overwhelming nature of the advantage gained by Japan with the command of the sea, the drag upon Russia's strategy constituted by the fortress of Port Arthur, and the fear of complications on the western frontier, which forced her to retain her best troops in Europe. The handicap that her inferior railway communications were to her arms is obvious, and less remarkable than the immense improvement in them effected during the course of hostilities.

Of the author's opinions, that of most interest to his own countrymen is probably the one we have already mentioned—that the war was, for Russia, prematurely concluded. To us, however, the value attached by him to a "national" war as opposed to an "army" war is instructive while the forethought and care with which the possible price of Empire in the twentieth century was worked out by the Russian War Ministry is enlightening, for who has estimated the probable cost in blood and treasure of the expansion or maintenance of the British Empire during the next hundred years? His views also as to the correct policy to be pursued by Russia on the Afghan and Persian frontiers, and generally with regard to Great Britain in India and the Middle East, are certainly important.

One last point, and one which is much to the credit of General Kuropatkin, is that he was able to follow where he had once led, and after having been in supreme command, was content to accept a subordinate position, and do his duty in it, rather than return to Russia before the war was over. It is refreshing to find no word of repining over his supersession, nor any direct or indirect complaint of his treatment by his Sovereign.

These pages are an exact translation of the portion of the work comprised within them. The only liberty that has been taken with the original is that some of the frequent repetitions—of which the author is a past master—and certain passages which are nothing but long lists of names and places, have been eliminated. There is still much repetition in the translation, but this has been allowed to remain, in order that the English version might adhere as closely as possible to the shape of the original. As the translation had to be made mostly from a faint carbon copy of typescript, the work was attended with considerable difficulties. The many faults in style and arrangement can perhaps be explained by the fact that the original had evidently not been corrected in proof by the author. The fact, also, that no copies of the maps referred to by the writer (if such exist) have been available has added very much to the difficulty of the cartography of this translation. As the Russian system of transliterating the place-names in Manchuria differs considerably from that used by the English, French, German, or Japanese, it has been impossible without large-scale Russian maps to identify every village or locality mentioned in the narrative. Those that have been fixed are shown on the maps that have been prepared, and in all cases, whether a place has been located or not, the name has—as far as possible—been spelled according to "Wade's System of Transliteration."[4] By this means it is hoped that, when better English maps become available, some of the places not at present identifiable may be located. The large map is a reprint of that issued with vol. ii. of the "Official History of the Russo-Japanese War," and has been used by the permission of the Controller of H.M. Stationery Office. A list of the most important actions, showing their names spelled according to the Russian and English methods, has been added.

In order to elucidate certain references to the Russian troops and to the mobilization of the military districts, it may not be out of place to give briefly the system of mobilization which existed in Russia in 1904. The law of universal military service has existed in that country for many years, and when war broke out with Japan recruits were enlisted from the age of twenty for twenty-three years' service in the army, of which five were passed in the regular army, thirteen in the reserve, and five in the militia. The period in the reserve was divided into two "categories." The 1st Category comprised those recently passed into the reserve, and the 2nd the older men. If a "general" mobilization were ordered, the 1st Category reservists of all districts were the first to be summoned to rejoin the colours. In case of a "partial" mobilization, however, the mobilization was by districts instead of categories, and in such a case men of both categories were to be ordered up from certain districts. The latter was the system employed in the war against Japan. The authorities, for reasons explained in the book, hesitated to employ the system of general mobilization, and so denude European Russia of all the 1st Category reservists. They therefore drew largely on the older men.

The unfortunate results of this action are made clear by General Kuropatkin. Again, as regards the troops sent from European Russia, a distinction must be made between "reinforcements" and "drafts." The former term has been used to signify formed units sent to the front; the latter term is applied to bodies of men despatched to make good the wastage as required.

A. B. L.
E. D. S.

London,

March 1, 1909.

AUTHOR'S INTRODUCTION

In the first three volumes[5] of my work accounts are given of the three principal battles of the war—Liao-yang, the Sha Ho, and Mukden. Though compiled from the best information obtainable, it is impossible for such a book to be entirely free from inaccuracies; for not only is our knowledge of what was done by the Japanese extremely limited, but it is derived from unofficial sources. At the time these volumes were written, moreover, there were few reports available from our own individual corps and armies, and what we had were sketchy in character. The most complete information, on the whole, was that given in the regimental reports, upon which we almost entirely depended; but even these were far from perfect. Commanding officers naturally have a soft spot in their hearts for their own troops, and the separate narratives gave very different accounts of what was done by units of one and the same division or army corps. Great importance has therefore been attached to such documents as copies of written orders for operations, dispositions and marches, casualty lists, and ammunition returns. Not that the latter could be accepted without careful scrutiny, as the ammunition lost on the march was often included in the total rounds fired. But, in spite of the admitted incompleteness and the partiality of the sources of information, the facts narrated in my first three volumes present ample material whereby to gauge the *moral*, the tactical fitness, and the armament of our troops—in short, to judge of the readiness of our army for war.

The account of the battle of Liao-yang was written in Manchuria by Colonel Ilinski, of the General Staff, who was then on my staff, and was sent in November, 1904, to headquarters in St. Petersburg. This narrative, supplemented by additional material from the pen of the author, forms the first volume. The second, "The Battle of the Sha Ho," was drawn up under my guidance in Manchuria by Colonel Bolkhovitinoff, of the General Staff. The third, "The Battle of Mukden," and the fourth, "The Summary of the War," I wrote myself, the former in Manchuria and the latter at my country home. For the collection of material, the compilation of statistics, and most of the cartography for the third volume, I am indebted to Colonel Sivers and Lieutenant-Colonel Havrilits, of the General Staff, whilst Lieutenant-Colonel Krimoff, of the same branch, has undertaken this work for the fourth volume. Without the able and unremitting efforts of these officers, the completion and printing of this book, consisting of 2,000 pages, with plates, maps, and plans, would have dragged on for years.

Although the ordeal of war through which our country and our army passed in 1904–1905 is now a matter of history, the materials so far collected are insufficient to enable us to estimate fairly the events which preceded the war, or to give a detailed and complete explanation of the defeats that we sustained. It is essential, however, that we should take immediate advantage of our recent experience, because it is only by ascertaining the nature of our mistakes and the failings of our troops that we can learn how to improve.

In times past, when wars were carried on by small standing armies, defeat did not touch the everyday interests of the whole nation so profoundly as it does now, when the obligation to render military service is general, and most of the soldiers are drawn from the great mass of the people. If a war is to be successful in these days, it must not be carried on by an army, but by an armed nation. In such a contest all classes are seriously affected, and failure is more acutely felt than it was formerly. When the national pride has been humiliated by defeat, attempts are usually made to ascertain the causes and persons responsible. Some attribute failure to general, others to specific, reasons; while some blame the system or the régime, others blame the individual. Discontented political factions are quick to make use of a national disaster as a weapon against the Government, and so with us the party hostile to the Russian Government not only strove to injure it after the war, but did so—much to the disadvantage of our arms—during the actual course of military operations. This party would indeed have been genuinely glad to see us suffer defeat, as there would then have been a hope of undermining the prestige of the Government, and so bringing about a revolution. Their motto was, "The worse things are—the better," and hundreds of thousands of proclamations were distributed among the troops going to the front—especially those from the west—urging the soldiers on to defeat, not victory. In Russia many journals, though not the organs of the above party, contributed materially to its success by abusing both the army and the Government. Again, many of the correspondents at the front, ill-informed as to our own operations, and worse informed as to the enemy's, did not scruple to despatch reports founded on entirely unreliable information, and so, by exaggerating the importance of every reverse, shook public confidence still more. Many officers, too, wrote home from the field,[6] and tried to show their smartness by hasty criticism, by making inaccurate statements, and by discussing affairs in a pessimistic tone. Little was written of what really happened in the actual fighting-line—of the deeds of those many heroes who lay face to face with the enemy for months together, and fought on without losing confidence in eventual victory. The gallant private soldiers, modest young officers, commanders of companies, squadrons, batteries, and regiments, did not write—they had no time to scribble of their labours and exploits—and there were few pressmen who elected to witness their deeds: it would have entailed sharing their hardships and their dangers.

Of course, there were brave men among the correspondents, and men who were genuinely desirous of rendering assistance; but, lacking as they were in the most elementary military knowledge, their efforts were, not unnaturally, of little value where complicated operations were concerned. The persons really most capable of forming a judgment upon what they saw, and of putting matters in their proper light before the reading public, were the foreign military attachés. Many of them were in every sense picked men. They were interested in our soldiers, shared all their dangers and hardships, and, in return, gained their affection and respect. But while none of their reports were seen in Russia for a long time, many of our Press correspondents, who stayed in the rear and saw only the reverse side of war, revelled in harrowing accounts of the orgies and dissipation that went on in Harbin, and presented to the public an absolutely distorted picture of the life of the army. The result was that our Press to a great extent played into the hands of our foreign and domestic enemies; instead of which, it might have called into being with the news of our first defeats a wave of patriotism and self-sacrifice, and, as the difficulties at the front grew thicker, might have appealed to the Fatherland for fresh efforts, cheered the faint-hearted, and summoned all the best of the country's manhood to fill the gaps in our ranks caused by the enemy. What it did accomplish was to instil a hatred of the war into the masses, depress those departing for the front, undermine the private soldier's confidence in his officers, and weaken the authority of those in command. Truly the army had little encouragement to issue victoriously from its difficulties. On the contrary, the troops sent forward from Russia carried with them the seeds of fresh disaster in the seditious proclamations with which they were loaded.

A large number of valuable works upon different subjects suggested by the late war have appeared, many of them written with a sincere desire to do justice to the army; but, owing to ignorance of what really happened, they contain numerous and serious mistakes. Passions are now calming down, and it is possible to separate into different categories the charges levelled at our forces and their representatives during and after the war. These accusations, in so far as they refer to the War Department, were mainly as follows:

That the army was not ready for war with Japan.

That, having taken insufficient steps to prepare for war, the War Department did not attempt to prevent it.

That the leaders of the army did not make the best use of the men and material placed at their disposal during its course.

I shall endeavour in my fourth volume both to refute these accusations conclusively and to emphasize the principal lessons for our future guidance to be drawn from the campaign.

The work of the War Ministry of an Empire like ours ought not to be of a haphazard nature. Its success must depend on the amount of money allotted to military needs and the manner of expenditure of these funds. The country spends large sums on the army, thus starving numerous other urgent demands, and an unsuccessful war naturally leads to the conclusion that this expenditure has been thrown away. But, before forming any judgment, it is necessary to be in possession of full details of what had to be undertaken, and of the financial means available. The problems which confronted our War Department were the inevitable result of the policy pursued by it in former years; they were, so to speak, the legacy of the nineteenth century to the twentieth. That the size and cost of an army must be in direct proportion to the growth of a nation and the military activity of its neighbours, is a fact that cannot be ignored if we wish to rest assured of the safety of our Empire. To us, in our comparatively immature state of civilization, the burden of the armed peace necessitated by the immense growth of armaments in Europe seems almost unbearable, and our available funds are inadequate to meet all the initial and recurring financial demands. It has only been possible to satisfy the most urgent. To decide which were most important among such things as the re-armament of the artillery, the construction of fortifications and barracks, the accumulation of reserves, and the improvement of the condition of the troops, etc., was a complicated and difficult enough matter for the War Department; but the decision upon larger questions, such as which frontiers were most in danger of attack or on which side our policy of expansion called for another forward step, was beyond its scope. The solution was dependent on the general political programme, and this was, in its turn, the result of the policy followed in former centuries, and the outcome of the internal condition and needs of the Empire.

On January 1, 1898, when I took over the duties of War Minister, I found many schemes actually in progress, and numerous others—worked out and marked as urgent—for the execution of which money had not been available. Thanks to the ability and energy of my predecessor, the army was in a high state of efficiency as compared with former years, and I thus found myself in a favourable position to draw up a scheme of work for the next quinquennium.[7] But, as has been explained, the policy of my department was bound up with that of the Ministries of the Interior, of Finance, and of Foreign Affairs, and there had been a difference of opinion between the late War Minister and his colleagues on some most important points. As there was no co-ordinated programme between the War and Navy Departments, I was forced to spend my first two years in office in framing an exhaustive statement for our guidance. In this I traced out and summarized the achievements of Russian arms and what the tasks before them had been in the eighteenth and nineteenth centuries, showed which had been finished and which had been left over for completion to the twentieth century, and pointed out the sacrifices made by the nation towards this result. I reviewed the condition of each of our frontiers, indicated the numbers and organization that would be necessary for military operations in the different probable theatres of war, and estimated the power of offence of our most likely adversaries. Having thus arrived at some logical conclusions as to what had to be faced in the coming century, it remained to draw up definite proposals for the improvements necessary in the organization for war of the army.

The General Staff Academy assisted me in my work, Colonel Mishlaivski helping in the history, Major-General Zolotareff in the military statistics, and Colonel Gulevitch in the administration. Information on strategical matters was furnished by the General Staff. This analysis was completed and submitted to the Tsar in the spring of 1900, and a few copies—with the secret strategic matter omitted—were, with his permission, sent to the Ministers of Finance, Foreign Affairs, and the Interior, to the State Comptroller, and a few selected officials. The programme for the period 1898–1902 was framed by me upon the conclusions drawn from this statement. In 1903 a general report of all that had been carried out by my department during the previous five years was printed and submitted to the Tsar. This document showed the funds available, the total requirements which had been carried out, and those left undone owing to the lack of money. Later on in the same year a programme for the period 1904–1908 was submitted and approved. Thus, for the twelve months immediately preceding hostilities work was carried out according to a strictly defined programme, from the printed record of which the results attained can be judged. In the same way that we in the War Ministry were forced to have recourse to the lessons of the past when framing our programme for the future, so in this work is it necessary, in order to explain properly what was done in the years 1898–1904, to refer to the conclusions upon which the programme for this period was based.

My fourth and last volume consists of twelve[8] chapters. In the first chapters I shall include some necessary extracts from my analysis of 1900, and my report of 1903 upon the work of the War Ministry for the quinquennium 1898–1902, omitting, of course, confidential matter. The last chapters will be based on papers relating to the recent war, on my diaries, and on articles that appeared in the Press.

I have been so intimately connected with the important events in the Far East, and have been so largely responsible for the failure of our military operations, that I can hardly hope to take an entirely dispassionate and objective view of the men and matters that I shall deal with in the present work; but my object is not so much to justify myself by replying to the charges that have been brought against me personally, as to furnish material that will make it easier for the future historian to state fairly the reasons for our defeat, and thus enable us to avoid similar misfortunes in the future.

CHAPTER I

An historical résumé of the problems which confronted the Russian War Department during the past two centuries.

During the eighteenth and nineteenth centuries the chief work accomplished by our armed forces was that necessitated by the expansion of our Empire towards the north, west, and south, in her struggle to reach the shores of the Baltic and Black Seas. During the first years of the twentieth century our forces have been similarly engaged in an approach towards the ocean, for, some years before the recent war with Japan—but after she had defeated China—we occupied Manchuria and pushed forward our advanced troops into the Kuan-tung Peninsula and on to the shores of the Pacific. During the war we had to repel Japan's advance while we maintained the position taken up by us as far back as 1897. In the event we have lost both Kuan-tung and Southern Manchuria, and have been driven back in the Far East, with the result that we are now in immediate contact on the mainland with Japan, who is in military occupation of Korea, Kuan-tung, and Southern Manchuria. For Russia this has been more than a surprise. It has been a disaster. But now that the first outburst of natural grief has subsided, there is some possibility of being able to trace the various causes to which our military misfortunes are due, of drawing attention to the most important, and of appreciating at their correct value the many hasty judgments pronounced upon military events by the Press. The complexity of the chain of circumstances which led up to hostilities, and the intricacy of the military operations which followed, demand some detailed investigation into the nature of the peculiar conditions which denied success to our arms in Manchuria. A proper understanding of the difficulties will, I think, be materially assisted by a review of certain events in our past military history.

It was only after a severe struggle and a violent upheaval that Russia became one united Empire in the seventeenth century. At the commencement of the eighteenth there were, in our immense expanse of territory amounting to some 265,000 square miles (of which 79,000 were in Europe), only 12,000,000 inhabitants; and our frontiers, though only partially defined, were already 9,333 miles in length. Our army was about 150,000 to 200,000 strong, but was unreliable as a fighting force owing to inferior organization and training. Of the total State Budget—some £1,200,000—half was taken up for the maintenance of this force. The proper defence of our long frontier necessitated an immense army, for our boundaries were not strengthened by any natural features, while our neighbours were powerful kingdoms, such as Sweden, Poland, and Turkey, nomad Tartars, Caucasian mountaineers, and the Chinese, about whom little was known.[9]

In the eighteenth century, besides creating a regular army, we had to carry on the following work, handed to us as a legacy from the preceding hundred years:

In the north-west we had to continue the efforts of Tsars John III. and IV. to drive Sweden from the Baltic littoral, and so push forward our frontier to the coast-line.

In the west, to proceed with the work of Tsar Alexie-Michaelovitch, and wrest White Russia and Little Russia from Poland.

In the south, to follow the course indicated by the Grand Dukes Sviatosloff and Oleg, of advancing to the Black Sea coast and creating unrest in Turkey, as a preparation for our further move forward.

In the south-east, to carry on the struggles of Tsar Theodore-Ivanovitch and Boris Godunoff to convert the Caspian into a Russian inland sea, and obtain a firm foothold on the ridge of the Caucasus. In Asia, to extend the Empire in two directions—towards Central Asia, for protection against raids, and towards Russia's natural outlet in the East, the Pacific Ocean.

During this century it was only the first three of these projects that we really set ourselves to carry out. Our attempt in 1717 to gain possession of Khiva ended in complete failure, which for a long time arrested our advance in Central Asia; while in Siberia, thanks to the peaceful attitude of the Chinese and Japanese, and to the weakness of the Kirghiz, we were enabled to protect our 6,000-mile Chinese frontier with an insignificant number of men. Of the three tasks seriously attempted, the first—that of gaining possession of the Baltic sea-board—was the most difficult. For twenty-one years had that able commander, Charles XII. of Sweden, fought with a small but veteran army against the might of Russia led by Peter the Great. Even the genius of the latter did not avail to avert our complete defeat at Narva in 1700, but his determined efforts to create an army well trained and numerically superior to the enemy were crowned by our victory at Poltava just nine years later. This struggle—the Great Northern War—only came to an end in 1721 with our annexation, under the Treaty of Nishtabtski, of Ingermanland (the province of St. Petersburg), Esthonia, Livonia, and a small part of Finland, altogether 3,500 square miles. The reasons of our defeat at Narva were that we put too few men—50,000—in the field in the first instance, and that they were unreliable. During the course of the war the army was increased in numbers to 136,000, and at Poltava Peter the Great had a very large superiority in numbers, besides the assistance of experienced subordinates and veteran troops. During the whole war we put in the field a total of 1,700,000 men. Our access to the Baltic cost us 120,000 killed and wounded, excluding missing, and 500,000 invalided, but in gaining it Russia won a place among the great Powers of Europe. Our progress towards the Black Sea proved almost as difficult, and necessitated four wars with Turkey. In the first—in 1711—we again committed the same initial error as we had against Sweden, and started operations with insufficient numbers, with the result that, in spite of the presence of Peter the Great, we were surrounded on the Pruth. Not only did we fail in our object, but we were forced by the Turks to surrender Azov, and to raze our fortifications on the Lower Dnieper; but we brought up our total numbers during the fourth war (1787 to 1791), by gradual increases, to 700,000 men, and eventually defeated the Turks. Our maximum number in any one campaign was 220,000. By the Treaty of Jassy[10] we obtained the Crimea and the area between the rivers Bug and Dniester. This final four years' struggle cost us 90,000 killed, wounded, and missing, and about 300,000 invalided; the total number of men put in the field during the century in order to gain access to the Black Sea being 1,500,000. The prosecution of the third task—namely, that of regaining Little Russia and White Russia—was the cause of three struggles with Poland, after the last of which she ceased to be an independent State. In these campaigns the largest army taking the field on our side was 75,000 strong. The total numbers on our side taking part in the three wars were 400,000, our casualties being 30,000 killed, wounded, and missing, and 75,000 invalided. It is plain, therefore, in which directions our efforts at expansion during the eighteenth century proved most costly. The brunt of these struggles was borne by our army, though our fleet, under Peter the Great—its founder—played a conspicuous and gallant part in the conflict with Sweden.

The commencement of the nineteenth century found Russia a strong Power as compared with her condition a hundred years before. During the past hundred years the Empire had extended in area from 265,000 to 331,000 square miles, and the population had increased to 37,000,000. The revenues had also grown considerably, from £1,200,000 to £5,500,000; but the finances of the State had been severely shaken by incessant warfare. Though £2,200,000 had been spent on military requirements, the whole frontier was still in an unsettled state, and required special watchfulness on account of the many politico-military questions which might arise with Sweden, Prussia, Austria, the Caucasus, and Central Asia.[11] The efforts which had been made during the latter part of the preceding century to develop our army had not been fruitless. It had improved in quality and in professional knowledge, had produced such men as Rumantsieff and Suvoroff, and had grown in numbers; but still its size was out of all proportion to the country's financial position. Economy was unknown in military affairs. The administration was defective, there was no higher tactical organization than the regiment, and the training given was not uniform. The steps taken by the Emperor Paul II. to rectify these defects were without success, and the war establishment was reduced from 500,000 to 400,000. Theoretically, the army was distributed over twelve inspection areas or military districts; but when the western districts became incorporated in the Empire, and we thereby became directly involved in the political problems of Europe, the greater portion of our troops was required to garrison the country west of the Dnieper. In 1799 about 100,000 men were stationed across the frontier,[12] approximately 130,000 formed two armies in the south-western districts,[13] and in the north some 50,000 were distributed around the capital; the rest were scattered throughout the country, about 25,000 being on the Siberian and Caucasian frontiers. Though a continuation of what had gone before, the military problems of the nineteenth century had to be faced under more complicated conditions. In the north-west Russia had still to put the finishing touch to her effort towards an outlet on the Baltic by gaining possession of the northern shores of the Gulf of Finland and the eastern shores of the Gulf of Bothnia. In the west the Poles had to be kept in subjection, and our frontier defended from Prussia and Austria. We had to maintain the position we had won, and also to oppose Napoleon's army of a million men. In the south we had to make permanent our footing on the shores of the Black Sea, and to guard its coasts from oversea attack. In the Caucasus and the Far East everything remained to be done. The consolidation of our position in the two latter directions, so as to protect, before all else, the Russian population of the southern districts, demanded an energetic advance.

It was upon the army that a large share of the execution of these projects naturally fell. Firstly, the beginning of the century was remarkable for our colossal struggle with France, of which Suvoroff's campaign in 1799 was the commencement. We advanced against Napoleon as the ally of Austria and Germany, whom he was in the process of destroying; but the campaigns ended in our utter defeat at Austerlitz in 1805, and Friedland in 1807. The war in our country of 1812–14 was a continuation of the first two Napoleonic wars, and, notwithstanding the invasion of Russia by an immense army, and the fact that our troops were driven back beyond Moscow, Napoleon was defeated, Europe was freed from his yoke, and Poland became an integral portion of the Russian Empire. The determination with which Peter the Great and Alexander I. conducted their struggles against such opponents as Charles XII. and Napoleon is in the highest degree instructive. In both cases we commenced hostilities with inadequate numbers, suffered complete initial defeat at Narva, Austerlitz, and Friedland, but nevertheless continued the contest. In both cases our troops were reinforced, and gradually became trained and seasoned; leaders were created by the war itself, and our numbers increased until we obtained superiority over the enemy, and finally ended the struggle victoriously by winning the battle of Poltava in the one case, and by marching into Paris in the other.

One result of these wars was the final definition of our present boundary with Poland, which will soon have been established for one hundred years. Any alteration of it, as will be shown later, would not only be distinctly detrimental to our interests, but could only be brought about by a European conflict, which would entail such appalling sacrifices that any change would be on the whole as disadvantageous to Germany and Austria as to Russia. Thus we can at once dismiss the defence of our present Polish frontier from the probable tasks of the twentieth century. Still, the Poles, split up as they are amongst three great Powers, with their well-known national aspirations, have not up till now become reconciled to their fate, and the internal pacification and administration of Poland will doubtless prove one of the problems of this century.

Though our most difficult piece of work in the eighteenth century had been the attempt to gain an outlet on the Baltic, the completion of this task in the nineteenth met with little opposition from Norway and Sweden. The campaign with the latter country in 1808–09 lasted fifteen months, and ended with our annexation of Finland. During its progress the army was never stronger than 44,000 men, the total number put into the field amounting to 65,000. Our casualties were 7,000 killed, wounded, and missing, and 9,000 invalided; total, 16,000. It is interesting to note that we were in superior strength in forty-three engagements, of which we won twenty-nine and lost fourteen. Although after this war we annexed Finland as an integral part of our Empire, we paid too little attention to its internal affairs, the result being that there grew up close to our capital a large hostile country, of which the population, though small in number, was stubborn and independent in character, and was imbued with ideals entirely differing from our own. The final incorporation of Finland in the Empire has been left for our statesmen of the present century.

The consolidation of our position on the Black Sea, which we had gained in 1791, was proceeded with energetically, but was not completed, in spite of three wars waged with Turkey—in 1806–12, 1828–29, 1877–78. The first ended in our annexation of a portion of Bessarabia. By the second we acquired the mouths of the Danube and a strip of the Black Sea littoral, 370 miles long. The interference of the European Powers in Russian affairs, in order to weaken us in the Near East, led to the Crimean War of 1854–56, which resulted unfortunately for us, as we lost our Black Sea fleet and the possession of the mouths of the Danube. At the time of the Crimean War we had a numerically strong army, and much excellent material both among the officers and the rank and file. A great number of the former were of the nobility; the men were long-service soldiers (twenty-five years); while the warrant and non-commissioned officers were experienced men, and wielded considerable authority. But after the successful wars we had waged earlier in the century the army had deteriorated in war-training and fallen behind in armament. All ranks had been deeply bitten by Arakcheeff's views of military science, the senior ranks being specially weak. That an army was intended for war was quite forgotten. Spit and polish and parade smartness were considered far more than battle efficiency, and more attention was paid to the "manual exercise" and to ceremonial movements than to anything else. The best proof of the views held at this period was the way in which commanding officers of all arms permitted the rifles to be filed and burnished, so that, in performing rifle exercises, a thousand rifles would flash and ring together as smartly as one. An officer's military career depended on the interest behind him. Without influence only those got on who most slavishly performed the wishes of their commanders, however cruel or barbarous. The national movement towards greater personal freedom, initiated by Emperor Alexander I. after the Napoleonic wars, had penetrated to the rank and file of the army, but had now been replaced by an Administration which paralyzed every activity or impulse towards initiative throughout the country, and acted like a blight on every grade of the population, civil as well as military. Everyone was, so to speak, dressed in a tunic buttoned right up to the chin, and looked as if he had "swallowed a poker." The whole country, army included, could say nothing but "Very good," "Quite so," and "All correct." The private soldier was treated with cruelty, and was badly fed; peculation and dishonesty of all kinds were rampant. Not only did commanding officers largely augment their pay from the money granted for the purchase of forage, but this was winked at as being only natural. As had always been the system, the commands of regiments were given to the younger sons of the nobility, to enable them to exist, while the favouritism shown to the Guards was the curse of the service. Any display of initiative by soldiers was punished, and the Press was afraid to speak; a discussion in a military paper of questions of dress even was considered to be harmful "free-thinking." The result was that while we were outdistanced in *matériel* by the armies of Europe, we made no progress in *moral*, despite our large numbers. Holding such views as, for instance, that the main use of a rifle was to make a pleasant noise in the "manual exercise," we naturally did not worry about re-armament, and entered upon the war of 1854–56 armed with smooth-bore weapons against our opponents' rifles. The spirit of our fleet, fresh from its victory at Sinope, and having such men in command as Lazareff, Nakhimoff, Korniloff, and Istomin, was excellent, and its numbers were strong; but, technically, it was even more behind the other fleets of Europe than our army was behind the land forces of our neighbours, and against our sailing-ships in the Black Sea the Allies brought a fleet of steam-vessels. The peace strength of the standing army in 1850–60 was more than 1,100,000 men, but the greater part of it was stationed in the western frontier districts, in the Caucasus, and in the large cities. The peace strength of the Allied armies amounted to: France, 400,000; Great Britain, 140,000; Turkey, 450,000. Only a portion of these forces took part in the war, but nevertheless Russia was beaten.

As regards our preparedness in our first campaign on the Danube, an officer who took part writes in his recently published Memoirs:[14]

> "The conflict with the West in the Crimean War of 1854–56 ought not to have taken us by surprise. Rumours of war were prevalent in the summer of 1852; and, on account of these rumours, particular anxiety was felt concerning the inefficiency of our transport and military equipment generally. Indeed, the late Emperor Nicolai-Pavlovitch, at his autumn inspection at Elisavetgrad, personally warned the troops of the proximity of hostilities. Finally, in June, 1853, our troops crossed the Pruth and occupied the Danube Principality, and in October Turkey declared war. Our brilliant victory and the total destruction of the enemy's fleet at Sinope aroused the enthusiasm of the whole nation, but gave France and great Britain a *casus belli* against us. Then began the long series of sad and scandalous disasters to the Russian arms. The Danube campaign of 1853–54 could not possibly have been successful, for it was carried out with no definite object. Either because we did not fathom Austria's real intentions, or else believed that she would remain neutral, we tried to meet her demands, and by so doing tied our own hands. Our defence of the left bank of the river was not favoured by one single piece of good fortune, and our offensive operations were soon abandoned under pressure from Austria. The campaign brought us neither honour nor gain, and while once more confirming the gallantry of the Russian soldier, it exposed the criminal incapacity of his commanders and the many abuses which had crept into the Service. In June, 1854, we returned with shame and anger to our own country from the walls of undefeated Silistria, and the Allies turned their glances towards the Crimea."

The disembarkation of the allied armies, only 50,000 strong, seemed madness in face of our force of 1,000,000 men and our strong fleet. However, Prince Menshikoff, the Commander-in-Chief, and a professional sailor into the bargain, allowed the landing to take place without hindrance at Eupatoria on September 14 and 15, though he had at his disposal sixty vessels, amongst them some steamers. Though the fleet could not, of course, have counted with absolute certainty on victory, we had it in our power then to wreck the enemy's plan of operations by dispersing their convoys of transports. The Allies were on the sea from September 8 to September 14 between Varna and Eupatoria, but we were unable to find them. At the Alma we had 33,000 men (42 battalions, 16 squadrons, 84 guns), and offered a determined resistance; but though we were operating in our own country, we did not know the locality, and General Boskey, leading his column by a path of whose existence we were ignorant, fell upon our left flank. This attack decided the day, and our troops were routed.[15] Then on September 26 began the eleven months' struggle for Sevastopol. Our exhausted fleet landed a number of guns and lent some experienced commanders to the army— chief of all, Nakhimoff, Korniloff, and Istomin. Operations now assumed the character of siege warfare, in which our troops played their part most nobly; but it must be remembered that the army of the Crimea was twice severely beaten: on November 5, 1854, at Inkerman, and on August 17, 1855, at the Tchernaya. Regarding the Battle of Inkerman, the above-quoted writer says:

> "Prince Menshikoff, with the arrival of the remaining two divisions of the 4th Infantry Corps, had, in addition to the Sevastopol garrison, an army of 40,000 men under him, but he lost the great battle of Inkerman on November 5, 1854. Its object was to seize Sapun Ridge, as a first step to raising the siege of the town, after which he would have driven the Allies towards Balaclava and then out of the Crimea. The battle was well planned, every arrangement was made to insure victory, but the result was, owing to the incomprehensible mistakes of individual commanders, a bloody and decisive defeat.

*   *   *   *   *

> "Ten thousand casualties, a loss of *moral* among the troops—the soldiers' lack of confidence in their leaders, as well as Prince Menshikoff's distrust of the army under his command—were the results of this disaster which for so long doomed our force to play a passive rôle. The ultimate issue of the Crimean campaign was really settled by this; the moment for the relief of Sevastopol had been missed, and our field operations lost every trace of initiative. A moral deterioration set in which led to unheard-of irregularities in our army."

Menshikoff was replaced by Prince Gorchakoff, but things became no better. The troops at the Alma[16] were commanded just as they had been at Inkerman. While individual commanders did not help one another, the attack delivered from Sevastopol did not support the operations on the Alma. On

September 8 the Allies delivered an assault, and seized Malakhoff Hill. Though they were driven back with great loss from other portions of the position, we were compelled to withdraw from the northern side during the night of the 10th. This retirement was decisive, and peace was declared—a peace dishonourable to us, for by it we were deprived of the right to maintain a fleet on the Black Sea, and lost the mouths of the Danube. This result was all the more painful as the Allies were inferior to us in strength, and, had we been determined to continue the war at all costs, would have been obliged to make up their minds to conquer the Peninsula. Even had they succeeded in taking it, we ought, remembering Peter the Great's counsel in the Northern War, and Alexander I.'s example in the war of the Fatherland, to have continued the struggle.

Our weak points were the incapacity of our seniors and of our staff, and particularly the inefficiency of the supply services. Of the different arms, the infantry, artillery, and sappers were the most reliable, while the cavalry, despite its numbers, played a small and inglorious part. It was very difficult to maintain communication with our own country in the rear, especially in the winter, when the roads were bad. The transport of supplies to the front encountered such great obstacles, and was so badly arranged, that the troops had not only to undergo great hardships, but were often in actual want of food. The medical services also were shockingly organized. Drunkenness and gambling amongst both officers and men, especially at a distance from the advanced positions, were of everyday occurrence, and looting and robbery of every kind became universal. But this was the seamy side of affairs, and did not imply that the whole army or the whole nation were rotten, for, despite all the mistakes of our commanders, the men kept up their spirit, and were quite ready to fight on until victory should eventually crown their efforts. The war produced Nakhimoff, Korniloff, and Istomin, who met heroic deaths, whilst amongst the survivors stood out the names of Khruleff, Todleben, Sabashinski, and others. Of the regimental commanders, most proved in every way fitted for their duties, and many junior officers of all arms became seasoned veterans whom the private soldiers would follow anywhere. The men were patient, enduring, brave, and ignorant.

The finances of the country, moreover, were not crippled by this war. Throughout the operations only two loans were raised, amounting to £10,000,000; £43,000,000 of paper-money were issued, and £19,000,000 taken in State banks. Altogether the war cost us £72,000,000. Even in 1856 general belief in our power and resources was not shaken, and our credit stood high, in spite of our disasters in the field. We, therefore, could and ought to have continued the struggle. If we had done so, the Allies would, as I have said, have been obliged to undertake the conquest of the Crimea. In proportion as they advanced from the coast their difficulties would have increased, while our army, gaining numbers and experience, would have become more and more formidable, and would in the end have hurled them back into the sea. In his notes on the war our historian, Solovieff wrote as follows:

"At the time of the accession of the new Emperor, the minds of all were full of the painful ending of the Crimean War. Alexander II. was forced to begin his reign with the conclusion of a peace such as no Russian Emperor had accepted since the peace after the Pruth, and the new Emperor felt to the full the weight of the burden imposed upon him. Foreign affairs were by no means in so critical a state that an energetic ruler could not have emerged from the war without loss of dignity or material advantages. In the interior of Russia there was no exhaustion; the nation was by no means driven to extremities. The new Tsar, whom everyone desired to love, could undoubtedly, if he had appealed to this feeling and to the national patriotism, have aroused a tremendous enthusiasm which would have supported any action he chose to take. The Allies not only felt the burden of the war, but were desperately anxious for its close, and a firm announcement by the Tsar to the effect that he intended to continue fighting until an honourable peace was concluded would undoubtedly have compelled them to fall back.

*   *   *   *   *

"... But for this course of action, breadth of view, daring, capability, and energy were necessary—qualities which the new Emperor did not possess. It would even have been sufficient if he had had round him advisers who would have lent him some support, but there was not a man of any moral or intellectual strength in his entourage. He was surrounded by those who, haunted by the groundless fear of having to fight the whole of Europe, had been partly responsible for Nicholas's retreat. The only voices to be heard now were those that cried: 'Peace! peace at any price!' And so, after the fall of Sevastopol, peace was concluded at a moment when that place might have played the same rôle as Moscow did in 1812. After the sacrifice of the fortress we should have announced that, far from being over, operations were only just beginning! With the Allies would have then remained the onus of finishing the war."

Dissatisfaction with the results of the campaign was universal, and penetrated all grades of society. The root of the evil was seen to lie in our serfdom, so the Tsar Alexander II., the most humane of men, himself headed a movement for the emancipation of the serfs. They received their freedom.

This event was of extraordinary importance, constituting, in truth, an epoch in Russian life, which affected all spheres of activity, not excluding that of the War Department. A new language was heard on all sides. Indeed, it is difficult now to realize the animated, convincing, and liberal tone of the articles which appeared in the *Voenni Sbornik*. But, alas! everything soon returned to its former state. The Polish rebellion of 1863, the attempt to assassinate the Tsar, and the open conspiracies of a few evil-minded people, served as a pretext for the adherents of the old régime to strive for the reduction of the rights that had been granted. Their efforts were crowned with success, and a reaction set in which was particularly violent as regards educational and agrarian affairs. The War Department, however, was under the enlightened guidance of General Milutin, who, as far as possible, reduced the effect of this reaction upon the army; the department, indeed, was on this account for some time looked upon with suspicion. Though the Crimean War did arouse to some extent the latent patriotism of the masses, it was waged at too great a distance from the heart of the people to have earned the title of a national struggle.

It is unthinkable that any great nation could ever have become reconciled to the terms of such a peace as that signed by Russia in 1856, when she engaged to abstain from maintaining a fleet in the Black Sea, and to give up the mouths of the Danube, won by her in 1828–29. However involved, therefore, its causes may appear, the war of 1877–78 was in reality but a continuation of our two-hundred-year-old struggle towards the Black Sea, on this occasion complicated by the necessity of assisting our kindred in the Balkans—the Servians and Bulgarians. Though we did not make the most of our opportunities, the time for preparation allowed us by the Turko-Servian War really decided the issue of that between ourselves and Turkey. It is true we mobilized and concentrated the army in Bessarabia before the declaration of war, but we delayed so long in making this declaration that the Turks also had time for preparation. The severe reverses we suffered after our initial successes showed that our opponents, who were now armed with the breech-loading rifle and organized on the European model, were no longer the foe that we had faced in 1828, whose mobs of armed men were easily routed by small bodies of our troops. As usual, we put too few men in the field at first; but the Emperor, upon the advice of General Milutin, pressed masses of reinforcements to the front, among them the Guards and the Grenadiers, the flower of our army. Our comparatively short line of communication enabled this to be done with considerable rapidity. It was at Plevna, in August, 1877, that we suffered our last heavy reverse, and by October the Guards and Grenadiers had arrived at the front. Including the Roumanian, Servian, Montenegrin, and Bulgarian militias, we succeeded in placing superior numbers in the field, our armies amounting altogether to some 850,000 men in both theatres of operations, and in spite of the enemy's gallant opposition, we advanced up to the very walls of their capital. But it was not a lightly-won victory. To break down the stubborn defence of the Turks, who were ably commanded at Plevna, we were forced to put thrice their number into the field. Dubniak Hill, which was very weakly fortified, was only taken by the Guards, who were five or six times as strong as the enemy at that particular point, after a desperate fight. Though their earth-works were mostly of field profile, and without any obstacles, such as wire entanglement, mines, and abatis; though the defenders had no bomb-proof shelters; and though we were three to one in men, and put many more guns in action, we were unable to seize Plevna by assault, but had to resort to a blockade. Our Commander-in-Chief, however, was ably supported on the European side by such distinguished leaders as Gurko, Skobeleff, Radetski, and Todleben, whose troops soon became seasoned, and brought victory to our arms. In the theatre of operations in Asia the Grand-Duke Michael Nicolaeff was assisted by Lazareff, Heyman, Ter-Gukasoff—all energetic and able soldiers. Under them our Caucasian force did gallant service. While the force under Kridner and Zotovi was being driven back from the weak Plevna position, they were engaged in night assaults on the fortress of Kars. The defence of the Shipka Pass and of Bayazet, on the Turkish side, are among the most brilliant achievements in our military history.

This war again showed up many blots in our organization. The supply and medical services were very inefficient. The work of the cavalry and artillery on the European side was not up to expectation. The whole burden of the campaign was borne by the infantry, and right well did this Arm issue from the ordeal. In some engagements units lost as much as one-third or even half their strength, and yet were able to re-form and continue the action. Nor was there anything to complain of as regards the reservists. Their long halt at Kishineff enabled them to shake down and to amalgamate with the serving soldiers. Certain units, however, just brought up to strength with reservists, and sent into action before they had had time to be properly trained and disciplined, were not on every occasion as steady as they should have been; but, generally speaking, our troops upheld their reputation for gallantry, steadiness, endurance, and discipline. But we were stronger in defence than in the attack. Although this campaign—our first experience after the introduction of the law of universal military service—ended successfully, it emphasized the inferiority of our arrangements for rapid mobilization and concentration as compared with those of our western neighbours. The men were called up upon no regular mobilization scheme or system, and the reserve units were formed haphazard, and, owing to the inefficiency of the railways running to Roumania, the general concentration was slow. Our information about the enemy was insufficient and unreliable—it was due to our ignorance of their strength that we took the field with such weak numbers. Our re-armament was not completed owing to lack of funds, and we started operations with three different patterns of rifle. We did not have enough maps, and the reconnaissance sketches which had been made—of the Shipka position, for instance—were left behind in St. Petersburg. Our artillery *matériel* was technically inferior to the enemy's, our 4-pounder gun in particular being useless. The engineer services and stores were insufficient, and their distribution was bad. Thus, in the fights at Plevna on September 12 and 13, when Skobeleff and Imeretinski led the main attack on the enemy's fortified position, with an army corps consisting of twenty-two battalions, there was only a detachment of some thirty sappers, which I myself had by chance been able to collect! Siege material was not forthcoming in sufficient quantity, and what there was was of obsolete pattern. I have touched upon the cavalry duties on the European side, which were, with few exceptions, unsatisfactorily and selfishly performed throughout the war. The work of the artillery, which on the Caucasian side was splendid and self-sacrificing, in Europe often left much to be desired. There were instances of batteries retiring because a few men had been wounded. Many of the most senior commanders were unfit for their positions, and capable artillery or cavalry leaders were few and far between. The staff work, particularly that of the General Staff, was seldom good. There was far too much correspondence before a battle, while to report the most important events, or to inform subordinates of what was happening, was a duty frequently forgotten in the stress of action. During the actual combat touch was not properly maintained either laterally or to the rear, and as a result there was little co-operation between the different arms, the brunt of the fight being thrown almost entirely on the infantry. The light railway communication (via Roumania) was inadequate in capacity and badly organized. There were no rest-camps along the line, and in winter, when the roads were cut up, the transport of every kind of supplies was almost impossible. The attitude of our troops in Bulgaria towards the inhabitants was not always humane or just. Payment for produce brought in was made irregularly, or not at all, owing to the improper system whereby forage allowance was treated as the perquisite of a commanding officer. Away from the front disorder and debauchery were common. Owing to our hurried advance in insufficient strength, we were obliged to evacuate areas of the country once occupied, and the people who had at first received us with open arms as liberators were forced either to retire with us or be slain by the returning Turks. Consequently, for a time there was a general revulsion of feeling; the Bulgarians lost all faith in us, and began to turn towards the enemy. Up to a certain point it was the Crimea over again. Strong in defence, we were weak in power of manœuvre, and our attacks consequently suffered from clumsiness: this was notably the case at Plevna. On the other hand, there is no doubt that we were greatly assisted by the comparative unreadiness of the Turks for any offensive operations; otherwise our cordon in Bulgaria might have easily been broken in August or September, before reinforcements reached us. We should then have been obliged to fall back behind the Danube. Only the jealousy and incompetence of the Turkish leaders, and the interference from Constantinople, saved us from misfortune. In spite, however, of all our want of organization, in spite of all our shortcomings, we defeated the Turks, capturing whole army corps at Plevna, Shipka, and Kars, and finally marched victoriously to the walls of Constantinople itself. This was the last great war in which we were engaged in the nineteenth century, and immediately after it, in 1879, our military self-esteem received a severe blow in Central Asia. Repeated raiding by the Turcomans, carried out even in the neighbourhood of Krasnovodsk, necessitated a special expedition into the Turcoman Steppe. The experienced and veteran leader, General Lazareff, was appointed to its command, but at his death, on the eve of the departure of the force from the line of the Artek towards Geok Tepe, the command unfortunately passed to the next senior— General Lomakin—who was quite unfitted for such responsibility. The expedition ended in disaster. The force reached Geok Tepe, the weakly fortified Turcoman stronghold, and made an attempt to storm it which was unsuccessful, though our troops consisted of the magnificent Caucasian regiments. We were forced to abandon several hundred breech-loading rifles, and to retire with great loss to the fortified posts on the line of the Artek. We had to make greater efforts, and had to organize quite a large force— measured by the standard of Asiatic warfare. General Skobeleff, an especially able and energetic man, was given the command of it, and after a severe fight he defeated the Turcomans and seized Geok Tepe. We twice met with reverses in the different night attacks made by the enemy, being overwhelmed by sheer numbers after desperate hand-to-hand fighting; we lost three guns and the standard of one of the most distinguished of our Caucasian regiments.[17] But Skobeleff succeeded in instilling into the minds of all that, whatever the loss or sufferings, they should continue to fight to the bitter end. So we won. This expedition showed, however, that the time had passed when columns composed of a few companies, like those under the command of Generals Cherniaeff and Kaufmann, could defeat greatly superior numbers of natives. Besides being very brave, the Turcomans were armed with captured Berdan rifles, with which they managed to inflict severe loss upon us. Of the small force of under 5,000 which attacked Geok Tepe, we lost about 1,000 in killed and wounded. The very last action in which our troops took part in the nineteenth century was the affair at Kushk in 1885,[18] when a small Russian force defeated the Afghans at the expense of forty-three men.

The result of the Turkish War of 1877–78 was that we regained the mouths of the Danube, and obtained possession of Batoum and Kars. In our contests with Turkey in the nineteenth century our primary object was the freeing of the various Balkan nationalities still subject to Turkey. But this question touched too closely the interests of the other nations of Europe, who opposed us, by force at Sevastopol, and diplomatically at the Berlin Congress. The lack of simplicity in our aims also militated against our success, for in our anxiety over the fate of the minor nationalities we lost sight of our own material interests. Consequently, the results attained in this century on the Black Sea did not on the whole correspond to the sacrifices we made. In the three wars with Turkey we put 1,700,000 men into the field (bringing the strength of the army up to 850,000 men in 1878), and lost in killed, wounded, and missing 126,000; sick, 243,000; a total of 369,000. If we take into account that we put 1,300,000 men into the field during the Crimean War, and that our casualties in killed, wounded, and missing were 120,000, and in sick 220,000, it appears that the acquisition of the Black Sea littoral, the mouths of the Danube, and the right to maintain a war fleet on the Black Sea, cost us 3,000,000 men put into the field, a loss in battle of 250,000, and 460,000 invalided. Yet, in spite of all these sacrifices, the gateway out of the Black Sea remained closed to us and open to our possible foes. In 1878 we were virtually in possession of this gateway, but now it is guarded against us not only by the Turks, but by the Germans. The task of preserving our position on the Mediterranean from the Black Sea has passed to the twentieth century.

To obtain possession of the Caucasus we had to fight twice with Persia in the nineteenth century, and were at war for sixty-two years with the mountaineers of the Caucasus. Before arriving at our present frontier in Central Asia we had been making expeditions for thirty years. Our operations both in the Caucasus and in Central Asia were productive of many gallant feats. Though in the former we crossed swords with a particularly brave opponent, and had to contend against extraordinary natural difficulties, we were in greatly superior numbers and far better organized than the enemy, and from a purely military point of view the contest did not present at all the same difficulties as the wars against the Turks. During our operations in Central Asia, from 1847 to 1881, we never had more than 15,000 men in the field at one time. The total number sent out was some 55,000, of whom we did not lose as many as 5,000 killed and wounded, and 8,000 sick. Our work in these two directions can be said to have been completed in the nineteenth century, for, as will be shown later, not only is no realignment of our present frontier necessary, but no change is possible without risking serious conflicts with Turkey, Persia, Afghanistan, and, probably, Great Britain. But the character of the Caucasian and Central Asian peoples will demand constant watchfulness and a strong hand in order to prevent racial and religious risings.

In spite of the small force maintained in Siberia, we considerably altered our frontier line in the east during the nineteenth century, and in the twentieth century we must be careful to preserve the peaceful relations which have lasted for 200 years between the Chinese and ourselves.

During that period we lost our possessions in America by making them over to the United States for a small sum of money. We also practically forced the Japanese to give us the southern portion of Saghalien in exchange for the Island of Kurile, and annexed Kamchatka, the Amur and Ussuri districts, and finally the Kuan-tung Peninsula. The Ussuri district was awarded to us by the Peking Treaty of 1860, more or less as a reward for the assistance we gave China in the drafting of the Peking Treaty with the French and British after their capture of Peking. Similarly, our movement in Manchuria was, so to speak, a *quid pro quo* for our mediation and intercession on China's behalf after her unsuccessful war with Japan. Thus, while our advance to the Baltic and Black Seas cost two centuries of work by the army and many lives, we were able to reach the Pacific seaboard in 1897 without any bloodshed. But the success so easily gained was pregnant with the seeds of disaster.

During the last two centuries the expansion of the Empire implied a gradual realignment of all our frontiers, except on the greater part of that between us and China, which, from the valley of the Katuna to the mouth of the Schilka, remained unchanged for 200 years. The western frontier had moved from a distance of 300 miles from Moscow in 1700 to one of 670 miles. In the north-west and south we had reached natural boundaries in the Baltic and Black Seas. In the same period we had pushed forward our confines a considerable distance from the Caucasus and in Central Asia. The following figures show us roughly what the two main struggles, between the years 1700 and 1900, have cost us in men: In our efforts to reach the Black Sea we lost 750,000 out of 3,200,000[19] men put in the field against Turkey, while the conflict with Sweden for an approach to the Baltic cost us 700,000 out of the 1,800,000 combatants employed. This is sufficient to convey some idea of what sacrifices we must expect from our army in any attempt on our part to reach the shores of the Pacific and Indian Oceans during the present century. Moreover, the growth of our territory has forced us to include within it many and different foreign and even hostile races, and our frontier is to-day (1900),[20] from a military point of view, therefore less soundly established than it was in 1700. Though the population of the Empire has increased from 12,000,000 to 130,000,000, it must be remembered that we have now on and within our borders more than 40,000,000 who are only partly connected to us by racial ties, but are more or less alien both by religion and by their historical past.

Within the same period peace reigned in Russia for 71⅔ years. During the remaining 128⅓ years there were thirty-three foreign and two internal wars, which can be classified, according to the political objects for which they were fought, in the following order:

1. For the expansion of the Empire—twenty-two wars, lasting about 101 years.

2. In defence of the Empire—four wars, lasting 4¼ years.

3. In the interests of general European politics—seven wars and two campaigns, taking 10 years.

4. Civil wars—two wars, lasting 65 years.

5. For the suppression of revolts—6 years of military operations.

These conflicts exposed to the horrors of war some 10,000,000 of people, of whom about one-third were lost to the nation, nearly 1,000,000 being killed and wounded.

The gradual change in the war establishment of the army (excluding militia, second line troops, and reserve) can be traced from the following figures:

In 1700, with a population of 12,000,000, we had a war strength of 56,000 men—*i.e.*, 0·47 per cent. of the population. In 1800, with a population of 35,000,000, we had a war strength of 400,000—*i.e.*, 1·14 per cent. In 1900, with a population of 132,000,000, we had 1,000,000—*i.e.*, 0·75 per cent. It must, however, be noted that the army had only just been formed in 1700, and that very shortly afterwards its war strength rose to 150,000—*i.e.*, 1·3 per cent. Thus, notwithstanding the introduction of a new system of recruiting our forces (the law of universal military service), and their gradual growth, the proportionate burden imposed upon the nation in keeping the ranks filled was at the beginning of the twentieth century about one-half of what it had been 100 and 200 years before. This is all the more remarkable, as in 1700 and 1710 the army had not been properly developed, and was considerably below its strength in 1800, owing to the reforms of the Emperor Paul Petrovitch. The great difference between the peace and war establishments first arose in 1855, on account of the Crimean War, but it became permanent upon the introduction of universal military service.

As regards the work that would probably fall to the Russian armed forces in the twentieth century, I wrote the following in a report I made, as War Minister in 1901:

"With the limitations of human understanding, it is not possible to look ahead a hundred years, and we cannot, therefore, lay down what our army will have to undertake in the twentieth century; but by analyzing the past and reviewing our present position among the great Powers of the world, it is both possible and essential to estimate the nature of the work that will come before our army in the next few years at least. In the last two centuries Russia's main work was connected with the expansion of the Empire. *From this it seems that the matter of our frontiers is still the most urgent.* It is, therefore, important to answer the following vital questions: Are we content with our present frontier? If not, where and why are we not? This is a matter which must not be considered only from our own point of view. If we are content with our position, and are not anxious to advance or retire our frontier, it is certainly improbable that we shall undertake any wars of aggression in the twentieth century; but in arriving, by great efforts and the immense sacrifices of 200 years, at a position satisfactory to ourselves, we have, perhaps, so placed our neighbours that it may be their object in the coming century to regain the territory of which they have been deprived. If so, the danger of war will not have been removed; it will have been changed in nature from that of an offensive to a defensive struggle."

CHAPTER II

Russia's frontiers in Europe and Asia—Conclusions as to their suitability to the needs of the Empire.

The second chapter of a report, made in 1900, when I was Minister for War, contained a strategical review of our frontiers. The general conclusions arrived at may be summarized as follows:

1. *Swedish Frontier.*[21]—This is 1,000 miles long, and traverses a rugged, inaccessible, and sparsely populated country. Starting from the extreme northern point of the Gulf of Bothnia, and running due north, it acts as a sharply defined ethnographical line between the Scandinavians on the west and the Finns on the east. The southern portion quite corresponds to our requirements, but the northern is too artificially drawn, and is disadvantageous to us, as it cuts Finland off from the Arctic Ocean, and gives all the coast to Norway. We would naturally like to see a realignment of this portion, but the advantages to be gained are too insignificant to warrant our quarrelling about them. Still, the situation on this section of our border cannot be considered to be all that is to be desired.

It has been shown in the preceding chapter what efforts and sacrifices have been made by Russia in order to gain access to the Baltic Sea and the Gulfs of Finland and Bothnia. We had to fight four wars with Sweden, and put 1,800,000 men into the field, and only won at last after losing some 130,000 men in killed and wounded. The main factor in our success was the influence on events exercised by Peter the Great, for it was his victory at Poltava which opened the way for us. At the beginning of the eighteenth century the Viborg province was, to a certain extent, Russianized: Russian villages and churches were to be found in it, and our language was the predominant tongue. In 1809, by the peaceful Treaty of Friederichsham, Finland passed for ever into the Empire. All that then remained to be done was to take advantage of our victories, and quietly but firmly incorporate the conquered province with the rest of Russia. But we did not do this. Being fully occupied elsewhere—in fortifying our foothold on the Black and Caspian Seas, in advancing towards the Pacific, in a long struggle in the Caucasus, in wars with Poland and in Central Asia—we paid little attention to what was going on in Finland, and rested content with the outward peacefulness, order, and submission of its people. The Finns took advantage of this, and from 1810 to 1890 unceasingly worked against us, hoping always to succeed in obtaining complete autonomy. In 1811 the Viborg province, won by us at so great a cost, was again made over to them, though they have not to this day completely obliterated in it all traces of Russian citizenship. Then, with the assistance of certain of our statesmen, we learned by degrees to forget that Finland had ever really been an integral portion of our Empire; we were gradually taught to feel that she ought to be administered according to the Swedish Constitution of 1772, and, finally, that she was not really a Russian province, but an autonomous State. In 1880 the law of universal military service was enacted. This gave Finland a national army—not a large one, it is true, but one which, by a well-thought-out system of reserves, enabled her to put in the field an armed force of 100,000 men near the Russian capital. Thus the Finns, without shedding a drop of blood, but by working cautiously, continuously, and systematically for eighty years, have succeeded in again shutting us out from the Gulfs of Finland and Bothnia, and have, to a great extent, robbed us of the fruits of our victories. Therefore, as the kingdom[22] of Norway and Sweden is weak, and as Finland, which stretches almost to the walls of the Russian capital, and screens not only it, but the whole of Northern Russia, is of immense importance to us, we ought, instead of planning any rectification of the Swedish frontier, to think how best to remove the causes of friction between the two countries. Sweden could only hope to take Finland from us if the Finns' dream of independence came true; she could only risk operations against us in that country if the inhabitants joined her or were at least sympathetic. Consequently, to insure our safety on that frontier, it is our duty to smooth the way as much as possible for the early unification of Finland and Russia.

The following is a quotation from my report:

> "However just our claims to the possession of Finland may be, it must be acknowledged that our mistaken policy with regard to her, lasting for eighty years, cannot be rectified all at once. Hasty action in dealing with matters which touch the domestic life of a people can only irritate and intensify difficulties. A firm and, at the same time, cautious attitude, extending, perhaps, over many years, is essential in order that we may be able in the end to take our proper place on the shores of the Gulfs of Bothnia and Finland. We must be particularly careful how we introduce any change into the people's mode of life, and must frankly admit that Finland has reached a more advanced state of civilization than many of our provinces, although this has been done mainly at the expense of the Russian people. We should respect Finnish culture, in the hope that when Finland is united to us it will assist and not harm us."

2. *Western Frontier.*—From Cape Polangen on the Baltic Coast to the mouth of the Danube in the Black Sea Russia marches for 738 miles with Germany, 761 with Austro-Hungary, and 467 with Roumania.

The northern and southern extremities of this frontier line are fairly straight. In the middle, from Raigrod to Litomerj, it runs due west, and bending round, continues for 390 miles to Myslowitz, along the southern and eastern frontiers of Germany, and thence for 213 miles along the northern frontiers of Austro-Hungary. It juts out into these States, forming our Warsaw Military District, important both by its position and its strategic significance. This area, formerly the kingdom of Poland, was joined to Russia by the Treaty of Vienna in 1815. By holding this area we can envelop the southern frontier of Eastern Prussia and the northern frontier of Galicia. Operating from this theatre, we can cut off those provinces from their neighbours by advancing towards the Baltic Sea on the north, or the difficult Carpathian range on the south. On the other hand, the district is itself liable to be cut off by offensive movements from north and south, directed on the fortress of Brest-Litovsk. Its position, therefore, makes it of decided importance. Were we more ready for war than our neighbours, it might constitute a source of strength to us. If, on the other hand, Germany and Austria together are able to throw greater numbers into the field, and can concentrate more rapidly than we can, it will merely be a weak spot.

The German frontier, 738 miles in length, follows no natural feature. Beyond it lies our nearest neighbour—a nation with whom we have been in close social and economic relationship ever since we got into touch with European life. At the present time (1900) five separate lines of railway connect different parts of Russia with Germany's Baltic ports and with Berlin; our annual trade with her amounts to £32,200,000 (the average of the five years from 1893 to 1897), or, in other words, to 26·5 per cent. of all our foreign trade. The yearly exports (five-years average) amount to £16,400,000, or 25·1 per cent. of all our exports; the imports to £15,800,000 (28·6 per cent. of our imports). In 1897 alone our German exports totalled £17,520,000, and our imports £17,980,000. Thus the economic connection between the two countries is very close. Our interests are reciprocal, and, consequently, economic reasons alone necessitate a preservation on our part of the present friendly relations. But it is of no use disguising the fact that the part played by the German Government at the Berlin Congress gave us reason to change a policy which had always been favourable to Germany, and her entry into the Triple Alliance, which was directed against us, was the origin of our *rapprochement* with France. The whole of the frontier is artificial, and quite exposed to invasion from either side. From the Baltic to Filippovo it acts as an ethnographical dividing-line between the Lithuanian races in the east and the Germans, German Lithuanians, and Poles on the west, and separates our Poles from the German Poles. Though there exists no obvious natural boundary between us and Germany, the racial one has the same effect as a natural boundary. By a systematic policy Germany has succeeded in so Teutonizing the one Slav country of Eastern Prussia that it now constitutes one of the most loyal provinces of the House of Hohenzollern. The same policy, with less successful results, however, is being applied to Posen. On our side we are making great efforts to colonize the Warsaw Military District and the north-western countries bordering on Germany, so as to bind them closer to us. If we have not been so successful in our efforts as our neighbours, it is mainly due to the backward state of our civilization. Our vacillations, also, as to the best policy whereby to attain the desired result are responsible for the slow progress made.

By the expenditure of vast sums of money, Germany has made ready in the most comprehensive sense to march rapidly across our borders with an army of 1,000,000 men. She has seventeen lines of railway (twenty-three tracks) leading to our frontiers, which would enable her to send to the front more than 500 troop-trains daily. She can concentrate the greater part of her armed forces (fourteen to sixteen army corps) on our frontier within a few days of the declaration of war; while, apart from this question of speedy mobilization, she has at her command far greater technical resources, such as light railways, artillery, ordnance, and engineering stores, particularly for telegraphs, mobile siege-parks, etc., than we have. She has also made most careful preparation for a determined defence of her own border provinces, especially those of Eastern Prussia. The first-class fortresses of Thorn, Königsberg, and Posen are improved yearly, entrenched camps are built at the most important junctions, and material lies ready stacked for the rapid semi-permanent fortification of field positions.

The crossing-places on the Vistula have been placed in a state of defence, as have also the various towns and large villages. The whole population, indeed, is making ready for a national struggle. Since the Crimean War we also have worked hard to prepare the Vilna and Warsaw areas for hostilities, but as Germany has done considerably more in thirty years than we have in fifty, she has outdistanced us. Her principal and most overwhelming superiority lies in her railways; to her seventeen lines running to our frontier we can only oppose five. This advantage is overwhelming, and gives to her and Austria a superiority which can be counterbalanced neither by large numbers nor bravery. The fact remains that Germany, by spending milliards—part of which were supplied by the war indemnity of 1871—has prepared for hostilities, both in the shape of an energetic offensive and also a determined defensive. If a war should happen to go against us, she might attempt to annex the whole of the Warsaw Military District, or even part of the Vilna District (on the left bank of the Dwina), for the peoples of these countries might considerably augment her military strength. On the other hand, those who analyze the possible consequences of such a war cannot see what advantage Germany would derive from such expansion. It is incredible that 100,000,000 Russians would ever become reconciled to the loss of territory which is bound to the Fatherland by historical ties, and which has cost so much Russian blood. Such thinkers are convinced, on the contrary, that we should concentrate ourselves on winning it back at the very first chance. If we were better prepared for war, or in a case where Germany's main forces were diverted in another direction, the Warsaw Military District would constitute a *place d'armes*, cutting deep in between her and Austria, whence we might, with equal ease, advance rapidly on either Berlin or Vienna. The former is 200 and the latter 213 miles from our frontier; St. Petersburg and Moscow are 533 and 733 miles respectively from the German, and 900 and 800 from the Austrian, frontier. If, however, we were successful in such a campaign, and sought to expand the Empire further, military considerations would point to the annexation of the whole of Eastern Prussia up to the Vistula. Astride this river, with possession of both its banks and of its mouths and of the River Niemen, we should hold a very commanding position as regards Germany, and should have considerably improved our military frontier. But these advantages of position would be more than outweighed by the many disadvantages attending such an increase of territory. There would arise for us a question of lost provinces comparable to that of Alsace-Lorraine; but it would be of a more acute nature, for the German nation would always be watching for an opportunity to regain—by war if necessary—territory with which the ruling dynasty was so intimately connected. It may be assumed, therefore—

That, taking the armed forces of both nations as they exist to-day, and making allowance for their comparative readiness, an invasion of our territory by German armies is more probable than a Russian invasion of Germany;

That an invading German army would meet with fewer difficulties than ours if we marched into Prussia;

That certain territory might be taken from us;

That we might take Prussian territory from Germany, but that the population of the conquered provinces would always be hostile to us, on account of the difference in their state of civilization, national ties, and traditional sentiment;

That both Russia and Germany are such great nations that neither could possibly accept a loss of territory nor rest until it had been regained; and

"That, taking everything into consideration, it would not suit Germany, and it would certainly not suit us, to go to war for the sake of altering the existing frontier."

3. *Austro-Hungarian Frontier.*—Austro-Hungary, 243,043 square miles in area, is larger than Germany, and in 1900 its population was 45,600,000; but while the German nation is exceedingly homogeneous and patriotic, the people of Austro-Hungary consist of many races. Of its population, 24·1 per cent. is

German; the numerous Slav groups comprise 47 per cent. (Bohemians, Moravians, and Slovaks, 16·9 per cent.; Croatian-Servians, 11 per cent.; Poles, 8 per cent.; Rusins, 8 per cent.; Slavonians, 3 per cent.); Hungarians, 16·2 per cent.; Roumanians, 6·6 per cent.; Jews, 4·5 per cent.; and Italians, 1·6 per cent. As regards the feeling of these various races towards Russia, the Germans who live at a distance from our frontiers are not hostile; the Hungarians, if not open enemies, are, at any rate, unfriendly on account of the part we took in suppressing the rebellion of 1849, and their latent dislike is fanned by the greatest of the Slav groups, the Poles. The rest of the Slavs are sympathetic with their kinsmen in Russia, but the main motive for this sentiment is fear lest they should be absorbed by the Germans or Magyars.

The Austrian frontiers are nowhere simple, but ever since the conclusion of the Triple Alliance she has turned her attention—in a military sense—almost exclusively to her Russian frontier. On glancing at the map, one's first thought is that the natural boundary between the two countries should run along the Carpathian range, but the actual frontier is a long way on the Russian side of it. Galicia forms, so to speak, a glacis of this main obstacle (the Carpathians) running down towards Russia, and it has recently grown up into a splendidly prepared entrenched camp, connected to the other provinces of Austro-Hungary by numerous roads across the Carpathians. It is strongly fortified and stocked with supplies of every nature, both for a protracted defence or an advance in force into Russia. Austria can now concentrate 1,000,000 men in this area within a very short space of time. For 760 miles we have a common frontier, and the upper reaches of the Vistula—from Nepolomnitsa to Zavikhost—and a small stretch of the Dniester, with its tributary, the Zbruoz, form a natural boundary in this direction. These rivers, however, possess no strategic value. The frontier is crossed by four lines of railway:

(*a*) At Granitsa, on the Warsaw-Ivangorod line.

(*b*) At Radziviloff.

(*c*) At Volochisk.

(*d*) At Novoselits.

Our economic relations with Austro-Hungary are not so important as those with Germany. For the five years 1893–97 the average value of our trade has amounted to only £5,800,000 per annum, or 4·5 per cent. of our total trade; of this, the exports are £3,500,000, and the imports £2,320,000 (4·8 and 4·2 per cent. of the respective totals). In 1897 our exports were £3,900,000, and imports £19,000,000. Though almost half the races of Austro-Hungary come of kindred stock to our people, and though much of our blood was shed in the nineteenth century in order to maintain the reigning house of

Austria on the throne, war between the two nations is by no means impossible in the event of a general European conflagration, for brothers by blood and religion will march against brothers. Such a war, which would, except in the imagination of a few Polish dreamers, be a calamity for all the Slav races, could not be popular with the Austrian-Germans, however much their interests may be opposed to ours. In Austro-Hungary it is the Hungarians and Poles alone who hate us, having, as is well known, many and good reasons for siding with our possible foes. Upon the subject of a change of our frontier after war with Austria, I wrote in my report of 1900 as follows:

"In the event of a successful war with us, the Austro-Hungarian Government—under pressure from the Poles—would probably insist on the annexation to Galicia of those Russian border-lands where the Poles predominate. Some of the Polish and Hungarian patriots even aspire to moving the Russian frontier back to Brest and the Dnieper.

"It is certain that Russia would never accept any loss of territory, even after defeat, and would do her utmost to win back as quickly as possible any which had been taken. On the other hand, after a successful war against Austro-Hungary, and the probably ensuing break-up of that Empire, Russia will be confronted with the problem of whether she should take more territory, and if so, what? There would then recur the cry for the 'rectification of the frontier.' The Carpathian Mountains seem formed by Nature for a boundary, so that the whole of Galicia might become part of Russia.

"But we must put the position before ourselves clearly and in good time. Is such an increase of land and population necessary to us? Should we be the stronger for such annexation, or, on the other hand, should we be creating a source of weakness and anxiety for ourselves? Seventy or a hundred years ago a transfer of Galicia might very likely have been of advantage and have added to our strength, though even that is problematical, for it is by no means certain that Austria would not have tried to win it back; she would have had an excellent opportunity in 1855. But now, after Galicia has for so long existed apart from us, it could only be torn from Austria by force, and therefore unwillingly. Neither the Poles of Galicia nor its Russian population are anxious to become Russian subjects. We must not lose sight of the fact that for the Slavs of Austria, including the Rusins, we can only be a means to an end (emancipation), not an end in ourselves. Even the Bulgarians and Servians might turn against us. Nor are the Austrian Slavs in real need of our help. Every year they are gaining, by persistency and peaceful methods, more and more civil rights, which are gradually placing them on an equality with the Germans and the Hungarians. Notwithstanding their grave economic position; notwithstanding the grip the Jews are getting on the land, or the taxes, which are heavier than in Russia, and the inequality of rights of Poles and Rusins, the people of Galicia consider themselves far more advanced than their Russian neighbours. In their opinion it would be a retrograde step to become Russian subjects. This is also a point we must always keep clearly in our minds, lest we imagine that we have only to move into Eastern Galicia for the people to rise against the Austrians—their eternal oppressors. If, on the contrary, we allow ourselves to be led away by the prospect of rounding off our possessions by means of natural boundaries, we shall certainly lay up endless trouble and expense for ourselves in the future. Joined to Russia, Galicia might in a lesser degree become an Alsace-Lorraine for us, just as Eastern Prussia would be."

In the matter of railway development the Austrians also have left us far behind. While they, by means of eight lines of rail (ten tracks), can run 260 trains up to the frontier every twenty-four hours, we can only convey troops up to the same point on four lines! As any of their troops on the frontier would be in advance of the Carpathians, this range was formerly looked upon as an obstacle to retirement and to communication between Galicia and the rest of Austria. But in the last ten years it has been pierced by five lines of railway, and preparations have been made to lay three more. Notwithstanding our unreadiness, the Austrians, even if egged on by the Germans, would not lightly attack us, for they well know that they would meet a determined foe and be committed to a national war. On the other hand, we must not deceive ourselves with any idea that we could easily defeat the Austrians. Their army, which is of great size and splendidly equipped, would base itself upon the strong entrenched camp in Galicia, and could, if properly commanded, throw superior numbers into the field against us. I recorded the following conclusions upon the Austrian frontier in my report of 1900:

"*It would be advantageous to neither Austria nor Russia to engage in war in order to bring about an alteration of the existing frontier.*

"It is satisfactory to be able to draw such conclusions regarding our frontiers with these two powerful States. Having no desire for our neighbours' land, and being at the same time quite prepared to make any sacrifice for the defence of our own country, we may hope that if we on our side have no reason to force on a war, our neighbours will, on their side, use every means to avoid beginning one with us."

4. *Roumanian Frontier.*—For 466 miles south of Austro-Hungary we march with Roumania. The frontier runs along the River Pruth and the northern branch of the delta of the Danube. It is there formed by a natural line of water; it fully meets our requirements, political and military, and therefore calls for no change. The young kingdom of Roumania, consisting of some 51,000 square miles, with a population of 5,000,000, is one of the second-class Powers of Europe. Our trade with her amounts roughly (taking the average from 1893–97) to £1,020,000 per annum, constituting O·8 per cent. of our foreign trade. Our exports amount, on the average, to £750,000 per annum (1·3 per cent. of our total exports). Two lines of railway run to the frontier from our side: one to Ungens, whence it continues on to Jassy; the other to Reni, whence communication extends to Galatz by road, there being no bridge across the Pruth. Although Roumania owes her very existence to Russia, the close relations into which she has entered with Germany, and still more with Austro-Hungary, and her evident anxiety to develop her army and fortify her frontier on our side, point in no uncertain manner to the possibility of her taking up arms against us in a European war. The reason may be that she wishes, in the event of such a conflict, to wrest from us Bessarabia, half the population of that province being Roumanian.

5. In *Trans-Caucasia* we march for 325 miles with Turkey and 465 with Persia. The territory of the former is in three continents, and amounts to 1,581,400 square miles, with a population of 40,000,000. Our trade with her (taking the same years as before) reaches £2,110,000 per annum, or 2·1 per cent. of our total foreign trade. The frontier was fixed after our victorious campaign of 1877–78. As it runs for the most part along natural boundaries, such as watersheds, it not only effectually guarantees the integrity of our possessions from any Turkish attempt at aggression, but it gives us an advantageous route by which to advance on Erzeroum, the most important point in Asia Minor, and the only fortress of any strength nearer than Scutari. Thus, the present frontier may be accepted as being quite satisfactory from our point of view, and no change is necessary.

In Europe we have no long land frontier with Turkey, as Roumania and Bulgaria lie between us. The only point at which we are in direct touch with her on the mainland is in the Caucasus, and this is the only point where we can engage her by a direct advance across the frontier. But though we are content with our position, we must not forget that Turkey, given a favourable opportunity, might make an effort to regain the territory we have taken from her. To make our position on her frontier safe, we should pacify the

Caucasus, improve the conditions of the people and our organization of troops there, and strengthen our command of the Black Sea.

6. *East of Turkey* we march with Persia for 465 miles in Trans-Caucasia, to the east again for 275 along the Caspian Sea, and further still to the east on land for 593 miles up to Zulfikar on the Heri Rud. Including the Caspian shore, we have a common frontier with Persia of 1,333 miles.[23] Our trade with her has gradually increased in the last ten years from £2,000,000 in 1888 to £3,500,000 in 1897. Of all our land-borne commerce, this is only exceeded by our trade with Germany, Austria, and China. In nine years our exports have risen from £900,000 to £1,600,000, and our imports from £1,100,000 to £1,900,000. Our exports have, however, been artificially stimulated by very heavy rebates on the export tax on sugar and cotton, and the imports diminished by the high taxes on tea brought through Persia (from China and India) and an almost prohibitive tariff on foreign manufactured goods. Her situation on the Indian Ocean, upon the shortest route to India from Europe, combined with the undeveloped state of her resources and her military weakness, makes Persia the natural arena for any struggle between the great Powers for predominance in the Middle East. Hitherto Russia and Great Britain have been the principal competitors, but Germany is now apparently ready to join in the race, for she is making serious efforts to establish her footing in Asia Minor. The fact that we are neighbours over an immense length; our long-standing peaceful relationship;[24] the privileges we enjoy from the Treaty of Gulistan, which give us a word in the internal administration of the country, and permit us to maintain exclusive supremacy on the Caspian, which washes the defenceless shores of Northern Persia; and, finally, our complete military superiority, can be said to confer at present on Russia an effective political predominance in the country. As regards economic predominance, we have in our hands only the trade of the three northern provinces; throughout the rest of the country it does not belong to us. In the southern provinces it is almost entirely in the hands of Great Britain. By seizing points on the coast of the Indian Ocean, by constructing railways[25] and developing her trade with Persia, Great Britain apparently aspires not only to make certain of supremacy in the south, but gradually to capture the trade of the central provinces, and even to compete with us in the north. Germany will also soon be a serious competitor of ours; she already controls the important trade route from Trebizond to Tabriz. The following is the conclusion I recorded in the report I have quoted from above:

"Our Persian frontier has been settled and delimitated along its whole length, and neither for strategic nor other reasons is any change desirable; nor do we wish to obtain any further concessions of land from Persia. On the contrary, not only would the acquirement of fresh districts filled by alien peoples, and the consequent expense of administration, be of no advantage to us, but any action likely to undermine the friendly feelings now underlying all our dealings with the Persians would be distinctly detrimental to our interests. From the military standpoint, there appears to be no need to realign the frontier. It separates kindred races only for a short distance—*i.e.*, the Persians and Turkomans in Lenkoran and along the Artek. Following natural landmarks for the rest of its length, it acts as a racial division—in Trans-Caucasia between the Armenians and Turks; in Azerbaijan between the Persians, Turko-Tartars, and the Kurds; in Central Asia between the Turkomans and Russians of Trans-Caucasia, and the Kurds and Persians of Khorasan. For the last fifty years our trade with Persia, taking imports and exports, has increased enormously, and it is now our duty to preserve and develop it, and to take every step in order that the northern markets may, year by year, become more completely dominated by us; but a further growth of trade is only possible if the people of the country feel secure and internal order is maintained. By the conquest of the Turkomans twenty years ago we guaranteed peaceful development to the people of Khorasan, and we are now reaping the fruits of our victory at Geok Tepe, for our trade in Khorasan alone amounts to about £10,000,000 a year. If, therefore, the necessity should arise in the future, it will certainly be our duty to assist the Persian Government to maintain order in those portions of country nearest to our border. Consequently, our most urgent duties in Persia are, at present, the maintenance of order in the provinces nearest us, and of our command of the markets in the north of the country."

7. *Eastwards* again from the Persian frontier runs that of Afghanistan, which has not long been delimitated. It is 1,259 miles long, and traverses a desert as far as the Oxus, and then runs along that river. This frontier is satisfactory, and well defined.

Bounded on the west by Persia, on the south and east by Baluchistan and the Indian Empire, Afghanistan contains the immense range of the Hindu Kush Mountains, with their numerous ramifications. In size it is some 217,800 square miles, with a population of 5,000,000 to 6,000,000, of which 56 per cent. are Afghan and 44 per cent. non-Afghan tribes. As it lies between our territory in Central Asia and Great Britain's Indian Empire, it has long been an object of interest to the British, who have desired to establish in it an exclusive supremacy. Being afraid of an attempt on our part to march on

India, they have followed our every move in Central Asia with a vigilant eye. So long ago as 1873 they tried to arrive at an agreement with us whereby, if they refrained from interference in Bokhara, we, on our side, should undertake to abstain from any intervention in Afghanistan. Since then they have moved forward several steps on the frontiers of the country, and have even annexed a portion of it. But in proportion as they have advanced beyond the Indus, they have, instead of assuring more peace upon the border, met greater difficulties, with the result that their present position on the north-west frontier of India is unsettled and unsatisfactory. Afghanistan has not only not become British, but under twenty years of Abdur Rahman's energetic administration has become stronger—so much so that it is now really an independent empire,[26] with a sound military organization. As regards the country's sentiments, it is as hostile to us as it is to the British.

Since 1873 we also have greatly added to our possessions in Central Asia. We conquered Turkomania and the Khanate of Khokand, defeated the inhabitants of Khiva, and turned it into a trading centre; and although we did not annex Bokhara, by running a railway through it and including it within our fiscal area we secured absolute supremacy. In this way we pushed our frontiers on to Persia and Afghanistan, and, having drawn our boundary along natural features, we now possess a clearly defined line along the whole of which we are blessed with peace. The conclusion I came to regarding the Afghan frontier was expressed as follows in my report of 1900:

"If we compare the success of British policy in India since 1873 with the results of our progress in Central Asia, we have reason to congratulate ourselves. We are at present better and more peacefully established than they are. There would not be any advantage in changing our present position for a worse one, which we would certainly do if we annexed part of Afghanistan. Since the non-Afghan peoples of Northern Afghanistan wish to be taken over by us, it would seem natural that we should annex Afghan Turkestan and the Herat province. Such annexation would bring us over 2,000,000 new subjects, of whom the majority are industrious and skilled tillers of the soil; would advance our frontier to the Hindu Kush, which has long been the dream of many Russians; and would give us possession of the far-famed Herat, a place most undoubtedly of great strategical importance. At first sight the gain seems indisputable; but from a closer study of the subject, it is clear that the result of the realization of these schemes would be to create for ourselves immense difficulties in the present and possible danger in the future. In the first place, the geographical boundaries would not coincide with the ethnographical. For, in moving our frontier up to the edge of the Hindu Kush, we should be forced to take over tribes of Afghan descent, and yet at the same time exclude some non-Afghan races kindred to those we had already taken over. This in itself bristles with difficulties. Where the inhabitants of the valleys are peasants, Uzbegs, and Tajiks, they would probably submit to us without opposition, but the hillmen, even those of non-Afghan descent, would fight fiercely for their liberty. Even after conquering them, we, like the British in India to-day, would have no peace. Continual risings would take place along our new frontier, the hillmen from Afghanistan proper would begin to raid just as the tribes do on the Indian border, and continual expeditions would be necessary. We should be compelled in the end, just as the British have been, to move the frontier forward repeatedly, and to absorb more territory. So it would go on until our frontier eventually coincided with that of British India. Immense sums of money would be required for the organization and administration of the country taken over, for the construction of roads and fortified positions for large numbers of troops, and to meet the cost of expeditions, etc. Finally, it must be remembered that the people of Afghan Turkestan and Herat, who now look on us as their liberators from Afghan oppression, might, when taken over, change their feeling towards us. The consequence would be that, instead of keeping neighbours well disposed towards us, and ready to assist us when called upon, we should be acquiring fresh responsibilities in the shape of discontented subjects, who would require military garrisons for their control."

In 1878—*i.e.*, twenty-seven years ago—when I was in the Asiatic Section of the Headquarters Staff, I was convinced of the necessity for Russia and Great Britain to work together harmoniously in Asia, and I was opposed to every plan of offensive operations towards India. After our brush with the Afghans at Kushk in 1885, when relations with Great Britain became very strained, and a rupture might have occurred at any moment, we made preparations to concentrate an army in Central Asia in case the British should declare war. I was nominated for the appointment of Chief of the Staff to this force, and at the committee meetings, over which General Vannovski presided, I expressed my opinion openly as to the necessity for a peaceful agreement with Great Britain. I pointed out that the interests of the two Powers on the continent of Asia were identical, for both had to reckon with the natural desire of conquered nationalities to overthrow their masters, and that it would therefore be far more rational for our troops in Central Asia to assist Great Britain in her struggle with the local peoples than for us to advance towards India with the object of raising it against the British. When

I was in command of the Trans-Caspian district from 1890 to 1898, I did everything within my power to maintain peace on the Afghan border, and, after I had succeeded in obtaining the construction of a railway to Kushk, I urged the necessity of coming to an agreement with Great Britain, so that, by joining up the railway systems of India and Turkestan, we might once for all put an end to our rivalry in the Middle East. I still continued to advocate an agreement after becoming War Minister, and my résumé on the Afghan frontier in the report already quoted concluded with the following words:

"I cannot but express my firm conviction that the connection of the Indian and Central Asian railway systems by a line from Chaman to Kushk, via Kandahar and Herat, would create a line of international importance. Such a line would in the future assist the peaceful delimitation of our sphere of influence in Afghanistan, and if Great Britain will abandon her policy of everywhere putting impediments in our path, would facilitate a *rapprochement*[27] based upon the mutual interests of the two nations. Absolutely convinced as I am that the possession of India would in twenty years' time be a misfortune and an insupportable burden for Russia, I consider it both natural and right that we should establish an *entente* with Great Britain, so that in case of any great rising in India we should be on the side of the British. The twentieth century must see a great conflict between the Christian and the other nationalities in Asia. It is essential for the welfare of humanity that we should in such case be allied with the Christian Power against the pagan races."

My opinions on the Chinese, Korean, and Japanese frontiers I will, on account of their importance, quote verbatim, where possible, from my report:

"From the Pamirs almost to the Pacific, we march with China for 6,074 miles. China is about 4,267,000 square miles in extent, and contains about 400,000,000 inhabitants, so that it has the largest population in the world. The great mass of the people are Buddhists, about 20,000,000 are Mohammedans, and about 1,150,000 Christians. Our trade with China, which has been gradually increasing during the last ten years, has risen from £3,100,000 in 1888 to £4,560,000 in 1897.

"Notwithstanding the immense length of this frontier, our exports are insignificant; but it is to be hoped that the railway-line through Manchuria, with its branch to Port Arthur, will alter this unprofitable state of affairs in our favour.[28] Although we have had relations with China for two centuries, and although our frontiers are identical for over 6,000 miles, they have not once been violated by military operations. The number of troops kept in Siberia has always been exceedingly small. This has been due to the generally peaceful disposition of the Chinese, to the position of the River Amur, and other natural obstacles—lofty mountain ranges and vast steppes—and to the absence of any really close tie between China and her subject races nearest to our frontier.

"Our occupation of the Ussuri district necessitated raising new bodies of troops for garrison purposes. Finally, the Chino-Japanese War and its consequences compelled us to take further and rapid action to strengthen our forces in the Far East. This war showed up the extreme political weakness of China on the one hand, and the great power and energy of Japan on the other—facts of immense significance in East Asian affairs. Our frontier with China is of such length that we naturally cannot remain indifferent to this development. Japan betrayed an intention of taking possession of Korea, our neighbour; we were therefore compelled, by force of circumstances, to establish a sort of temporary protectorate over it, and, by an agreement with Japan, Korea was declared to be independent, and was ostensibly left to itself. But we did not confine ourselves to this. For the great services we had rendered China in the war, we obtained on commercial pretexts a concession for a railway through Manchuria from Trans-Baikalia to Vladivostok, and as the immediate consequence of this, we found it necessary to try and get a concession of part of the Kuan-tung Peninsula, with the ports of Dalny and Port Arthur.[29] This forward policy compelled us to augment our forces in the east with troops withdrawn from European Russia, thereby weakening, to a certain extent, our position in the west.[30] Notwithstanding the more active line we have taken up, and the inclusion of the whole of Manchuria within our sphere of influence, we must remember that we are at present quite content with our frontier, and that to change it by the annexation of any portion of Manchuria, for instance, would be in the highest degree undesirable.

"On the extreme western side our boundary, running along the lofty spurs of the Tian-Shan Mountains, is so strong by nature that, although the people of Kashgaria on one side of it are racially akin to our native population in Eastern Turkestan on the other, there would be no gain in altering the boundary. Further north the border-line bisects the basin of the Ili, peopled partly by tribes of the same race. Annexation of the fertile province of Kuldja, projecting like a strong bastion to the east, would, on the contrary, have been of some advantage to us, as it would have facilitated defence, and would have acted as a menace to the Chinese. Such an advantage is of minor importance, however, and not enough to warrant impairing our relations with China. All the way to Manchuria the boundary-line runs across the Mongolian steppes, where its position is sufficiently strong for us to cope both with local conditions and with China's lack of control over her border tribes. Finally, in the extreme east—in Manchuria—the frontier is less assured, and, owing to the construction of a line of railway to connect the Ussuri district with Trans-Baikalia by the shortest route through Manchuria, our position has become disquieting.

"As regards the position of the Chinese province between the Amur district on the north, the Ussuri district on the north-east, and the Kuan-tung Peninsula on the south, the question naturally arises: What shall we do with it in the future? To annex it would be very unprofitable, not to mention the fact that the seizure of this—one of the most important provinces of China—would for ever destroy the ancient peaceful relationship between China and ourselves. It would result in many Manchurians settling in our territory, in the Amur and Ussuri districts, which now are only thinly peopled by Russians, and our weak colonies would be swamped by the flowing tide of yellow. Eastern Siberia would become quite un-Russian, and it must be remembered that it is the Russians alone who form, and will form in the future, the reliable element of the population. Such an inrush of Chinese into the Pri-Amur district would undoubtedly improve the standard of its agriculture and convert its deserts into flowering gardens; but, at the same time, surplus land in Siberia, every acre of which we ought to preserve for our own people, would be passing into the hands of non-Russian races. The population of Russia of the twentieth century will need it all. As this will probably amount to some 400,000,000 in the year 2000, we must begin now to set aside land for at least a quarter of this number. It would, therefore, be preferable if Manchuria remained an integral part of China. But if we decide against its annexation, we ought undoubtedly to take every means to obtain absolute commercial control, consolidating our position by constructing lines through it, such as the Trans-Baikal-Vladivostok and Port Arthur railways. We should not obtain any further concessions from China, but our policy towards her in the near future should be—

"1. Not to permit any increase in, nor development of the training of, her armed forces, particularly in the north, and to forbid the presence of foreign military instructors in that quarter.

"2. To develop our social and commercial relations with her as much as possible, in the northern provinces to commence with.

"3. To avoid as far as possible any dispute on her soil with other European nations, to insure which we should confine our attentions to North China, and undertake no railway enterprises south of the Great Wall, more especially in the Yang-tsze Valley.

"The last portion of our frontier marches with Korea, a country with an area of 80,000 square miles, and containing a population of at least 11,000,000, amongst whom are only some 2,000 to 10,000 Chinese, 45,000 to 55,000 Japanese, and some 300 Europeans.[31] The position of Korea is peculiar; she is subordinate both to China and Japan, and yet, since 1897—by the agreement between ourselves and the latter Power—her independence has been acknowledged. Extreme caution is therefore demanded in our dealings with and our policy concerning her. Though we feel no necessity to annex the country ourselves, we can under no circumstances consent to the establishment in it of an energetic Japan or any other Power. For the present, a Korea, weak, independent, but under our protection, is for us the simplest solution of the question. The immediate establishment of a Protectorate would not only necessitate all sorts of expense, but might drag us unprepared into war. And so in this case, just as in Persia and in North China, we must work systematically towards gradually acquiring absolute economic control of the country. The occupation of the Kuan-tung Peninsula, the permanent fortification of our position there, and the completion of the roads running through Manchuria, are steps in advance, and important ones, in this problem of the future. *At present we are in no way ready to take an active line in Korea, and must, at any cost, avoid stirring up a conflict with Japan on account of Korean affairs.*

"We are certain to encounter Japan's strenuous opposition in our endeavour to obtain control of the Korean markets, even if it be only in the shape of political or mere trade competition, and if we cannot altogether avoid a conflict, we shall in all probability have to fight her in the beginning of the twentieth century."

From this very brief survey of our frontiers it is seen how we are for over 11,000 miles in touch with nine States, and nowhere wish any realignment of our frontier. This is highly satisfactory, and if we are content with our present boundaries, and concern ourselves in the present century solely with the consolidation of the position we have gained during the past 200 years, the danger of war with our neighbours seems remote. For the present generation such a course is absolutely essential. Immense were the sacrifices made by our forebears in adding to our great Empire, but the struggle which is even now necessary to preserve the existence of our frontier regions is so severe that it is retarding still further the naturally slow economic development of the mass of the people in Russia itself. Our border districts exist, in fact, at the expense of the interior of the country, and have up to the present been a source of weakness rather than of strength to the Empire at large. So over-burdened is the present generation with the many requirements necessary for their administration and defence, that to undertake at the same time any fresh foreign enterprises may soon become quite beyond our powers. But with a growing population, will our Empire be content with the existing frontiers, or will Russia have to solve further problems of expansion? And what will they be? Such was the question I put to myself in submitting my report. I considered it natural that Russia, "without increasing her extent either in Europe or Asia," should try in the twentieth century to gain access to warm seas, which are ice-free all the year round, such as the inner Mediterranean seas and the outlets which are open all the year round into the Pacific and Indian Oceans. As regards the difficulties and dangers in undertaking these schemes I said:

"However natural our wishes may be to possess an outlet from the Black Sea and access to the Indian or to the Pacific Oceans, such aims could not be realized without inflicting grave injury upon the interests of almost the whole world. In fact, so much is this the case, that in the pursuit of such aims we must be prepared to fight combinations of any of the following nations: Great Britain, Germany, Austria, Turkey, China, and Japan. It is not the actual move on our part to any of the above-mentioned places that is feared by others, but the consequence of such a move—if successful. The possession of the Bosphorus and the passage into the Mediterranean would enable us to take decisive action as regards the Egyptian question, and to make the Suez Canal international,[32] and our presence on the Indian Ocean would be a continual menace to India. But the chief disturbing element in the minds of the more advanced nations of Europe and America (which are now the factories and workshops of the whole world) would be the fear of our competition in the marts of the world. Having in our hands the main lines of railway connecting the Pacific Ocean and the Baltic Sea, with feeder lines from the Bosphorus, the Indian and Pacific

Oceans, we could, with our inexhaustible natural wealth, control the industry of the globe."

Such has been the recent growth of armaments among all nations that the difficulties which will confront us in any effort to reach warm seas in this century will absolutely put into the shade any faced by us in the past, and the powers of the present generation may well prove unequal to the effort required to gain what is, after all, only necessary for our children's children. Indeed, a comparison of fighting strengths leads to the inevitable conclusion that not only is the present generation too weak to undertake fresh tasks to secure what is necessary for the existence of the 400,000,000 of our future population, but that the relative greater power of our probable enemies makes it extremely difficult to guarantee the integrity of the Empire. The following is the reference to this point in my report:

> "Within the last fifty years the military resources of our neighbours have so increased, and Germany and Austria, more especially, are so much better prepared to invade us, that our western frontier is now exposed to greater danger than it has ever been in the whole of our history.

> "Our military position on the Turkish frontier also is no longer as favourable as it was in the beginning of the nineteenth century. This is particularly the case now that Germany seems to be taking so much interest in Turkish affairs. Again, the defence of the Caucasus has also become difficult. So, too, on the Afghan frontier we now have powerful neighbours, who in organization and armament are more on a level with our troops in Turkestan than they were in the beginning of the last century. An Afghan invasion of our territory is by no means an impossibility, a fact which complicates considerably the defence of Turkestan.

> "China is at present alone in having no army worthy of serious consideration, and she is impotent against us in the Pri-Amur[33] or Kuan-tung districts. But in the place of a weak China has arisen a powerful Japan, whose armed forces may prove a danger to our troops in the Far East until sufficient reinforcements can be sent out.

> "Still, notwithstanding our great length of frontier to be defended and the immense development in the military power of our neighbours, the difficulties in the way of defeating us on our own soil are so obvious and so great that, if we confine our actions to self-defence, no enemy will be likely to attack us."

Finally, an analysis of the strength and resources of our nearest neighbours forced me to the conclusion that *"our western frontier has never in the whole history of Russia been exposed to such danger in the event of a European war as it is now, and that accordingly the attention of the War Department in the first years of the present century should be confined to strengthening our position on that side, and not diverted to aggressive enterprises elsewhere."*

CHAPTER III

The expansion in numbers of our army in the eighteenth and nineteenth centuries, the suitability of our peace and war establishments, and the growth of our neighbours' forces—The growing complication of our defence problems towards the end of the last century.

In the year 1700 our forces numbered 56,000; in 1800, 400,000; while in 1894 our war strength amounted to 2,000,000; but the growth in the nineteenth century was attended by great fluctuations as compared with the gradual increase in the previous 100 years. The universal dissatisfaction with the results of the Crimean War first brought about the awakening of public feeling which ended in the emancipation of the serfs, and the great efforts in the direction of economy made at that time led directly to the reduction of the army. Even while the guns were booming at Königgrätz in 1866, our standing army in Europe was cut down from 600,000 to 372,000 men. It was not long, however, before the Franco-German War opened our eyes to possible dangers from the west. Up to that time we had been living upon tradition, upon experiences of the days when war was waged by standing armies, and did not call for the mobilization of the whole of a nation's forces; when armies moved by road, and several months elapsed between the declaration of war and the first decisive engagement. By her rapid concentration and by her ability to throw an immense army so quickly across the French frontier in 1870, Germany showed also what she would be capable of doing in our direction. We had for a long time neglected to keep up the fortifications on our western frontier, lest we should give Germany cause to suspect that we distrusted the long-standing traditional good feeling between the reigning Houses. The speed, however, with which she disposed, first of Austria, then of France, her immense increase in power, and her evident ambition not only to protect herself, but to gain the hegemony of Europe, together formed a menace against which we were forced to take strong measures. Accordingly our army was again increased as quickly as possible, and between the years 1869 and 1880 the peace strength of the forces in European Russia rose from 366,000 to 535,000 men, arrangements at the same time being made for the mobilization of a field army of 1,500,000. But during the same period our neighbours were able to perfect their own arrangements still more, both in the number of men mobilized and the speed of their concentration. From a force whose strength was the same in peace and war our war army now became so large that it merited the title of "national." But even a national army is not enough nowadays. For the successful conduct of a conflict against a powerful opponent, a struggle which calls for the exertion of every effort—moral, mental, and physical— the whole nation itself must take part. In other words, to achieve success with an army mainly composed of men called up for actual operations, the people must be in sympathy with it, must recognize the importance and magnitude of its task, and must back it up unreservedly.

The war of 1870–71 was prosecuted by the Germans in a truly national spirit. The attitude of all grades of society towards the racial struggle entered upon by their Government was one of the highest patriotism. The good tone and unselfish devotion of the troops was well supported by the wave of patriotic feeling which, starting with the Prussians, ran through all the German nationalities from King down to peasant. It is a platitude that the German school-teacher was the real victor in the war of 1870–71. This figure of speech can perhaps be more truthfully expressed in another way: the French were not conquered by the German troops, but by the German nation, which gave to the army both its sons and its moral support. There was no such close union between the French Emperor, the French army, and the French people. It was not France which fought Germany, but the French army. The result we know. When the country was overrun by the invader, the people, with few exceptions, did not exhibit a proper patriotic spirit, nor did they assist the soldiers to wage a national war. Some of the intelligent sections of the populace, indeed, thought fit to carry on an internal strife directed towards the overthrow of their Government whilst the war was actually in progress, and as soon as the Imperial forces were beaten and the Emperor taken prisoner, they succeeded in their effort.

In this sense we fought against Turkey under favourable conditions in 1877–78. The sympathies of our people for the closely related Slav races in the Balkan Peninsula had been aroused by the preceding struggle of the Servians against the Turks, and we were, moreover, fighting our traditional enemy. Consequently, many volunteers and large sums of money found their way from Russia into Servia. Society, worked up by the Press, was deeply moved, and brought pressure upon the Government to declare war, while active operations were of course the one desire of our soldiers. The eventual declaration of hostilities was hailed with acclamation. As has been explained, the slowness of our concentration in Bessarabia permitted the further training of our troops, especially of the reservists, and of the selection of the best men for command, and we consequently moved into Turkey fairly well prepared. Our troops were in the best of spirits, and their belief in victory boundless. But valuable time had elapsed, and the resistance of the Turks was far more determined than anything we had expected. However, we reinforced rapidly, broke down all opposition, and eventually reached the walls of Constantinople. It really seemed as if we were on this occasion about to take full advantage of what had been done by our army, and place the protection of our Black Sea coast on a permanent basis. But we hesitated and delayed operations in front of the enemy's capital, and so allowed the fruit of our military success to be snatched from us by the ill-timed action of diplomacy. Great Britain's incorrect appreciation of the Eastern Question in 1877, combined with our distrust of Austria, and, most important of all, the fact that we were tired of war in high quarters, led to results quite out of proportion to the sacrifices we had made. When the Agreement of San Stefano was replaced by the Treaty of Berlin, the national feeling of optimistic patriotism gave way to general dissatisfaction. Victors in war, we had been beaten in politics.

Within twenty-five years Russia waged two European wars, which were prematurely concluded. In 1850 at Sevastopol we acknowledged ourselves beaten at a moment when our enemies were themselves powerless to proceed. In 1878, though we had reached the very walls of Constantinople, we did not occupy it, and though we had conquered the country, we acknowledged that we alone were not strong enough to guarantee the peaceful development even of those districts of the Black Sea littoral which had belonged to us before. But these results, though surprising and disappointing to the army and the nation at large, brought their compensations. It was the Berlin Congress that proved to us in unmistakable terms that we were alone on the Continent of Europe, and showed how necessary it was for us to set our house in order on the western border, if we did not wish to be taken unawares by neighbours already prepared. But it was no simple matter to improve our military position on that side—especially towards Germany—so that it might be on a level with that of our possible adversary. It meant large expenditure in the construction and improvement of fortresses, the making of roads, and the collection of reserves of supplies, at a time when our financial resources had been crippled, and the War Department, instead of having increased funds at its disposal, was receiving a smaller grant than before the war. In our generosity we had taken so small an indemnity from Turkey, and had allowed payment to be spread over so long a period, that it could not be used—as was France's indemnity to Germany—as an "iron fund" towards the expenses of the war and the betterment of the army. About this time, also, the feeling of disquiet caused by the state of our western frontier was increased by fresh complications arising on the Asiatic side of the Empire.

The first time we made any effort to use our position in Central Asia indirectly in furtherance of our general policy was in 1878, when we sent a force to Djam (near Samarkand), with the object of causing embarrassment to Great Britain, then at war with Afghanistan. This attempt to force Great Britain to give us a free hand in the Near East by means of pressure applied elsewhere (on the Afghan frontier) was not successful. By Stolietoff's mission to Kabul the Afghans were assured of Russian assistance against Great Britain, but when the British marched into their country in force we held aloof. When the Amir Shere Ali died, the country was again thrown into complete disorder. From Samarkand Abdur Rahman went into Afghanistan, and endeavoured to enlist the sympathies and obtain the assistance of some of the tribes in his attempts to gain the throne; he also tried hard to obtain our support. But it was the British who gave him assistance, and, whether for good or evil, he remembered this fact during the whole of his reign, and was our enemy. In 1877–79 we might easily have converted Afghanistan into a friendly "buffer State" between us and India, but in spite of General Kaufmann's representations we failed to seize the psychological moment, and the "buffer" subsequently created by Great Britain was one hostile to us. Thanks to this short-sighted policy of ours with regard to this country, we lost prestige in Central Asia for some time, and numerous English emissaries charged with the task of stirring up the warlike Turkomans against us penetrated into the steppes of Turkestan. Raids by Turkomans into our territory on the eastern shores of the Caspian became more frequent and more daring, eventually reaching even as far as Krasnovodsk. We could no longer hold our hand, and decided to send an expedition into the steppes to seize Geok Tepe. The failure of the first expedition under Lomakin, and the heavy losses suffered at Geok Tepe under General Skobeleff, were signs that we might expect serious trouble in Central Asia, and would therefore have to increase our garrisons there, and also—which was more important—to improve the communications with Russia. The example of what happened to the Italians in Abyssinia showed what even pastoral tribes, if patriotic and well led, can do against European regular troops. It became increasingly clear that to leave our districts in Central Asia, 1,335 miles by road from Orenburg—Russia's outpost—with such small garrisons as they then had, was, under the then complicated conditions, to court disaster. We therefore began the construction of the Central Asian railway system, which reached completion only two years ago.[34] These lines cost a large sum, which had to be provided at the expense of our preparations on the western frontier and in the Far East; but the wisdom of our action was amply proved in 1885 during the frontier trouble, ending in the defeat of the Afghan troops at Kushk.[35] After negotiations with Great Britain, which at some periods became almost critical, a *modus vivendi* was reached, and our present frontier with Afghanistan, delimitated by a special mixed Boundary Commission, has not been violated for the twenty years of its existence. I repeat that it is my firm conviction that this frontier is in every way satisfactory to us, and to alter it by advancing to Herat[36] would in no way be beneficial. The period of small expeditions, always ending in some slight increase to our territory, ceased with the delimitation of this frontier. Of the two nations who now march with us in Central Asia—the Persians and the Afghans—the latter possesses such large armed forces that we should need a considerable army to carry out any advance into their country, irrespective of any assistance that might be given to them by Great Britain. On the other hand, the defence of our own extensive territory has become a very difficult matter, chiefly owing to the spread of the Pan-Slav[37] propaganda, and were the Afghans to attempt an invasion on the pretext of liberating our subject races, partial risings of the population are quite possible. We must, therefore, maintain sufficient troops in those regions, not only in case of war, but also to prevent internal trouble. In this way our position in Central Asia has become more complicated during the last forty years—in fact, ever since we took Tashkent. Now, instead of the five or six battalions with which we conquered the country, we have two whole army corps in Turkestan.

Just as had been the case when the Emperor Alexander II. came to the throne, a great effort in the direction of military economy was made after the accession of Alexander III., and the army was reduced by 28,000 men; but the conclusion of the Triple Affiance and the rapid growth of our neighbours' armaments brought about a fresh increase in the army, as well as a *rapprochement* between ourselves and France, who was equally menaced. To the creation of new units by Germany and Austria we replied by raising fresh troops or by transferring men from the Caucasus and the interior to the western frontier. In this severe race of preparation for war we were unable to keep up with our western neighbours, not so much in point of mere numbers as in necessary organization. We were too poor and too backward, for modern mobilization entails heavy drafts upon the whole reserve forces of a State, and is deeply felt by the whole nation. This is what that distinguished German writer, Von der Goltz, implied when he wrote that modern wars must be waged by armed nations, not by armies. Other things being equal, success is assured to the side which can quickest concentrate superior numbers in the field. These forces must not only be under competent leaders, but must be well supplied, reinforced, and equipped. It was chiefly in this respect that we soon felt our inferiority. By forming cadres without any strength, or with a very small strength, we are able, thanks to our large population, our numerous reserves and militia, to mobilize an immense number of troops of sorts—regulars, reservists, reserve units, and militia. But owing to the shortage of officers and lack of supplies, these units would vary much in their value for war. While our advanced troops only could be concentrated as quickly as those of our neighbours, the reserve troops could be mobilized but slowly, the reserve units would be quite inadequate, and, finally, the militia would not be embodied at the same time as the others, and even then only with great difficulty. But though we had plenty of men and horses, *matériel*—particularly technical stores—was insufficient (telegraphs, telephones, balloons, pigeon post, light railways, explosives, tools, wire, etc.). Owing to the constant advances in scientific knowledge, and to the continual demands made for increased strength in construction, fortresses are no sooner built than the whole of their masonry has to be remodelled. We could not, therefore, keep our armaments and defences up to date, and they were largely obsolete. Though our siege artillery had received a certain number of good and modern guns, it was not equal to our neighbours' in mobility, and we did not possess nearly enough technical troops, such as sappers, and mining and railway companies. There was no organization either for peace or war of the auxiliary services for the line of communications; the depôt troops it was proposed to form would not have been sufficient; and there were no means of keeping up the numbers of officers and doctors. But our greatest danger lay in the inferiority of our railways.

After 1882 we made great advances in efficiency, but only arrived at such a point that we were able to carry out a concentration on the frontier in double the time it would have taken our neighbours, so that not only were we condemned to the defensive, but our forces coming up in succession would be destroyed in detail. Since the lesson of 1870–71, we had become reconciled to the fact that we should never be able to catch up Germany in speed of mobilization, but we had flattered ourselves that in this respect we were ahead of Austria. Some ten or eleven years ago we were undeceived on this point also. The Austrian War Department had succeeded in working wonders in preparing the probable area of operations on our side for both attack and defence, and, owing to the many strategic lines of rail constructed through the Carpathians, this range had ceased to be a dangerous obstacle in rear of their advanced position.[38] Besides the sums allotted for the ordinary expenditure on the army, both the Austrians and the Germans had had recourse to extraordinary and special grants; thus their storehouses were filled, their fortresses well built and equipped, and their roads constructed. Not only did our lack of funds handicap us in these directions, but our backward state of development proved an insuperable bar, especially as regards the construction of railways. With our neighbours, the directions in which strategic lines of rail were required coincided generally with their economic alignment. With us the two requirements were at variance, and each strategic line proposed on our side met with the opposition of the Finance Department as being economically unsound.

In the Far East we had little trouble for many years. Though our frontier with China was 6,000 miles long, it was not till 1880—twenty-seven years ago—that the increase in Japan's military power and the awakening of China compelled us to think about strengthening our position in that quarter.

In 1871, when the western provinces of China[39] were convulsed by the Mohammedan rebellion, we occupied the province of Kuldja in order to safeguard our own borders. The inhabitants—the Dunganites and

Taranchites—who had previously completely defeated the Chinese and some of the Kalmuits, gave us very little trouble, and laid down their arms on our definite promise to make them Russian subjects. But while our soldiers were doing their work on the spot, our diplomats in their offices miles away, without consulting any of those with local knowledge, such as Kaufmann or Kolpakovski, thought fit to promise the Chinese that as soon as they quelled the revolt and arrived as far as Kuldja, that province could be restored to them. As a matter of fact, we hoped, of course, that they would be unable to defeat Yakub Beg, and so would never gain possession of Kashgaria, and yet we were helping them towards this very object. The position was a curious one, and in 1876, when I, as Russian envoy, was in Yakub Beg's camp near Kurlia[40] negotiating as to the delimitation of the boundary of Fergana, just conquered by us, he himself remarked on it. He very justly reproached me with the fact that while I was dealing with him, another officer of the General Staff, one Lieutenant-Colonel Sosnovski, was, with the knowledge of the Russian authorities, supplying the Chinese troops moving against him. His statement was absolutely correct. After Yakub Beg's sudden death the Chinese quickly got possession of the whole of Kashgaria, advanced up to the southern edge of Kuldja, and asserted their rights to that province also. While Kaufmann urged most strenuously that we ought not to return the province to them, we procrastinated. In 1878, when I was at the head of the Asiatic Section of the General Staff, I put a memorandum before my Chief, Count Heyden, in which I pointed out the great strategic value of Kuldja to us. I also stated that, if we felt bound by our loosely given engagement to return this province to China, we should most certainly be justified in demanding compensation for the expenses incurred by us during our eight years' occupation. I suggested a sum of £10,000,000 in gold, as being suitable and also opportune for the construction of the Siberian Railway. My contention was supported by Kaufmann, but our diplomatists were against it. A special committee, consisting of M. Giers, Minister for Foreign Affairs; Admiral Grieg, Minister of Finance; Generals Kaufmann, Obrucheff, and myself, under the presidency of Count Milutin, was appointed to go into the question by the Emperor Alexander II. M. Giers and Admiral Grieg were in favour of returning Kuldja to China without demanding any compensation. Admiral Grieg asserted that Russia was in no particular need of money, and both Ministers held that we were bound by the promise to China—a promise lightly made by our diplomats without the knowledge of the men on the spot—while the other engagement made with the Dunganites and Taranchites in 1871 could be forgotten. After prolonged discussions, it was decided to return Kuldja to China, and to ask for £500,000 as compensation. The member who was most opposed to obtaining a large sum of money from China was, of all people, the Finance Minister; he apparently overlooked the possibility that would be conferred by this sum of carrying out the construction of the Siberian Railway ten years sooner. For this oversight we paid later. Meanwhile the Chinese assumed a stiff attitude, and threatened to seize Kuldja, moving troops towards it to Urumchi, Manas, Kunia-Turfan, and other points. We, in reply, hastily strengthened our position by sending up troops from Tashkent towards Kuldja. In 1880 we fortified the Barokhorinski ridge, separating it from parts of Chinese Turkestan in the occupation of the Chinese. I was in command of our advanced guard, and saw how gladly our troops would have obeyed the order to advance. They were disgusted at the thought of having to abandon the splendid country of which we had been in occupation for nearly ten years, and at the idea of breaking faith with the people to whom we had promised protection, who were even then crowding round our camps in alarm at the rumour that we were going to hand them over to the Chinese. Of course, at the time this question was decided we entertained a very exaggerated idea of the value of the Chinese troops themselves, and also of China's military resources.

Events afterwards moved rapidly. We commenced the construction of the railway through Manchuria, and occupied the Kuan-tung Peninsula, thus alarming not only China, but Japan.

Thus, during the last quarter of the nineteenth century matters became more involved on all sides. Not only did we have to meet the preparations of Austria and Germany on the west, and threatened trouble in our frontier districts near Roumania, Turkey, and Afghanistan, but from 1896 to 1900 we had, in addition, to face the problem of safeguarding the position we had suddenly—and, for the War Department, unexpectedly—taken up in the Far East in our advance to the Pacific Ocean. The magnitude of the task of protecting 11,000 miles of frontier, and of keeping up forces so as to be in a position to fight different combinations of no less than nine adjacent States, conveys some idea of the colossal expense involved.

CHAPTER IV

Deductions drawn from the work of the army in the past 200 years, which may serve as some guide for the line our military policy should take in the beginning of the twentieth century.

During the eighteenth and nineteenth centuries the energies of the country were mainly absorbed in expansion and consolidation. In the prosecution of these objects we were engaged in many wars, and the experience thereby gained should help to indicate what is in store for the War Department in the future. The following appear to be the principal deductions that can be drawn from the past:

1. The duties in connection with our movement towards the shores of the Baltic and Black Seas, the expansion of Russian territory to the west (White Russia, Little Russia, Poland), to the south (Caucasus), to the east (Central Asia), were carried out by the army. From the analysis of our frontiers already made in Chapter II., it will be seen that, thanks to what has been done, *Russia is in no need of any further increase of territory. This conclusion is in the highest degree important and satisfactory. At the same time, our military position does not now compare so favourably as formerly with that of our neighbours, principally owing to our lack of railways, and our western frontiers are exposed to great danger through the perfect state of preparation of Germany and Austria.*

2. For only seventy-two years in the preceding two centuries did we enjoy peace; during the remaining time Russia was engaged in thirty-three external and two internal wars. On an average, therefore, wars occurred every six years. They were particularly frequent during the first half of the nineteenth century, while in the latter portion, if the campaigns in the Caucasus and in Asia be excepted, we were only twice engaged in hostilities—in 1853–55 and in 1877–78. We entered the present century after twenty-two years' continuous peace, a longer interval than had occurred for 200 years; but during this time many possible causes for hostilities had arisen on all sides. Not only had the Empire become oppressed with the burden of armed peace, but the strain was so tense that there were grounds for fearing lest "guns should begin to shoot of their own accord." The commencement of each of the three past centuries are full enough of sad memories for Russia; it might, therefore, have been expected, taking into consideration the military forces which were straining at the leash, that the beginning of the twentieth century would not be free from war clouds. It only needed a spark on one part of the frontier to kindle conflagration everywhere. Serious potential causes for hostilities existed on the western, Turkish, and Afghan frontiers, and in 1895 there was an actual *casus belli* on the Chinese border. In such circumstances

international affairs required the most delicate handling, in order to avoid creating any additional excuses for war.

3. If the Caucasus be excluded, we were engaged on our own soil in only six campaigns, lasting for six and a half years, out of all the struggles during this period, the remainder being waged beyond our frontiers. This conferred great advantages on us, and showed the high state of our preparation in those days as compared with that of our enemies. The offensive has such immense advantage over the defensive that we should always strive, by being as ready as our neighbours, to be in a position to attack.

4. In the twenty-six battles of the nineteenth century, the casualties out of 1,500,000 combatants amounted to 323,000—i.e., almost 22 per cent. The heaviest were at Austerlitz—21,000 out of 75,000 engaged; at Borodino— 40,000 out of 120,000 engaged; and at Sevastopol—85,000 out of 235,000 engaged. The following table shows our total losses in the two centuries:

PROBABLE LOSSES IN THE FUTURE

	Numbers Engaged.	Casualties		
		Killed and Wounded.	Sick.	Total.
Eighteenth century	4,910,000	350,000	1,030,000	1,380,000
Nineteenth century	4,900,000	610,000	800,000	1,410,000
Total	9,810,000	960,000	1,830,000	2,790,000

While the numbers engaged, therefore, were practically the same in both centuries, the losses in killed and wounded in the nineteenth were almost double those in the eighteenth; this indicates the more deadly character of war in the former period, and shows also that the losses became greater as weapons became perfected.[41] If we assume that Russia will probably have to put the same number of men in the field in the twentieth century as in the past, and that the growth of casualties will be in the same proportion, we must be prepared to face losses amounting to 2,000,000 killed and wounded—*i.e.*, 40 per cent. of those engaged.

5. To keep pace with our neighbours' continually improving preparation, there is no doubt Russia will be compelled to increase her war establishment. In our victorious combat with Turkey in 1827–29, the greatest strength to which our army ever rose in one campaign was 155,000 men, while in 1877–78 the highest figure reached was 850,000. Our maximum in the Prussian War of 1756–62 was only 130,000. I am thankful to say we have lived at peace with our western neighbour for 150 years; but if we were to fight in the west without allies now, ten times that number would be insufficient to defeat the German army, and—what is the main thing—crush the patriotism of the armed nation behind it. It follows, therefore, that we must not only be prepared in the present century to take the field with forces that are huge in comparison with those of former days, but also to face the colossal initial expenditure and recurrent cost demanded by their creation and maintenance.

6. In the eighteenth and in the first half of the nineteenth century our army was a long-service one, formed on the European model, well armed, and in spite of its lack of training, quite equal to the forces of Sweden, France, or Prussia, while we were superior in organization, armament, and training to our chief foe—Turkey. About the middle of the last century we began to fall behind the western nations in equipment and in all the technical means of destruction. At the battle of Borodino our firearms were not inferior to those of the French, but at Sevastopol we had only smooth-bore muskets, excellent for making a noise, for performing rifle exercises or bayonet fighting, but inaccurate, and of short range.

7. It became only too clear during our last wars—in 1853–55 and 1877–78—that many of our senior officers were unfit for their work under modern and complicated conditions. The juniors were brave and active within the limits of their duties, but insufficiently educated. Officers commanding units were, with some brilliant exceptions, quite incapable of making the most out of the fighting qualities of their troops; but weakest of all were our generals—our brigade, division, and army corps commanders. The majority were incapable of commanding all three arms in action, and knew neither how to insure cohesion among the units under them, nor to keep touch with the forces on either side. The feeling of mutual support was therefore with us quite undeveloped. Indeed, it often happened that while one of our forces was being destroyed, the commander of some other force close by remained inactive under the plea of not having received any orders.

8. Generally speaking, at the time of the Crimea and Turkish War (of 1877–78) our troops had practically no tactical training, and we did not know how to attain the best results with the minimum of loss. In the attack we advanced

almost in column, and suffered heavily; while very little use was ever made of the auxiliary arms—cavalry, artillery, and sappers—indeed, they were almost forgotten. But we had one strong point: we were not afraid to die, and only asked to be shown in which direction sacrifice was required of us.

9. Judging by the experiences of the wars of these two centuries, in order to insure success in the future we must be prepared to concentrate a superior force. Without superiority in numbers our troops were unable, especially in the attack, to defeat Swedes, Frenchmen, or, in the last war, Turks.

10. But, quite apart from the grave question of how best to make ready to oppose the armies of our western neighbours, 2 millions strong, the War Department has to take into account the 40,000,000 of non-Russian subjects, many of whom live in our Asiatic frontier districts and in the Caucasus, for their attitude really determines the number of men we must leave for the defence of those frontiers in case of a European war.

11. Finally, the work of the Department became still more complicated in the concluding years of the last century, owing to the greater frequency of the calls upon the troops to take part in the suppression of civil disorder in Russia itself. The discontent of all grades of the population has increased of recent years, and revolutionary propaganda have found in this dissatisfaction their most favourable soil; even the army has not escaped infection. It therefore appears that the maintenance of order in the interior of our country will not be the smallest task of the War Department in the coming century.

12. In the last twenty-five years not only Germany and Austria, but our other neighbours, have perfected the organization of their forces, and have arrived at a pitch of excellence which will enable them either to take up a strong defensive, or rapidly to carry the war into our territory; consequently, we have to face greater expenditure, and arrange for larger concentrations also on the Roumanian, Turkish, and Afghan frontiers. We were at peace for nearly two hundred years on the Chinese border, but events occurred within the last fifteen years of the last century which forced us to begin increasing our insignificant forces then in the Far East, although we quite realized that our best policy was to keep peace with China, and to avoid rupture with Japan. *Thus the chief duty of the War Department in the first years of the present century is the defence of our frontiers. Of these, our Austrian and German borders, being the most dangerous, should receive our particular attention.*

There is no doubt that to carry on an energetic offensive is our best protection. But our power to do this does not depend upon the action of our War Department alone: it depends upon the relative national efficiencies. The more fully developed and efficient a nation is, the more numerous are its war resources of every sort. But the one factor which nowadays determines more than all else the nature and direction of operations is the railways. In this connection we have noted the large number of lines at the disposal of our neighbours in the west, and that is precisely the front upon which we are handicapped almost to actual impotence by our backwardness. There are so many other urgent calls for the expenditure of money that the construction of purely strategic and economically unremunerative lines seems wasteful and the cost prohibitive. For this reason our strategy on this side calls for the greatest care and thought in order that we may conduct as active a defence as possible. The next thing to do after admitting our present disadvantages is to realize that it is upon this frontier that the largest portion of the funds available for military purposes should be spent, while the remainder can be apportioned between all our other frontiers. It is clear that we were in no position to spend money on the Far East, and after the forward moves made in that direction from 1896–1900, it was realized that in that quarter the purely defensive was our best policy. The *communiqué* of our Government of June 24, 1900, informed the whole world of our intention not to annex the territory we were then occupying in Manchuria, and gave us every reason to suppose that if we kept our engagements no trouble with China and Japan was likely.

13. Even in the concluding years of the last century Russia was not preparing for any further advance in the Far East, but was fully occupied with the defence of her western front and with the maintenance of internal order. Thus, our unexpected forward movement, first in Manchuria and then to the shores of the Pacific Ocean, found the War Department as surprised as it was unprepared. In such circumstances our promise not to annex Manchuria was a very necessary one, not only on account of our desire not to disturb our friendly relations with China, but because we were aware of our military unreadiness in that part of the world. In the report I submitted in 1900 regarding the duties of the Department in the early future, I said:

> "While we must be prepared to defend our interests upon the Pacific Ocean, in Afghanistan, Persia, and Turkey, and also to fight at sea, we cannot afford either the men or the money to be at the same time equal in power to our western neighbours. We have given to Germany and Austria a decided advantage by directing our attention to the Far East. This disturbance of the balance of power menaces the integrity of the Empire, and I sincerely believe that it will not be permitted to continue by the Tsar. As the War Department's first task, therefore, I propose to develop the efficiency of our forces on the western frontier, and to formulate a definite plan of operations for them."

From our Ally's point of view, also, it was only right to attend to this at once, for our comparative weakness on this side would in case of war allow the Powers of the Triple Alliance to contain us with quite a small force on our frontier and to crush France by overwhelming numbers.

14. Our land forces bore the brunt of the national struggles during this period. After Peter the Great's time the rôle of the Russian fleet in all the wars in which we were engaged was insignificant. In the last two great wars of the last century we particularly needed the co-operation of the fleet, but our sailors at Sevastopol fought on land, owing to our naval inefficiency. In the war of 1877–78 the Turks had no fleet on the Black Sea. Russia is undoubtedly a land Power; the small part played in the past by the fleet, therefore, was not accidental, but natural. If we had spent large sums in this period on our navy, we should only have made our position worse, for it was only by immense expenditure on the army that we were able to win. History has taught us that we should follow in our fathers' footsteps, and, considering the army as Russia's right arm, spend upon it the larger part of the sums allotted by the Ministry of Finance for general military needs. But our active ventures in the Far East forced us into naval expenditure, which was arranged for in the last years of last century by starving the army finances. The result is alarming. On this point I wrote in my report of 1900:

> "If in the future the fleet is to be increased at the expense of the army, and if the increase of our forces on the eastern frontier is to be made at the expense of those stationed on the western, then our already weak position in regard to Germany and Austria will become still worse. With the growth of our navy will arise questions of coaling stations and ports, and as our expenditure on these as well as on our ships grows heavier, it will entail retrenchment on our most important frontier—that in Europe. Once our fleet had destroyed the Turkish sailing fleet at Sinope, it became impotent, despite its high *moral*, for it then had to contend against steam, against which it was powerless."

15. In the war of 1877–78 we had an unfortunate experience. The Turks, whom we had conquered previously, although we had to fight against huge odds, were on this occasion organized on the European system by European instructors, and were better armed than we were. Their firearms had been made in the workshops of Germany and England, and were far superior to ours.[42] Now, other conditions being equal, not only does the better weapon tend to victory, because it causes greater loss, but because—and this is far more important—the knowledge of being better armed bestows confidence. Possessed of a weapon even but little inferior to that of an

enemy, men are inclined to ascribe their own faults to the superiority of the enemy's armament. There was in this respect no such difference between us and the Turks in 1877–78 as had existed in 1853–55; but still, after our first misfortune at Plevna, our army lost confidence in its rifles and guns, and ascribed its misfortunes to the superior armament of the Turks. Everything, therefore, points to the necessity of keeping up to date in armament. In the past our difficulty in keeping pace with the various improvements so rapidly introduced was increased by the fact that we not only had to re-arm the regular army, but had to create an immense stock of weapons for the reserve troops, militia, depôt troops, and again as a reserve for the whole of the forces.

16. In our wars with minor enemies (such as Turks, Caucasians, and Central Asians) we were victorious, owing to our great numerical superiority. In meeting nations of a higher civilization than our own (such as the Swedes and the French), we generally suffered very heavily at first, but won in the end, in spite of our comparative lack of skill, owing to our dogged bravery and determination. Peter the Great carried on the struggle for nine years from Narva to Poltava, and Alexander I. fought for the same period between Austerlitz and the entry of our troops into Paris. The objects of these wars were clear to our troops, and the men were inspired to fight on to the end at all costs. As a result, our troops did win. In the Crimea, and in 1877–78, not only was our object in fighting vague, but the wars were prematurely finished before the army or the nation had really put out their strength, and in spite of our sacrifices and losses, we were in both cases unsuccessful. Every war brings in its train much unhappiness to both sides, and the loss of a campaign is for a great nation a supreme misfortune and one overwhelming the machinery of government. Therefore, strive as it may against commencing hostilities, when once a country takes up arms it should continue to fight until it wins; otherwise it will lose the right to be considered a great nation, and will become a "collection of mere ethnographical material," from which other nationalities may be strengthened. The following words of my report of 1900 are as applicable to-day as when I wrote them:

> "Crises of world-wide importance arise suddenly, and are not prevented by the unpreparedness of a nation for war. On the contrary, the knowledge of unreadiness in any quarter only leads to a desire to take advantage of it in others. Therefore a struggle such as has never been seen in the world may come sooner than we think. It may burst forth even contrary to the wish of the Tsar, and against the interests of Russia. This would be a great calamity for the whole world. But particularly calamitous for Russia would be any cessation by her, before complete victory was achieved, of a war once started.

"*In the event of disaster in the first campaign, and after the first and serious consequences of war—famine, disease, paralysis of trade, and, above all, heavy losses—have made themselves felt, the Russian monarch's character will need to be of iron to enable him to resist the universal clamour that will be raised to accept defeat and make peace.*"

CHAPTER V

The work before the War Department in the concluding years of the last, and the early years of the present, century—Money allotted to it from 1898–1903—Inadequacy of these sums to meet the demands—Measures which it was possible to undertake—Steps taken to improve and consolidate our position in the Far East.

In the *Russki Invalid* (No. 143 of 1895) an article appeared in reply to one by Demchinski, which had been published in the *Slovo* under the title of "Were we Ready for War?" Demchinski endeavoured to prove that we spend more than other countries on national defence; that the amounts allotted for this purpose in Russia are ample; that the measures brought forward as necessary in order to prepare our army for war are merely a cloak for extortion; and that lack of financial control in our administration allows great openings for the misappropriation of funds. In replying, the article in the *Russki Invalid* quoted from the standard works of Professor Maksheeff upon the army estimates of Germany and Russia from 1888 to 1900. During these thirteen years the expenditure amounted to £358,100,000 in Germany, and £347,900,000 in Russia. Therefore Germany, with half our peace strength, spent in that period £10,000,000 more than we did. The enormous length of our frontiers, amongst other things, forces us to maintain twice as many men in peace as Germany. Even of the lesser sum for greater numbers that we spend, we are obliged to allot almost the whole to meet maintenance charges (food, uniform, etc.). So that not only do we spend less money than Germany on the whole, but we can afford proportionately less on "special or extraordinary services," which include those of preparing the army for war. On this important question the writer of the article in the *Russki Invalid* expresses himself much to the point:

> "As the ordinary expenditure is urgent, and cannot be postponed, it calls for no comment, being allotted, in fact, to measures to which we are already committed. With regard to the measures which come under the head of extraordinary expenditure, the case is different. They are not urgent in the sense that we are absolutely committed to them, and they are, therefore, as a matter of course, not urgent in the opinion of those unversed in military matters. Consequently these persons are inclined to refuse sanction to such measures, to postpone them, or, under the most favourable circumstances, to spread their execution over a considerable period. The result is bad for national defence and for the preparation of the army for war. Our forces might suddenly be called upon to take the field with inferior armament, with insufficient and unserviceable supplies, and

without well-organized communications. Upon analyzing the German army estimates, one is struck with the comparative magnitude of the initial and extraordinary expenditure, which shows that, although her army is half the strength of ours, she spends vastly more money on it than we do on ours."

Our comparative unreadiness for war, in spite of our possessing a large standing army, first became evident, as I have mentioned, as far back as 1870, when the Germans were able to throw an immense army across the French frontier in a fortnight, and conduct a victorious campaign with extraordinary speed. The Turkish War of 1877–78, again, exposed our weak points in organization and mobilization, and profiting by its lessons, many measures towards improvement were undertaken during Count Milutin's régime at the Ministry of War. The new grouping of the Powers and the formation of the Triple Alliance, also, were events which emphasized the necessity for us to set our house in order as regards defence. During the sixteen years from 1882 to 1898 Generals Vannovski and Obrucheff, guided by the opinions of the leading generals in command of troops, managed to increase the efficiency of the army and at the same time to strengthen our defences. On the western frontier a system of fortified positions was organized, and reserves of supplies collected at strategic points; but, owing to the inadequate development of our railway system, it became necessary, in addition, to increase the number of troops permanently stationed in the western military districts. Steps were also taken for the defence of the Baltic and Black Sea coasts. But our attention was chiefly, and quite rightly, confined to the west, and as small appropriations as possible were made for the Caucasus, Turkestan, and the Siberian Military Districts. Thus, in Siberia, from the Pacific to the Ural Mountains, we only had a few battalions, and not a single fortress; nor did we have any fortified posts in Turkestan. To strengthen the troops on the western frontier, indeed, we took troops from the Caucasus, and to find money for the formation of new units, we had to reduce the strength of those in Turkestan. This was done on the supposition that if we were strong on the German side, no one would attack us in the Caucasus or in Asia. In other words, our efforts were concentrated upon the most dangerous frontier. But even then, taking into consideration the many wants of the army, the sum available for our western side, though large, was insufficient to place us in all respects on a level with both Germany and Austria. Though great results were obtained as regards the acceleration of our mobilization, and some very useful strategic lines of railway were constructed, our speed of concentration could not be compared to that of our neighbours, with their better-developed railway systems. However economically the War Ministry treated those measures which were unessential, and could therefore be shelved temporarily, progress with the urgent services was not as rapid as could be desired. Confronted as it was, therefore, with many demands of the western frontier still unsatisfied, the Department, on the whole, could not but be a convinced opponent of a forward policy in the Far East, in Afghanistan, or in Persia. This practically represents the state of affairs and the feeling of the Department right up to the outbreak of the Chino-Japanese War in 1894.

In 1898 I succeeded General Vannovski as War Minister, General Sakharoff taking the place of General Obrucheff.[43] We fully recognized the necessity, when framing the estimates, of pursuing the same policy as our predecessors, and of placing first and foremost the improvement of our military position on the west, but we had by this time taken steps in the Far East which made it impossible to confine our expenditure in that quarter to the small amount of previous years. Events out there had moved rapidly, and were such as called for expenditure of men and money in Kuan-tung, Manchuria, and in the Pri-Amur region.

A schedule is drawn up for the allocation of the expenditure of the sum allotted to the War Ministry. In this, with the previous consent of the Finance Branch, the War Minister frames a general estimate for five years, in which the services are divided up according as the expenditure is to be capital or recurring. The estimates for new and important services entailing initial expenditure are, after being examined by the Military Council, scrutinized by a special committee before being approved. This committee is presided over by the President of the Department of State Economy, and the Finance Minister and the State Comptroller are members. The final list of measures to be undertaken during the five-year period are then submitted to the Tsar for sanction. The exposition of all the army's requirements constitutes one of the most important duties of the War Minister. Firstly, all general officers in command of districts[44] submit to the Tsar statements as to their requirements for the troops under their command, as well as those for works, such as fortresses, railways, etc. The heads of the chief departments—commissariat, artillery, engineers, etc.—draw up their estimates as to buildings, mobilization, and educational requirements, etc. These are classified according as they demand initial or recurring expenditure, and many of the more important items are examined in the Military Council or by special committees. This was the complicated procedure necessary in 1897 and 1898 to fix the total sum required by the War Department during the five years 1898 to 1903 for the maintenance of the army and the improvement of its military efficiency. The very limited amount allotted during the twenty years preceding this period had literally been doled out, not according to the needs of the army, but according to the amount available in the Treasury; consequently the need of money had gone on increasing cumulatively, until in 1898 we were face to face with a situation which demanded greater sacrifices than ever.

Early in 1898 a general statement had been drawn up by my predecessor's orders to show our urgent requirements. By this it was clear that, in order to satisfy all our wants, a *supplementary* allotment of £56,500,000 was absolutely necessary beyond the sum required for the five-year schedule. This amount included expenditure on two items of a very special nature: the re-armament of the field artillery with quick-firing guns (£9,000,000), and the increase of house allowances (£2,000,000). It must be remembered that the measures now put forward by General Vannovski did not even dispose of our many really important needs, for in his supplementary statement were included only those things that could not be postponed, or which had long ago been sanctioned, but not carried out for want of funds. Amongst the most important of these were the following:

1. The improvement of the organization of the army and increases to its establishment, including additions to the troops in the Asiatic districts, especially in Pri-Amur.

2. The betterment of the conditions of service of all ranks, particularly as to an increase to the officers' pay and house allowance, and the introduction of field kitchens.

3. The augmentation of reserve supplies in the Pri-Amur and Turkestan districts.

4. An increase in the artillery in the Siberian Military District.

5. The formation of extra engineer units and strengthening of fortresses.

The Finance Minister, to whom this demand for a further allotment of £45,500,000[45] additional to the schedule for the period of 1898 to 1902 was submitted, replied that the state of the country's finances would not permit of the money being given. After much discussion he agreed to grant £16,000,000 instead of £45,500,000, and this lesser sum was finally approved. So we actually received for this five-year period about £30,000,000 less than was required, or a deficit of £6,000,000 per annum. Such a policy could have only one result, that of placing us further behind our western neighbours in the military race, as in many directions it compelled the cessation of work necessary for the strengthening of our position both on our European and Asiatic frontiers. Besides this, large sums were required for the general improvement of the status of our troops on the peace establishment. In the first place, in order to obtain greater efficiency among the senior officers, it was essential to treat the whole body of officers in a more liberal spirit, so that zealous and capable men should be content to remain in the Service, and not wish to leave; to modernize and add to the number of our military educational establishments, so that as large a number of officers as possible should receive a general training of a standard equivalent to that given in the middle-class educational establishments. Our private soldiers were decidedly worse off than those of other armies as regards ready-money, food, dress, and equipment, and the expenditure required to improve their condition would of course be heavy. Again, our horses were not of a sufficiently good class, especially in the Cossack regiments and the transport. These were only the most pressing of the army's many needs.

Thus the legacy left to me when I assumed the duty of War Minister on January 1, 1898, was no pleasing one. The immense needs of the army were clear at a glance, but not clearer than the lack of funds wherewith they might be met. Consequently I had to examine all proposals most carefully in order to settle which could be carried out, and which must be indefinitely postponed. I have already expressed my views on the importance of our western frontier, but to carry out what was necessary for our military position on that side would have absorbed the whole of the additional £16,000,000 allowed on the supplementary estimate for all purposes during five years. Meanwhile there was the long list of almost equally pressing demands for the improvement in the senior ranks and for the consolidation of our position in the Far East, etc. The housing of our troops was in many cases so extremely bad that it was difficult to train the men, and this necessitated the construction of barracks at various stations. Finally, those services which had been started in the preceding five years had to be completed, particularly those touching the organization of reserve units. The Tsar investigated the relative urgency of these matters, and approved a scheme for 1899 to 1903, which, with the exception of the reorganization of the reserve troops and the further increase to our troops in European Russia, was carried out completely. The services approved by the Tsar were noted by the War Ministry. The following are a few, and show the form in which they were officially recorded:

1. With a view to possible complications in the Far East, the Tsar gave orders that our military position there should be strengthened.

2. The War Minister's recommendations as to the necessity of improving the general conditions under which officers served, in order to get greater efficiency among the seniors, were warmly supported by the Tsar, who issued orders that the matter should be taken in hand at once.

3. The Tsar was also pleased to order that the conditions of service of the soldiers should be made more liberal. Better quarters were to be constructed, and the issue of a tea ration was to be gradually introduced.

4. The Tsar was pleased to recognize the particular importance of the re-armament of the artillery, and instructed the Minister of Finance to provide funds for it by a supplementary grant.

The measures carried out by the War Department from 1899 to 1903 can be described in a few words:

The Pri-Amur Military District as at present defined had only been formed in 1883. Its garrison originally consisted of 12 battalions, 10 squadrons, 2½ Cossack battalions, 5 batteries, a sapper company, and 1 company of fortress artillery. Ten years later, in 1894, it had risen to 20 battalions of infantry. From 1895 we began to increase the troops in the Far East with some rapidity. Between 1898 and 1902 they were increased by 840 officers, 37,000 men, and 2,600 horses. Altogether in that period our forces had grown to 31 battalions, 15 squadrons, 32 guns, 1 sapper battalion, and 3 battalions of fortress artillery. Moreover, 5 railway battalions had been formed for work on the Eastern Chinese Railway, and the Frontier and other guards had been increased from 8,000 to 25,000. The general total increase in numbers in the Pri-Amur district, in Manchuria and in Kuan-tung, amounted to 60,000 men. The idea of the scheme of 1899 was to enable us to bring as soon as possible the establishment of the troops in these districts of the Far East up to 48 Rifle and 48 reserve battalions, 57 squadrons, 236 guns, and 3¾ sapper battalions, organized in three corps. Compared with the few battalions in Siberia and the Pri-Amur district only a short time before, this was a large force, and its organization at so great a distance was most difficult. It depended to a great extent on the amount of money available and local conditions, and took some years to complete. As this force could be rapidly concentrated, the idea was that it should constitute a strong advance-guard, under cover of which the reinforcements from Russia would be able to concentrate. The fate of a first campaign must obviously depend to a great extent on the rapidity with which these reinforcements could be transported, and yet in 1900 the Siberian Railway was not constructed as a first-class line, and the Eastern Chinese line was not finished. I reported in 1900:

"To bring our forces up to the total specified[46] will take six to seven years. This fact, coupled with the incapacity of our railways to cope with any heavy traffic, calls for the greatest care in our external relations, lest we permit ourselves to be drawn into war at a disadvantage, with an insufficient number of troops which could be only very slowly concentrated."

For various reasons, too complicated to explain, this advice was not acted on; the necessity for extreme care was not appreciated, and we were suddenly plunged into war when we were not ready. In 1902 our military position was good, and having begun to carry out our promises as to the evacuation of Manchuria, we had every reason to count on a continuance of peace in the Far East. But towards the end of that year there were signs of a possible rupture with Japan. The War Department was not blind to these, and the measures enumerated above, which, with the money then available, were to have been completed by 1906 or 1907, were, by the aid of a supplementary allotment, carried out within a year.

While hoping for peace, we steadily prepared for hostilities, and increased our troops in the Far East in 1903 by 38 battalions, and in the same year formed 32 new battalions in European Russia; so that by adding one to each of the East Siberian two-battalion[47] regiments, and thereby converting them into three-battalion regiments, all the 9 East Siberian Brigades could be expanded into 9 East Siberian Rifle Divisions, with 12 battalions apiece. The allotment of artillery and sappers to these divisions was carried out under a special scheme. Thus the force of 19 battalions which we had in the Pri-Amur district at the time of the Chino-Japanese War should have swollen in 1903 into one of 108 rifle and 20 reserve battalions. Behind these stood 40 more reserve battalions, held in reserve in the Siberian Military District. Altogether our Siberian possessions were to have contained in 1903 an army of 168 battalions of infantry, with a due proportion of other arms. The railway, however, did not permit us to transport these additional units until the spring of 1904, when hostilities had commenced. Yet they were eventually received, and the force in the Pri-Amur—which was practically defenceless at the time of the Chino-Japanese War—had grown into an army of four Siberian corps and two independent divisions, which received the first blows in the Japanese War. Though hastily improvised between 1895 and 1903, thanks to the great efforts made to render them reliable, to the fortunate selection of their commanders, and to their strong peace establishments, they proved to be our best troops. The principle upon which they were formed was the transference to them of complete companies chosen by ballot from the corps in Europe, and only under exceptional circumstances were the company officers permitted to be transferred from these new units. Each of the 32 battalions was formed from one of the army corps in Russia, one company being taken from each brigade, and picked officers were placed in command of each battalion. The soundness of the scheme upon which these units were created is borne out by the fact that at the Ya-lu the 3rd Battalions of the 11th and 12th Regiments, which had only just arrived to join their regiments, fought most gallantly. The 3rd Battalion of the 11th Regiment in particular, by making a counter-attack with the bayonet, inflicted severe loss on the enemy. In the spring of 1905 the regiments of all 7 East Siberian Rifle Divisions were turned into four-battalion regiments. In the 1st Manchurian Army, which I had the honour to command, were 5 of these East Siberian Rifle Divisions, and their 90[48] battalions were acknowledged to be the pick of all three armies. But to form all these new units we had to denude our German frontier to an alarming extent.

Besides increasing the number of men in the Far East between 1896 and 1903, we formed supply depôts, and hastily fortified Vladivostok and Port Arthur. Indeed, one quarter of the total sum allotted to all our fortress construction and maintenance from 1898 to 1902 was spent upon these two fortresses. Only on Kronstadt,[49] of all our land and sea strongholds, was more money spent than on Port Arthur. Many other difficulties besides those of finance confronted us in the provision of armament. It was vitally necessary that both Vladivostok and Port Arthur should have coast guns of the latest pattern, but it took a long time to get them delivered by the factories owing to the heavy orders already being executed for the Navy Department. As a temporary measure we were obliged to mount old-pattern guns. In a short time more than 1,000 pieces of ordnance were transported from European Russia to these two places. Progress was greatly delayed when the railway was interrupted during the rising in Manchuria in 1900, while work at Port Arthur itself was for a long time stopped by Admiral Alexeieff's order. Had it not been for these delays, the place would have been much better prepared in 1904 than it was. But to appreciate properly what was accomplished there in a short time two circumstances should be remembered:

A. Owing to our fleet being shut up in Port Arthur, the Japanese possessed the command of the sea, and were able to remove the armament from several of their naval fortresses to Kuan-tung for the siege operations; against these coast guns even masonry defences were of little use.

B. The delivery of these heavy howitzers and the landing of other siege material was greatly facilitated by the existence of Dalny, a place which had been created entirely at the instance of M. de Witte, without any reference having been made to the War Ministry or the officer commanding the Kuan-tung district, under whose control the locality actually was.

A large quantity of food-supplies was collected in Port Arthur, and even at the time of its premature surrender there was enough in the place to last for one and a half months. Moreover, the authorities on the spot were empowered to purchase locally, and as the resources of flour, barley, rice, and cattle in the district were unlimited, there was nothing to prevent them doing this. Many unreasonable reproaches have been hurled upon the War Department on account of the inadequate strength of the fortifications, but in the creation of this fortress great difficulties had to be overcome in a very short time. In estimating the ultimate strength of the place, it must not be forgotten that we only took possession of it at the end of 1897; that during

1898 and 1899 we had a very weak temporary armament on the sea-front; and that the cumbrous official procedure then in force made it impossible to spend quickly large sums on new fortress works. Firstly, the scheme had to be drawn up by the engineers on the spot, then it had to be sent to St. Petersburg to be examined by the Engineer Committee, and afterwards to be approved by the Tsar. In the case of Port Arthur, in order to accelerate this routine, special authority was deputed to the local authorities; while Major-General Velichko, a gifted and energetic Engineer officer, was sent to the Far East as the representative of the Headquarter Engineer Administration. Indeed, when the scheme of fortifications at Port Arthur was put before the Emperor for his approval, a large portion of the works had, contrary to the usual procedure, been commenced in anticipation of sanction. As everything was stopped by Admiral Alexeieff, who was commanding the Kuan-tung district, during the rising in Manchuria in 1900, we only had three years (1901, 1902, and 1903) to finish these tremendous permanent works. Considering the time available and the rocky soil, much indeed was done.

The armament, also, could not well have been provided more quickly. The ordnance had first to be made, and the orders for coast guns could only be executed slowly, as the Obukhoff factory was full of work for the Navy Department. The 10-inch and 11-inch Canet guns and large-calibre mortars ordered by the War Department were required simultaneously in all the Russian naval fortresses, especially in Libau, Kronstadt, and Vladivostok; but, as a matter of fact, Port Arthur and Vladivostok received most of them at the expense of our strength in the Baltic and Black Seas. While awaiting the demands for new ordnance to be complied with, we robbed other places, so as to bring up the Port Arthur armament to some hundreds of guns. In the first years of its occupation, also, everything for this place had to be sent round by sea. Notwithstanding all these difficulties, in four years (1899 to 1903) we succeeded in making Port Arthur so strong that the armament of its sea-front kept the whole Japanese fleet at a respectful distance, while the batteries on the land side withstood a severe test under the most unfavourable conditions. Not only were the enemy numerous and possessed of technical troops and material for the destruction of our defences, but being presented with a ready-made base in Dalny, they were able to land monster siege-guns. Once again, as at Sevastopol, our fleet was more useful on land than on its proper element. Yet the enemy lost twice as many men as the garrison, and Port Arthur held out almost twelve months from the commencement of the war. Even then its fall was premature.

Much attention was also paid to economy, and Treasury interests were by no means overlooked. The rapid concentration of troops, the large number of buildings that had to be constructed and the collection of supplies and stores for the commissariat and engineer departments, afforded ample scope for malpractices; but the appointment of selected officers at the head of these two great branches of the army, and of picked men as their assistants, was naturally productive of good results, and the reputation of these branches in no way suffered in the war.

I am confident that if future historians take into consideration the enormous distance of the theatre of war from the centre of Russia, they will not only be amazed at the results achieved by the War Department in strengthening our position there between the years 1895 and 1903, but will see how unfounded was the accusation that adequate steps were not taken to prepare for war. I repeat that, with such money as was available, and with the limited time at our disposal, a great and responsible work was accomplished, so much so that the Pri-Amur district, which was defenceless in 1895, was in 1903 so strong that a whole armed nation, in spite of its own great efforts and the entire uselessness of our fleet, was unable to touch our territory anywhere, with the exception of Saghalien. In 1900 I recorded my opinion that the Japanese would be able, in the event of war, to put into the field about 400,000 men with 1,100 guns. Of course, it was not possible for us to pour such a number of men into Manchuria and Pri-Amur. This would have necessitated many years, and the expenditure of millions, as well as the earlier construction of railway connection with the Far East.

The extent to which our strength in the Far East directly depended on railway efficiency is apparent from the fact that in our schemes of July, 1903, for the transport of troops, we could only count on two short military trains per diem. When instructions were given to carry four Rifle and one sapper battalions, two batteries, and 1,700 tons of military stores as quickly as possible to Port Arthur, it was calculated, according to the mobilization schemes, that it could not be done in less than twenty-two days, and we were unable to make use of the full carrying capacity of the newly built Eastern Chinese line for six months after the opening of the war. To improve it an immense amount of work in laying sidings and crossings, arranging for water-supply, ballasting the track, and the construction of buildings, was necessary. All this implied railing up a large number of sleepers, rails, building materials, and rolling-stock; construction trains were also required. During 1902 and 1903 the greater the number of troop-trains that ran, the less was the progress in the construction and improvement of the line. During the latter year the War Department took every advantage of the railway in order to increase our forces in the Far East, and it was only owing to the immense exertions of all the railway personnel that it was possible to transport the troops and military stores without stopping construction altogether. Notwithstanding the danger of such a course, we used the sea for the transport of troops as well as stores, and the great risk that we ran in doing so during the second half of 1903, after the viceroyalty had been formed, is illustrated by the fact that some of the consignments of preserved meat sent for Port Arthur fell into the hands of the enemy a few days before war was declared. It is clear, therefore, to what extent Bezobrazoff's project for the rapid concentration of an army of 75,000 men in Southern Manchuria [sent to me in the summer of 1903] could be carried out. The scanty population and the absence of local resources in the Pri-Amur prohibited the maintenance of a large force there in peace-time. Over the wide stretch of territory from Lake Baikal to Vladivostok there are only about a million souls, and of this total only 400,000 are in the Amur and Maritime districts. From this can be gathered what an impossible burden to the State it would have been to attempt to maintain a large army in such a desert. Consequently we endeavoured to keep in Siberia and Pri-Amur only such a number as would be sufficient, in the first instance, to contain the enemy, and to form a screen, under cover of which the reinforcements could be concentrated. The conditions are the same on the western, Caucasian, and Afghanistan frontiers: the local troops form, so to speak, an impenetrable veil, under cover of which the main forces can be concentrated.

Though this screen consisted, in the Far East, of 172[50] battalions, of which more than 100 could take the field, it was never, of course, intended that the issue of the war should hang upon their efforts alone; but our difficulty lay in bringing up our main forces soon enough, for, as the enemy could concentrate quicker than we could, our reinforcements might be destroyed in detail as they arrived. So poor was the traffic capacity of the railway that we were neither able to send drafts to the advanced troops nor to support them in time with adequate reinforcements. If the arrangements had been such as I shall detail later on, we should have had double the number of men at Liao-yang and Mukden that we did have, and the issue of the battles must have been different. But the Ministries of Ways and Communications and of Finance were unable to carry out their promises, and our army only succeeded in concentrating eight months later than it should have done. By September, 1905, we were at last able to collect an army 1,000,000 strong, ready in every respect to commence a second campaign, with troops and material of a nature to guarantee success. We had received machine-guns, howitzers, shells, small-arm ammunition, field railways, wireless telegraphy, and technical stores of all sorts, and the senior officers were mostly fresh. The War Department had, with the co-operation of other departments, successfully accomplished a most colossal task. What single military authority would have admitted a few years ago the possibility of concentrating an army of a million men 5,400 miles away from its bases of supply and equipment by means of a poorly constructed single-line railway? Wonders were effected, but it was too late. Affairs in the interior of Russia for which the War Department could not be held responsible were the causes of the war being brought to an end at a time when decisive military operations should really have only just been beginning.

The re-armament of the artillery was accomplished as follows. Owing to the introduction of the quick-firing gun in other armies, we were compelled to adopt it. The superiority of the quick-firer over the old pattern was obvious, for, apart from its greater range and accuracy, each quick-firing battery, by reason of the greater number of shells it fires, can cause destruction equal to that of a much larger number of non-quick-firing guns. After prolonged and exhaustive trials of different patterns, amongst which were those submitted by the French factories of St. Chamond and Schneider, the German firm of Krupp, and the Russian Putiloff, preference was given to the Russian design, and in the beginning of 1900 the first lot of 1,500 guns was ordered, further trials being also arranged for. Not everybody was convinced of the undoubted superiority of the new type of weapon, and General Dragomiroff, who had always been opposed to quick-firing artillery, still remained a strong opponent of its adoption. In 1902 an order for a second lot of guns of a modified and improved pattern was given. To test the weapon thoroughly and under war conditions, the 2nd Battery of the Guards Rifle Artillery Division, armed with this new 3-inch quick-firer, was sent, in August, 1900, to the Far East, where the Boxer campaign was then in progress. The division took part in four expeditions, two in the valley of the Pei-chih-li, one in the hills and sandy steppes of Mongolia, and one in the hills of Eastern Manchuria. It covered altogether about 2,400 miles of different sorts of country, under variations in temperature of from 35° to 22° Réaumur. Most of the marches were as much as forty miles in length. The battery came into action eleven times, and fired 389 rounds at cavalry, infantry, buildings, and fortifications at ranges from point-blank to 2,500 yards. The results attained were quite satisfactory, particularly if the arduous nature of the campaign, the season of the year, and the haste with which the battery was formed, be taken into account. Unfortunately, the test of shelling houses and field works was made against an enemy who made little resistance, so that faults in the ammunition which have recently come to light were not then discovered. Wishing to have as simple an equipment as possible, we adopted one pattern of shell, which was efficient with time-fuze against troops in the open, and could be used with percussion-fuze against troops under cover; but we omitted to take into account the weakness of the explosive employed as burster. The projectile which did splendidly against exposed targets was of little use for destroying such cover as buildings, timber, or breastworks. In March, 1902, the necessary grant was made for re-arming batteries of the 2nd Category, and the orders were carried out in our arsenals. The re-armament made such progress that at the time of the outbreak of the Russo-Japanese War the whole of our artillery, with the exception of some Siberian batteries, was armed with quick-firers. At this time a quick-firing mountain-gun was also invented, which proved very effective. Generally speaking, the re-armament of the artillery was quickly and skilfully carried out.

But besides the four points above mentioned,[51] to which the Tsar was pleased to give his particular attention, the War Ministry had to make great efforts in other directions connected both with the life of the army and its efficiency. Amongst these tasks was that of improving our communications by building strategical roads and railways. These were constructed in order of urgency, according to a special scheme, as funds became available. Great efforts were made to push on with both the Bologoe-Siedlce and Orenberg-Tashkent lines, which were of particular strategic importance; and in 1899 considerable improvements were carried out in the Krasnovodsk-Kushk line.

In 1902 we began to consider what would be required in the five years 1904 to 1909, and in 1903 I submitted to the Finance Minister a demand for a supplementary grant of £82,500,000 in addition to the ordinary Budget for these five years. He only found it possible to grant £13,000,000. Numerous pressing measures which had been already postponed in 1899 had again to be put off with a hope that perhaps in 1910 Russia would be able to find means for the safeguarding of her most vital interests—in other words, for the defence of the Empire.

In submitting his annual report on the War Ministry in 1904—the first year of the new five-year period—Lieutenant-General Rediger, in his capacity of War Minister and as an acknowledged authority, made the following true and important observations:

> "The existing defects in organization and equipment of our army are the direct result of the inadequate financial grants made ever since the war with Turkey. The sum allotted has never corresponded either to the actual requirements of the army or to the work it has had to do, but has been fixed entirely by the amount of money which seemed available. It has been made clear, in drawing up the scheme for the coming five years, that to satisfy only the most pressing needs a supplementary sum of £82,500,000[52] is required. Only £13,000,000 has been allotted. Thus the estimates for the current five years afford no hope of improving the existing situation."

Owing to the large requirements of a peace army of 1,000,000, and the necessity for protecting frontiers stretching for over 11,000 miles, the Ministry of Finance had undoubtedly great difficulty in meeting the demands of the War Department. The requirements of the navy were also continually growing, with the result that less was available for the land forces. But if the Minister of Finance[53] had confined himself to his rôle of collector of revenue whereby to satisfy all the needs of the State, it could never have been suggested that the money so collected was spent except in accordance with actual requirements, for the decision as to which demands were the most urgent would not have been within this official's province. As a matter of fact, our finances were managed in so curious a manner that the Finance Minister was not only the collector, but also the greatest expender of State moneys! Besides having to bear the ever-increasing outlay in his own department—for establishment, for expenses connected with the collection of taxes and the sale of Government liquor—he formed in his own Ministry subsections of the other Ministries, such as Ways and Communications, War, Navy, Education, Interior, Agriculture, and Foreign Affairs. So equipped, he planned, built, and administered the great Eastern Chinese Railway without any reference to the Minister of Ways and Communications; organized and commanded two army corps, one of Frontier Guards, and the other of guards for the railway, and actually chose the type of gun for their armament without reference to the Minister of War; initiated and managed a commercial fleet on the Pacific Ocean, and ran a flotilla of armed river steamboats, which might be regarded as the duty of the Naval Ministry. As regards the work of the Department of Education, the Finance Minister founded the higher technical institutions; as regards the sphere of Ministries of Interior and Agriculture, the Finance Minister had the most important administration—the so-called "alienated" strip of land set aside for the Eastern Chinese Railway—and the building of towns and villages, and the decision of questions concerning the taking up of land and its cultivation; as regards the Department of Foreign Affairs, the Finance Minister conducted negotiations with the highest representatives of the Chinese Administration, concluded treaties, and maintained his commercial and diplomatic agents in different parts of China and Korea. There is, I believe, a proverb to the effect that "charity begins at home."[54] Is it to be wondered at, therefore, that the grants for the pet projects of the Finance Minister were more liberal than those for corresponding services required by the other Ministries? The appropriations for public education were cut down, but many millions were spent in constructing huge buildings for polytechnic institutes in St. Petersburg and Kieff, magnificent blocks for the Excise Department, and perfect palaces for officials. Immense sums were spent on the creation of the town of Dalny, on the Eastern Chinese Railway and its palatial offices in Harbin, and on the services connected with it. For this latter enterprise, which was both a commercial and State proposition (private as regards management, and official as regards the supply of funds), the money was mostly obtained from the so-called "surpluses." These "surpluses" expanded in a manner unprecedented in the financial records, not only of our own country, but probably of the world, and in our case much to the detriment of the most pressing needs of all departments. The idea underlying the creation of a surplus was simplicity itself. While all demands for money made by the different departments were cut down, the estimated receipts from revenue were also reduced. The results were amazing. The excess of receipts over expenditure at a time when the most pressing requirements for national defence could not be met for lack of funds amounted in some years to over £20,000,000. The following table gives the "errors" in estimating made by the Finance Minister in calculating the revenue between 1894–1905:

| | The Revenue. | | Actual Excess over Estimate. |
	Estimated.	Actual.	
	£	£	£
1894	100,482,327	115,378,581	14,896,253
1895	114,295,700	125,581,878	11,286,177
1896	123,947,169	136,871,935	12,924,765
1897	131,836,649	141,638,609	9,801,960
1898	136,445,821	158,485,444	22,039,622
1899	146,912,820	167,331,306	20,418,485
1900	159,374,568	170,412,850	11,038,282
1901	173,009,600	179,945,715	6,936,114
1902	180,078,448	190,540,444	10,461,995
1903	189,703,267	203,180,081	13,476,813
1904	198,009,449	201,826,131	3,816,682
1905	197,704,561	202,443,193	4,738,631

This shows—

(*a*) That the difference between the estimated and actual receipts amounted in 1898 and 1899 to more than £20,000,000 *per annum.*

(*b*) That in eight years out of twelve the actual income exceeded the estimates by £10,000,000 *per annum.*

(*c*) That the revenue was little affected by the war, and that for 1904 and 1905 the excess of income over estimates was more than £8,000,000. Had the calculations as to receipts, therefore, been more accurate, it would have been quite possible to grant to the War Ministry the supplementary sum asked for, and thus to enable our preparations to have been more complete in east and west.

In conclusion, the main reason for our military inefficiency was the inadequate funds granted by the Treasury. Funds for the War Department were stinted—

(*a*) Owing to the greatly increased expenditure on the fleet.

(*b*) Owing to the large expenditure upon the projects of the Minister of Finance in the Far East, and owing to the underestimation of revenue. But in spite of this, I think it will be allowed that from 1898–1903, during which time it distributed its money according to a strictly defined plan, the War Department attained, on the whole, remarkable results in the strengthening of our military position in the Far East. The results in this direction of the ten years preceding the Russo-Japanese War can be gauged from the following figures. We had in the Pri-Amur district, Manchuria, and in Kuan-tung:

In 1884   12   battalions

In 1894   20   ,,

In 1903   63   ,,

In 1904   140   ,,

SKETCH MAP OF EASTERN ASIA, SHOWING POSITION OF
THEATRE OF WAR WITH REFERENCE
TO NEIGHBOURING TERRITORIES.

CHAPTER VI

The War Minister's opinion on the Manchurian and Korean questions from the year 1900 to 1903—What he did to avoid a rupture with Japan.

Not only was the war unexpected; it was against our interests, and contrary to the wishes of the Emperor. Had it ended victoriously, those who were responsible for it would have found themselves national heroes for having laid the train for our success in the Far East with such sagacity; but the premature peace forced on us by our internal troubles prevented a continuation of the struggle till victory was ours. All classes of society were convulsed by our misfortunes, and are now insistent in a desire to hear the truth as to the causes of the war, and to learn the names of those who turned a deaf ear to the Emperor's expressed wish for peace, and, by sins of commission or omission, so steered the ship of State as to bring about a rupture. The existing freedom of the Press has already permitted the publication of various opinions on these subjects, and amongst much fiction certain facts have now been revealed, the publication of which could only have been possible with the knowledge and permission of interested persons holding high appointments in the different Ministries.

The most important of many newspaper articles touching upon the causes of the war is one by M. Gurieff, entitled "The Outbreak of the Russo-Japanese War," and published in the *Russki Viedomost* in May, 1905. M. Gurieff evidently had access to many official documents, and the article reads as an *ex parte* statement, in which the author holds a brief for the defence of the Finance Minister, M. Sergius de Witte. As this lucubration must have been widely read, having been reprinted in foreign as well as in Russian newspapers and magazines; as it is still being quoted; and as the statements contained in it concerning the Ministry of War are not correct, and have led to a wrong construction being placed upon the actions of that Department, I feel constrained to state in as few words as possible the part played by the War Minister in Far Eastern affairs between 1898 and 1903.

The question of obtaining an outlet on the Pacific Ocean was discussed in Russia some time ago. It was thought that an exit to ice-free seas would eventually be a necessity in view of the immense growth of our population; but as two centuries had shown us the cost of moving towards the Baltic and Black Seas, it was felt that particular care must be exercised lest, in our desire to get access to the Pacific coast, we should be drawn prematurely into war. Our possessions in the Far East and Baikalia are inaccessible wastes, where everything in the way of development remains still to be done. Our trade with the Far East was in every way so insignificant, that not only did access to the Pacific Ocean appear unnecessary for the present generation, but it actually seemed that the expense and sacrifices entailed in obtaining this access would be a burden of a nature to hinder our national development in other quarters. During the latter half of the last century the War Ministry—in conjunction with the Ministry of Foreign Affairs—systematically opposed any extension of our frontiers in Asia in view of what was going on in Europe. Consequently the successive steps of our advance into the heart of Central Asia often took place in defiance of the opinions of and the orders issued from St. Petersburg. The occupation of Tashkent by Cherneff in 1864–65 was considered premature, for it brought us into direct touch with the Khanates of Bokhara and Khokand, and after the expedition to Samarkand in 1868, not only was Kaufmann not permitted to conquer the Bokhara Khanate completely, but Shaar and Kitab, which had been captured by us after severe fighting, were returned to the Emir. In 1873, after conquering the Khiva Khanate, we confined ourselves to taking only the right bank of the Oxus, while we preserved the Khan's authority. In 1875, when traversing the whole Khanate of Khokand, we deliberately confined ourselves to occupying the town of Namangan, leaving the rest of the Khanate in the possession of its feeble ruler. In 1881 the War Minister did not assent to our retention of the Kuldja province, which we had captured ten years before; and in 1882, after Skobeleff had seized Geok Tepe, he was strictly forbidden to advance on Merv. This consistent policy on the part of the War Ministry was in every case born of a fear of greater expenditure and fresh responsibilities which could only weaken our existing position on the western and Turkish frontiers. Above all was the Department opposed to starting complications with China or Japan. It accordingly viewed with alarm, and strongly opposed, the theory that "Russia is the most western of Asiatic States, not the most eastern of European," and that her future lies entirely in Asia. As has been explained, twenty years ago we were practically defenceless in the Far East. An enormous extent of country such as Saghalien was garrisoned by only three local detachments, totalling 1,000 men. Vladivostok had no defences, and its main communication with Russia—a trunk road 6,000 miles long—was in a military sense absolutely useless. It was only after 1882, when we yielded to China over Kuldja, and when Japan began increasing her army, that we began to augment the number of our troops in that quarter.

The Department was all the time keenly alive to the precarious nature of our communications between the Pri-Amur and Russia, and recruits and a large proportion of supplies were sent to Vladivostok by sea. Under such conditions it was, of course, quite out of the question to dream of any offensive operations or even schemes of offence; but the awakening of China and Japan caused much uneasiness for our safety east of Lake Baikal, and the project for the construction of the Siberian Railway through our own territory was welcomed as facilitating communication. The question of the construction of this railway-line was first discussed by a committee of Ministers in 1875, but the scheme was then confined to a line within the limits of European Russia as far as Tumen. In 1880 a resolution was passed sanctioning this portion. In 1882 the Emperor Alexander II., dissatisfied with this partial scheme, decided that the line should be laid right through Siberia. Surveys were accordingly made, and three alternative routes were put forward. In 1885, after examining these alternatives, the committee were unable to come to any conclusion as to the most advantageous, but they decided to set to work at once to construct the first portion of the railway. In 1886, upon receipt of a report by the Governor-General of Eastern Siberia, the Emperor wrote:

> "So far as I have read the report of the Governor-General, I am grieved to observe that the Government has up till now done practically nothing to meet the requirements of this rich but neglected country. And it is time—indeed time—that something should be done."

Notwithstanding such a strongly worded animadversion on the part of the Emperor, it was only in February, 1891, that the committee put on record its decision to build simultaneously the Ussuri Railway and the portion of the Siberian line from Mias to Cheliabinsk. In a rescript to the Tsarevitch, who was then on his voyage round the world, it was explained that the line would run "right across the whole of Siberia," and be called the Great Siberian Railway. The idea underlying this scheme was as simple as it was bold, and the line would undoubtedly have put life into a very slowly developing country, would have attracted a large number of colonists, and would thus have secured to us an important region. Of course, as it ran along the Chinese frontier for the greater part of its length, it would not have been free from danger; but the risk was diminished by the comparative inaccessibility of the part of Northern Manchuria adjacent to the railway and the weakness of China. Moreover, it was covered by the mighty Amur River.

After the Chino-Japanese War we, in conjunction with other Powers, compelled Japan to abandon Port Arthur and the Kuan-tung Peninsula, which she had just conquered. This, the first of the acts of Russia to excite Japan's hostility, was also by far the most decisive. A new state of affairs now arose in the Far East which made our complete military unreadiness seem alarming, especially as the Pri-Amur was at that time practically defenceless against an offensive movement by the Japanese. Throughout the immense expanse of this military district there were only nineteen infantry battalions, and we were at once obliged to start increasing our troops in the Far East and turning Vladivostok into a naval fortress; but the most urgent question was that of establishing railway communication.

Before the Chino-Japanese War no one imagined that the Siberian line would be laid anywhere but through our own territory. The weakness displayed by China at that time, however, formed an inducement to carry it through Manchuria, and thus shorten the distance by over 300 miles. In vain did General Dukhovski, Governor-General and Commander of the troops in the Pri-Amur district, protest and point out the risks of such a course. He argued that, if the rail passed through Chinese territory, not only would it be of advantage to the Chinese instead of to the Russian settler population, but it would be insecure. His views did not find acceptance, and this great artery of communication—of incalculable importance to us—was laid through a foreign country. The temptation to give as far as possible an international importance to this line by attracting all trans-continental through-traffic proved too strong for the modest claim for consideration of the Pri-Amur district, though it was one that concerned us very deeply. General Dukhovski's fears were soon justified. Part of the line was destroyed by a rising of the people in 1900, and our troops in Harbin were forced upon the defensive. We lost a whole year, wasted millions of money, and only too soon began to realize that, except a very limited quantity of the most perishable freight, no goods would be sent by rail. Sea transport was cheaper and safer. We were forced to abandon our dreams of international importance for the line, and to confess that it merely constituted a portion of the Siberian Railway, which, as it ran for 800 miles through a foreign country, would require special protection at great cost. Moreover, the Finance Minister's estimate of the saving—£1,500,000—to be effected by taking the line through Manchuria, instead of through Siberia, proved entirely misleading, as the mileage cost of the line worked out to a much larger figure than that of any railway undertaking in Russia! Not only was all idea of the line's international importance very quickly abandoned, but it soon became only too clear that its economic value, though important to the local Chinese population, would be very slight for Russia. Its *raison d'être* must then have been mainly strategic. But, if built on strategic grounds, surely a route through our own territory would have been preferable? This unfortunate enterprise, which turned out so badly for Russia, was the first outward sign of an active policy which was to have such great results. The occupation of Port Arthur, the creation of Dalny, the construction of the southern branch of the line, the maintenance of a commercial fleet in the Far East, and our business enterprises in Korea, were all links in the chain which was to bind these distant tracts so securely to Russia.

It is thought in some quarters that if we had confined ourselves to the construction of the northern line through Manchuria, there would have been no war; that it was the occupation of Port Arthur and Mukden and, in particular, our activity in Korea which caused it. In the opinion of others, the railway through Manchuria cannot be looked upon as merely the commencement of our activity, but must be regarded as the foundation of it all; for if we had run the line along the banks of the Amur in our own territory, it would never have occurred to us to occupy Southern Manchuria and Kuan-tung. It is quite true that the northern portion of the line passing through Manchuria could never have disturbed our friendly relations with China, and I am personally convinced that if we had been satisfied with this, Japan would never have started a war with us for the sake of Northern Manchuria. In any case, the line through Manchuria was built neither in the interests nor at the instance of the War Department, and was carried through in spite of the opposition of General Dukhovski, its representative on the spot. The Boxer rebellion in Manchuria showed up our military weakness, and the hope of the Finance Minister that the local guards raised by him would be able to protect the line without the assistance of troops supplied by the War Department was not realized. Even when the rising became general, he begged us not to despatch to Manchuria the troops which General Grodekovi and Admiral Alexeieff were holding in readiness in Pri-Amur and the Kuan-tung district. His advice was taken, but this delay in sending reinforcements to the railway cost us dear. Almost the whole of the line north of the Eastern Chinese main line, with the exception of the section near Harbin, as well as a great length of the southern branch, together with the stations of Kuang-cheng-tzu, Mukden, and Liao-yang, were seized by the rebels. The local railway guards, commanded by Generals Gerngros and Mischenko, behaved with gallantry, but, overcome by superior numbers, they were forced to retire from almost all the points they had occupied, and the greater part of them were concentrated at Harbin, where they were besieged by the insurgents. Finally, it was by direct order of the Emperor that the War Ministry took action in concentrating troops to put down the rising. Railway communication with Trans-Baikalia was then in existence, and the sea was also open to us, and by the autumn of 1900 we had collected by land and water an army of 100,000 men, and rapidly quelled the rebellion. The capture of Peking,[55] the headquarters of the Boxer movement, by the Allied troops under General Linievitch was also instrumental in restoring order in Manchuria, while the energy with which General Grodekovi organized and despatched columns into Manchuria itself, and so relieved General Gerngros in Harbin, is worthy of notice. Tsitsihar and Kirin were captured by General Rennenkampf; Mukden, by General Subotin.

Once order was restored, the War Department set to work to withdraw our troops from the province of Pei-chih-li as quickly as possible, and succeeded in doing so in spite of the disapproval of Count Waldersee;[56] all the reinforcements from Siberia and European Russia returned. The damage done to the railway was considerable, and all idea of its completion during 1900 was abandoned, and a whole year—the importance of which has been little realized—was lost. Had we been in sufficient strength to maintain order on the line in 1900, the railway would have been in a far greater state of readiness in 1904; the transport of reinforcements in 1903, and the concentration in 1904, would have been accomplished far more rapidly than it was, and we should in all probability have had two or three more army corps at Liao-yang than we actually had. The rising in 1900 clearly showed that it was impossible, with our main line of railway running for 800 miles through Chinese territory, to count on maintaining secure communication with Russia in the future. To insure our position it was necessary to build a line rapidly within our own territory along the left bank of the Amur, and at the same time to place Northern Manchuria in such a condition that it would not, with the aid of the line we had already built, continue to be a source of weakness to us in the Far East.

H.I.M. THE EMPEROR NICHOLAS II.

As the Manchurian and Korean questions were the causes of the war, it is necessary to touch on the War Minister's views with regard to them in some detail. The duties which Russia of her own accord took upon herself in Manchuria are based on the Government *communiqué* of September 1, 1900, in which a circular telegram from the Minister of Foreign Affairs, dated August 25, 1900, was quoted. In this telegram it was stated that our Government was mainly guided by the following axiom, amongst others, with regard to Chinese affairs:

> "The *status quo ante* in China must be preserved, and everything that may tend to a partition of the Celestial Empire is to be avoided."

It continued that if, owing to any action of the Chinese, we should be forced to send troops into Manchuria and to occupy Newchuang, such temporary measures were on no account to be taken as evidence of any self-interested schemes outside the general policy of the Imperial Government, and that, as soon as order was permanently restored in Manchuria and the railway protected—

> "—Russia would not fail to withdraw her forces, provided that no difficulty were placed in the way of such withdrawal by the action of the other Powers."

This announcement appeared at a time when we had over 100,000 men in arms in Asia. There can, therefore, be no question of our sincere intention—at that time—to evacuate Manchuria. In 1901 these promises were repeated by our Government in a similar *communiqué* of April 5. Neither the opposition of China nor the Anglo-Japanese Treaty concluded in 1902, which was unmistakably directed against us, were at the moment considered sufficient to warrant our abandoning all hope of fulfilling our promise to withdrew from Manchuria.

But so long ago as 1900 it had seemed doubtful whether we should be able to carry out this promise. In the first place, it was impossible to ignore entirely the advice of the authorities on the spot, who did not consider a withdrawal was either desirable or possible in our own interests. The action of the Chinese officials in Manchuria, the existence of bands of Hun-huses, and the serious military expeditions we had been forced to make in 1901— all strengthened the opinion of our commanders out there that we had been in too great haste to promise the evacuation of the country. Notwithstanding these doubts, a treaty was concluded with China in April, 1902. This was but the logical development of the official pronouncements made in 1900 and 1901. At first it was supposed that this agreement would lead to a definite settlement of our position in the Far East, but it soon became apparent that there was little ground for such hope. The immense expenditure from 1900 to 1903 on the railway, the army, and the fleet, gave birth to and nourished the fixed idea that our most vital interests would not be sufficiently guarded if we strictly observed the treaty made in April. China viewed us with suspicion, and was almost openly hostile; Japan was openly hostile; while all the other Powers distrusted us. Our foothold in Manchuria also seemed precarious, and in spite of hurrying on the construction and increasing its guards, the railway was by no means secure. Trains had to be escorted on account of the frequent raids by Hun-huses, and no trust could be placed in either the natives or their officials. All this showed that if we confined ourselves merely to protecting the line itself, it would be destroyed in many places at the first rising. Our position would then be serious in the extreme if we should be attacked on the western frontier while carrying on a war in the east. There is no doubt whatever that, if trouble had arisen in the west, and our troops had been withdrawn from Manchuria, a repetition of the Chinese disorders of 1900 might easily have occurred; our communications with the Pri-Amur would again have been interrupted, and we should have had to reconquer Manchuria.[57] With each month that passed the doubt as to our ability to carry out the terms of the treaty of April increased, and this difficult period of uncertainty turned to one of acute anxiety on account of the increasing hostility to us of China and Japan. Officially, we continued to give assurances that we should keep to our engagement, and we even carried out the first portion of it by withdrawing our troops from that part of the Mukden province up to the River Liao; but we were, as a matter of fact, already taking steps essential to our own interests, but absolutely at variance with the treaty.

Before the Boxer rising of 1900 I had expressed the opinion that Northern and Southern Manchuria possessed entirely different values for us, the greater importance of the former being due to the various considerations. In the first place, the country through which the main Siberian line passed was of special importance, because upon it depended the security of our communication, and because the experience of 1900 had shown the extreme weakness of its protection as organized by the Finance Minister. I therefore asked that a small force of four infantry battalions, one battery, and one squadron of Cossacks might be stationed on the line as a mobile reserve at Harbin, in addition to the local railway guards. Barracks for a force of this size were built, and were ready for occupation in 1903; but placing troops merely along the line itself—and a small number at that—would have been of no use if China had intended to make things unpleasant for us in Manchuria. The line would have been cut, and the culprits would never have been discovered, for the officials, who outwardly *kow-towed* to us, were all the time acting in accordance with instructions from Peking. The only thing we could expect was an influx of Chinese into Northern Manchuria, and the crowding of the tracts bordering on the Chinese frontier. Against this, even complete annexation of Northern Manchuria did not appear to me desirable, or likely to serve any useful purpose, as the Chinese population so annexed, possessing the rights of citizenship and settling along the left bank of the Amur, would have swamped the native population of the Amur and coast districts.[58] During the whole of the last century we had only succeeded in colonizing very sparsely with our own people that part of Siberia east of Trans-Baikalia to the sea, which means that the bonds binding it to Russia were extremely weak. In the Amur and coast districts, with a frontier of 1,600 miles bordering on China (from Trans-Baikalia to the sea), the whole population only consisted of 400,000. Northern Manchuria, of about 450,000 square miles in extent, includes the whole of the Kheilutsianski and the northern part of the Kirin provinces. According to available information, it had before the war only 1,500,000 inhabitants. This works out at three persons per square mile. The Boxer rising of 1900 indicated that, so long as the affairs of the people in Northern Manchuria continued to be controlled from Peking, we must expect risings and attempts to destroy the line, for the Chinese Government always had a ready reply to our protests: "It is the Hun-huses who are the culprits." Nor could we regard without apprehension the increases to the Chinese forces in Northern Manchuria, and the settling of Chinese on the waste lands adjacent to the Rivers Amur and Argun, where our people had for a long time been settled. It was necessary, therefore, that we should have, in some form or other, the right of control and of generally making our own arrangements in Northern Manchuria. Without this our weakly guarded railway might be a positive disadvantage, as it added to the vulnerability of our frontier line, which makes a large bend to the north between Trans-Baikalia and the Ussuri region, the whole of the Kheilutsianski and the northern part of the Kirin province running wedgewise into our territory. Only by the security of Northern Manchuria could we feel sufficiently at ease about the Pri-Amur region to start its development.

Now, Northern Manchuria is not next to Korea, and our permanent occupation of it would consequently not have threatened complications with Japan, nor were there in it important European interests which might have been disturbed. It was, however, undoubtedly important to China, with whom its forcible annexation by us might lead to complications. It therefore devolved upon us to find some method of consolidating our position in this region which would not cause a rupture with China. Thus I was strongly in favour of including Northern Manchuria in some way or the other within our sphere of influence; but I was at the same time absolutely opposed to any quasi-political or military enterprise in Southern Manchuria.

This region, up to the Kuan-tung district, includes the whole of the Mukden and the southern part of the Kirin province. Though only one-quarter the size of Northern Manchuria, the population was more than 8,000,000. This works out at more than seventy souls per square mile, as compared with about three for the latter. Mukden, sacred to the Chinese dynasty, might always be a source of misunderstanding with China, and our contact with Korea for 533 miles might easily lead to complications with Japan.

Southern Manchuria, contracting in a wedge-shape, borders on Kuan-tung, and has only 530 odd miles on the Korean frontier. The occupation of it, therefore, would necessitate having two fronts, one towards Korea and one towards China. If an enemy were superior at sea, he could threaten a landing along the 400-mile-long coast of Southern Manchuria. A landing in

Newchuang,[59] for example, would have taken all our troops south of that place in the rear. In discussing possible solutions of this problem, it might be suggested—in the event of any unfriendly action on the part of China—that we should obtain possession of Manchuria in the same way as we had secured the Kuan-tung Peninsula. If we did, this would secure our communication with the latter. Being convinced, as I have said, that the inclusion of Northern Manchuria within our sphere followed as the natural consequence of running the Siberian main line through Manchuria, I felt equally sure that any kind of annexation of Southern Manchuria would be dangerous.

In a special memorandum upon the Manchurian question which I submitted to the Tsar in October, 1903, I expressed myself as follows:

"If we do not touch the boundary of Korea, and do not garrison the country between it and the railway, we shall really prove to the Japanese that we have no intention of seizing Korea as well as Manchuria. They will then in all probability confine themselves to the peaceful furtherance of their interests in the Peninsula, and will neither enter into a military occupation of it nor greatly increase the strength of their home army. This will relieve us of the necessity of augmenting our numbers in the Far East, and of supporting the heavy burden otherwise necessary even should there be no war. If, on the other hand, we annex Southern Manchuria, all the questions that now trouble us and threaten to set the two nations by the ears will become more critical. Our temporary occupation of certain points between the railway and Korea will become permanent, our attention will be more and more attracted to the Korean frontier, and our attitude will confirm the Japanese in their suspicions that we intend to seize that peninsula.

"That our occupation of Southern Manchuria will lead to a Japanese occupation of Southern Korea there cannot be the slightest doubt; but beyond that all is uncertain. One thing, however, is certain. If Japan takes this step, she will be compelled rapidly to increase her military strength, and we, in turn, shall have to reply by enlarging our Far Eastern force. Thus two nations whose interests are so different that they would seem destined to live peaceably, will begin a contest in time of peace, in which each will try to surpass the other in preparations for war. We Russians can only do this at the expense of our strength in the west, and of the vital interests of the people at large—all for the sake of portions of a country which really has no serious importance for us. Moreover, if other Powers take part in this rivalry, the struggle for military supremacy is liable at any moment to change into a deadly conflict, which may not only retard the peaceful development of our Far Eastern possessions for a long time, but may result in a set-back to the whole Empire.

"Even if we should defeat Japan on the mainland—in Korea and Manchuria—we could not destroy her, nor obtain decisive results, without carrying the war into her territory. That, of course, would not be absolutely impossible, but to invade a country with a warlike population of 47,000,000, where even the women participate in wars of national defence, would be a serious undertaking even for a Power as strong as Russia. And if we do not utterly destroy Japan— if we do not deprive her of the right and the power to maintain a navy—she will wait for the first convenient opportunity—till, for instance, we are engaged in war in the west—to attack us, either single-handed or in co-operation with our European enemies.

"It must not be forgotten that Japan can not only quickly throw a well-organized and well-trained army of from 150,000 to 180,000 men into Korea or Manchuria, but can do this without drawing at all heavily upon her population. If we accept the German ratio of regular troops to population—namely, 1 per cent.[60]—we shall see that she can, with her 47,000,000 of people, maintain, instead of 120,000, a force of 400,000 men in time of peace, and 1,000,000 in time of war. Even if we reduce this estimate by one-quarter, Japan will be able to oppose us on the mainland with a regular army of from 300,000 to 350,000 men. If we mean to annex Manchuria, we shall be compelled to bring up our numbers to a point which will enable our troops in the Far East alone to withstand a Japanese attack."

From the above lines it will be seen how seriously the War Department regarded such an antagonist as Japan, and how much anxiety it felt concerning possible complications with that Power on account of Korea. Still, so long as we adhered to our decision to evacuate Southern Manchuria, and not to interfere in Korean affairs, the danger of a rupture was removed. In 1900 our Government had been obliged to respect the territorial integrity of China, and the question of evacuating Manchuria had been in principle decided in the affirmative; and if we were preparing to leave the country, we certainly could not at the same time be preparing it as a theatre of military operations.

As regards the evacuation, there was a difference of opinion between Admiral Alexeieff (the Commander of the Kuan-tung district) and myself as to the importance to us of Southern Manchuria. I believed that the occupation of Manchuria would bring us no profit, and would involve us in trouble with Japan on the one side, through our nearness to Korea, and with China on the other side, through our possession of Mukden. I therefore regarded the speedy evacuation of Southern Manchuria and Mukden as a matter of absolute necessity. The Commander of the Kuan-tung district, on the other hand, whose duty it was to defend that district, thought fit to contend that a permanent occupation of Southern Manchuria would be the best guarantee of our communications with Russia. There was also a minor difference of opinion between the Finance Minister and myself with regard to the withdrawal of our troops from Northern Manchuria. He thought that it would suffice to leave the Frontier Guards only for the protection of the railway. Guided by our experience in quelling the Boxer rising in 1900, I considered it necessary, after withdrawing our troops as quickly as possible from Southern Manchuria, to remove them from all populated places in Northern Manchuria which were off the line of rail, including Kirin and Tsitsihar, and to station a small reserve at Harbin on the line itself in case of disorder. This reserve need not have been stronger than two to four infantry battalions and one battery of artillery. Moreover, I thought we ought to continue to guard communication between Harbin and Khabarovsk along the Sungari, and between Tsitsihar and Blagovieschensk, by the maintenance of a few small military posts. These differences of opinion, however, ceased to exist with the ratification of the Russo-Chinese Treaty of April 1, 1902. By the terms of that convention our troops—with the exception of those guarding the railway—were to be removed from all parts of Manchuria, Southern as well as Northern, within specified periods. This settlement of the question was a great relief to the War Department, because it held out the hope of a "return to the west" in our military affairs. In the first period of six months we were to evacuate the western part of Southern Manchuria, from Shan-hai-kuan to the River Liao; this we punctually did. In the second period of six months we were to remove our troops from the rest of the province of Mukden, including the cities of Mukden and Newchuang. The Department regarded the arrangement to evacuate the province of Mukden with approval, and made energetic preparations to carry it into effect. Barracks were hastily erected between Khabarovsk and Vladivostok for the soldiers to be withdrawn into the Pri-Amur country; the scheme of transportation was drawn up and approved; the movement of troops had begun, and Mukden had actually been evacuated, when suddenly everything was stopped by order of Admiral Alexeieff, the Commander of the Kuan-tung district. His reasons for taking such action have not, to this day, been sufficiently cleared up. It is definitely known, however, that the change in policy which stopped the withdrawal of troops from Southern Manchuria corresponded in time with the first visit to the Far East of State Councillor Bezobrazoff (retired). Mukden, which we had already evacuated, was reoccupied, as was also the city of Newchuang. The Ya-lu timber concession[61] assumed more importance than ever, and in order to give support to it and our other undertakings in Northern Korea, Admiral Alexeieff sent a mounted force with guns to Feng-huang-cheng. Thus, far from completing the evacuation of Southern Manchuria, we actually moved into parts of it that we had never before occupied. At the same time, we allowed operations in connection with the Korean timber concession to go on, despite the fact that the promoters of this enterprise were striving to give to it a political and military character contrary to instructions from St. Petersburg.

VICE-ADMIRAL ALEXEIEFF.

This unexpected change of policy alarmed both China and Japan, and there is good reason to believe that the stoppage of the evacuation of the province of Mukden was an event of supreme importance. So long as we held to our intention of withdrawing all our troops from Manchuria, confined ourselves to the protection of the line by the Frontier Guards and a small reserve at Harbin, and refrained from intruding in Korea, there was little danger of a break with Japan; but we were brought alarmingly near a rupture with that Power when, contrary to our agreement with China, we left our troops in Southern Manchuria, and entered Northern Korea in pursuit of our timber enterprise. The uncertainty as to our intentions, moreover, alarmed not only China and Japan, but even England, America, and other Powers.

In the early part of 1903 our position became extremely involved. The interests of the Pri-Amur were by this time pushed completely into the background; even General Dukhovski, its Governor-General and Commander-in-Chief, was not consulted upon the most important points concerning the Far East. Meanwhile, immense enterprises involving many millions of pounds were being created and controlled on independent lines in Manchuria, on Chinese territory. The Minister of Finance (M. de Witte) was building and managing over 1,300 miles of railway. The alignment of the northern portion was, as I have explained, fixed in direct opposition to the opinion of General Dukhovski, our chief authority in those parts, while under the orders of the Finance Minister an army corps was organized for the protection of the line. So independent, indeed, was the latter in his conduct of purely military matters that a pattern of gun for the railway guard was settled, and the gun purchased abroad without reference to the War Ministry. To assist in the economic development of the railway, M. de Witte started a fleet of sea-going merchant ships; for work on the Manchurian rivers he ran a flotilla of river steamers, some of which were armed. Vladivostok was no longer considered suitable as a terminus for a trans-continental trunk line, so, regardless of the fact that the Kuan-tung district was under the War Department and immediately under the officer commanding the troops in it (Admiral Alexeieff), Dalny was selected and created as a great port without reference to either. Huge sums were spent on this place, which adversely affected the military importance and strength of Port Arthur, as it was necessary either to fortify Dalny or be prepared for its seizure and employment by an enemy as a base of operations against us—a thing which afterwards happened. I should add that the Russo-Chinese Bank was also in the Finance Minister's hands. Finally, M. de Witte maintained his own representatives in Peking, Seoul, etc. (Pokotiloff in Peking). It so happened, therefore, that in this year our Minister of Finance was managing in the Far East railways, a flotilla of merchant steamers, a certain number of armed vessels, the port of Dalny, and the Russo-Chinese Bank. He also had under his command an army corps. At the same time Bezobrazoff and his company were developing their concessions in Manchuria and Korea, and promoting by every possible means their timber speculation on the Ya-lu in Northern Korea. One incredible scheme of Bezobrazoff's followed another. His idea was to utilize the Timber Company as a sort of "screen" or barrier against a possible attack upon us by the Japanese, and during 1902 and 1903 his activity and that of his adherents assumed a very alarming character. Among requests that he made of Admiral Alexeieff were to send into Korean territory 600 soldiers in civilian dress, to organize for service in the same locality a force of 3,000 Hun-huses, to support the agents of the Timber Company by sending 600 mounted rifles to Sha-ho-tzu on the Ya-lu, and to occupy Feng-huang-cheng with a detached force. Admiral Alexeieff refused some of these requests, but unfortunately consented to send 150 mounted rifles to Sha-ho-tzu, and to move a Cossack regiment with guns to the latter place. This action was particularly harmful to us, as it was taken just at the time when we were under obligations to evacuate the province of Mukden altogether. As has already been stated, instead of withdrawing, we advanced towards Korea.

The Ministers of Finance, Foreign Affairs, and War (de Witte, Lamsdorff, and myself), all recognized the danger that would threaten us if we continued to defer fulfilment of the promised evacuation, and, more especially, if we failed to put an end to Bezobrazoff's activity in Korea. We three Ministers, therefore, procured the appointment of a special council, which assembled in St. Petersburg on April 18, 1903, to consider certain propositions which Bezobrazoff had made to its members in a special memorandum. These proposals had for their object the strengthening of Russia's strategic position in the basin of the Ya-lu. We three Ministers on the committee expressed ourselves firmly and definitely in opposition to Bezobrazoff's proposals, and all agreed that if his enterprise on the Ya-lu was to be sustained, it must be upon a strictly commercial basis. The Minister of Finance showed conclusively that, for the next five or ten years, Russia's task in the Far East must be to tranquillize the country, and bring to completion the work already undertaken there. He said, furthermore, that although the views of the different departments of the Government were not always precisely the same, there had never been—so far as the Ministers of War, Foreign Affairs, and Finance were concerned—any conflict of action. The Minister of Foreign Affairs pointed out particularly the danger involved in Bezobrazoff's proposal to stop the withdrawal of troops from Manchuria.

It pleased His Imperial Majesty to say, after he had listened to these expressions of opinion, that war with Japan was extremely undesirable, and that we must endeavour to restore in Manchuria a state of tranquillity. The company formed for the purpose of exploiting the timber on the River Ya-lu must be a strictly commercial organization, must admit foreigners who desired to participate, and must exclude all ranks of the army. I was then ordered to proceed to the Far East, for the purpose of acquainting myself, on the spot, with our needs, and ascertaining what the state of mind was in Japan. In the latter country, where I met with the most cordial and kind-hearted reception, I became convinced that the Government desired to avoid a rupture with Russia, but that it would be necessary for us to act in a perfectly definite way in Manchuria, and to refrain from interference in the affairs of Korea. If we permitted the schemes of Bezobrazoff and Company to continue, we should be in danger of a conflict. These conclusions I telegraphed to St. Petersburg. After my departure from that city, however, the danger of a rupture with Japan, on account of Korea, had increased considerably, especially when, on May 20, 1903, the Minister of Finance announced that, "after having had an explanation from State Councillor Bezobrazoff, he (the Minister) was not in disagreement with him so far as the essence of the matter was concerned."

In the council held at Port Arthur, when I arrived, Admiral Alexeieff, Lessar,[62] Pavloff,[63] and I cordially agreed that the Ya-lu enterprise should have a purely commercial character; and I added, moreover, that, in my opinion, it ought to be abandoned altogether. I brought about the recall of several army officers who were taking part in it, and suggested to Lieutenant-Colonel Madritoff, who was managing the military and political side of it, that he should either resign his commission or give up employment which, in my judgment, was not suitable for an officer wearing the uniform of the General Staff. He chose the former alternative.

All the military requests made by Admiral Alexeieff, after consulting with the senior officers in the Kuan-tung district, were carried out with great promptitude. My recommendations and orders were made in Port Arthur, and issued by despatch. In the autumn of 1903 I was thanked by him for acting on his recommendations so promptly. In view of the repeated assurances given me by Admiral Alexeieff that he was wholly opposed to Bezobrazoff's schemes, that he was holding them back with all his strength, and that he was a firm advocate of a peaceful Russo-Japanese agreement, I left Port Arthur for St. Petersburg in July, 1903, fully believing that the avoidance of a rupture with Japan was a matter entirely within our control. The results of my visit to the Far East were embodied in a special report to the Emperor, submitted August 6, 1903, in which I expressed with absolute frankness the opinion that if we did not put an end to the uncertain state of affairs in Manchuria, and to the adventurous activity of Bezobrazoff in Korea, we must expect a rupture with Japan. Copies of this report were sent to the Minister of Foreign Affairs and the Minister of Finance, and met with their approval. By some means unknown to me, this report was given publicity, and on June 24, 1905, the newspaper *Razsvet* printed an article, by a certain M. Roslavleff, entitled "Which is the Greater?" the object of which was to prove that I ought to be included amongst those responsible for the rupture with Japan, because, through fear of Bezobrazoff, I signed a paper drawn up in Port Arthur, which put the Ya-lu enterprise under the protection of Russian troops, and thus stopped the evacuation of Manchuria. This article has been reprinted by many Russian and foreign journals, and there has never been any refutation of the misstatements that it contains with regard to my alleged action in signing this imaginary memorandum.

In view of the special publicity this effusion received, and of the gravity of the accusations levelled against me, I will give a few extracts from it. M. Roslavleff quotes from my report to the Emperor the following sentences and paragraphs:

"Our actions in the basin of the Ya-lu, and our behaviour in Manchuria, have excited in Japan a feeling of hostility which, upon our taking any incautious step, may lead to war.... State Secretary Bezobrazoff's plan of operations, if carried out, will inevitably lead to a violation of the agreement that we made with China on April 8, 1902, and will also, as inevitably, cause complications with Japan.... The actions of State Secretary Bezobrazoff toward the end of last, and at the beginning of this, year have already practically caused a violation of the treaty with China and a breach with Japan.... At the request of Bezobrazoff, Admiral Alexeieff sent a force of mounted rifles to Sha-ho-tzu (on the Ya-lu), and kept a body of troops in Feng-huang-cheng. These measures put a stop to the evacuation of the province of Mukden.... Among other participants in the Ya-lu enterprise who have given trouble to Admiral Alexeieff is Acting State Councillor Balasheff, who has a disposition quite as warlike as that of Bezobrazoff. If Admiral Alexeieff had not succeeded in stopping a despatch from Balasheff to Captain Bodisco with regard to 'catching all the Japanese,' 'punishing them publicly,' and 'taking action with volleys,' there would have been a bloody episode on the Ya-lu before this. Unfortunately, it is liable to happen even now any day.... During my stay in Japan, I had opportunities of seeing with what nervous apprehension the people regarded our activity on the Ya-lu, how they exaggerated our intentions, and how they were preparing to defend by force their Korean interests. Our active operations there have convinced them that Russia is now about to proceed to the second part of her Far Eastern programme—that, having swallowed Manchuria, she is preparing to gulp down Korea. The excitement in Japan is such that if Admiral Alexeieff had not shown wise caution—if he had allowed all the proposals of Bezobrazoff to be put in train—we should probably be at war with Japan now. There is no reason whatever to suppose that a few officers and reservists, cutting timber on the Ya-lu, will be of any use in a war with Japan. Their value is trifling in comparison with the danger that the timber enterprise creates by keeping up the excitement among the Japanese people.... Suffice it to say that, in the opinion of Admiral Alexeieff, and of our Ministers in Peking, Seoul, and Tokio, the timber concession may be the cause of hostilities, and in this opinion I fully concur."

After quoting the above extracts from my report, M. Roslavleff says:

"Thus warmly, eloquently, and shrewdly did Kuropatkin condemn the Ya-lu adventure, and thus clearly did he see on the political horizon the ruinous consequences that it would have for Russia. But why did this bold and clear-sighted censor not protest against the decision of the Port Arthur council? Why, after making a few caustic remarks about Bezobrazoff, did he sign the paper which put the Ya-lu adventure under the protection of Russian troops, and thus stop the evacuation of Manchuria? Why did not the other members, who shared Kuropatkin's opinion as to the great danger of Bezobrazoff's adventurous schemes, and expected a rupture with Japan to be imminent, prevent, on the authority of those July councils at Port Arthur, Bezobrazoff's political and economic escapades? Why did they, on the contrary, with Kuropatkin, put their signatures to a document which admitted Bezobrazoff's enterprises as useful Government undertakings, ratify a treacherous policy in China, Korea, and Japan, and so lay the first stone in the monument of indelible shame erected by the war? Why? Simply because at that time everybody was afraid of Bezobrazoff."

Such accusations, which have had wide publicity, require an explanation.

The council held at Port Arthur, in June, 1903, was called for the purpose of finding, if possible, some means of settling the Manchurian question without lowering the dignity of Russia. There were present at this council, in addition to Admiral Alexeieff and myself, Acting State Councillor Lessar, Russian Minister in China; Chamberlain Pavloff, Russian Minister in Seoul; Major-General Vogak; State Councillor Bezobrazoff; and M. Plancon, an officer of the diplomatic service. We were all acquainted with the wish of the Emperor, that our enterprises in the Far East should not lead to war, and we had to devise means of carrying the Imperial will into effect. With regard to these means there were differences of opinion, but upon fundamental questions there was complete agreement. Among these were—

1. *The Manchurian Question.*—On July 3 the council expressed its judgment with regard to this question as follows: "In view of the extraordinary difficulties and enormous administrative expenses that the annexation of Manchuria would involve, all the members of the council agree that it is, in principle, undesirable; and this conclusion applies not only to Manchuria as a whole, but also to its northern part."

2. *The Korean Question.*—On July 2 the council decided that the occupation of the whole of Korea, or even of the northern part, would be unprofitable to Russia, and therefore undesirable. Our activity in the basin of the Ya-lu, moreover, might give Japan reason to fear a seizure by us of the northern part of the Peninsula. On July 7 the council called upon Acting State Councillor Balasheff, and Lieutenant-Colonel Madritoff of the General Staff, to appear before it, and explain the status of the Ya-lu enterprise. From their testimony it appeared that the concern was legally organized, the company holding permits from the Chinese authorities to cut timber on the northern

side, and a concession from the Korean Government covering the southern side of the Ya-lu. Although the enterprise had lost, to a great extent, its provocative character after the conclusions of the St. Petersburg council of April 18, 1903, became known in the province of Kuan-tung, its operations could not yet be regarded as purely commercial. On July 7 the company had in its employ 9 senior agents, of whom one was an officer of the army; 97 or 98 reservists, who went down the river in charge of rafts from Sha-ho-tzu to its mouth; some 200 Chinamen (from Chifu), and about 900 Koreans. Its affairs were managed by Lieutenant-Colonel Madritoff, although that officer was not officially in the company's service.

After consideration of all the facts put forward, the members of the council came to the unanimous conclusion that, "although the Ya-lu Timber Company really appears to be a commercial organization, its employment of military officers of the active list to do work that has military importance undoubtedly gives to it a politico-military aspect." The council, therefore, in order to deprive Japan of a pretext for looking upon the Timber Company as an enterprise of a military-political character, acknowledged the necessity of "at once taking measures to give the affair an exclusively commercial character, to exclude from it officers of the regular army, and to commit the management of the timber business to persons not employed in the service of the Empire." On July 7 these conclusions were signed by all the members of the council, including State Councillor Bezobrazoff. I declined to go personally into any of the economic questions concerning Manchuria, and said that the proper person to do this was the Minister of Finance. State Secretary Bezobrazoff was asked to work out the following points with the assistance of experts selected by him:

1. "What action should be taken and what economic policy should be followed in Manchuria in order to reduce the deficit on the Eastern Chinese Railway."

2. "To what extent the measures for increasing the revenue of the line and the economic policy in Manchuria, recommended by the experts, would affect the economic situation of the Pri-Amur region."

Another duty entrusted to this sub-committee was the compilation of a list of all the private enterprises which were being carried on in Manchuria. At the last meeting of the council on July 11 the sub-committee's report on the economic question was read out, and it was decided "to take note of its conclusions without discussion, and to attach them to the council's proceedings." Admiral Alexeieff suggested that to this should be added the words, "so that when considering the question of the further economic development in Manchuria, we should endeavour not to invest more State moneys in it." This addition was supported by all the members of the council, excepting State Councillor Bezobrazoff, who did not feel himself able to offer an opinion on the subject.[64] No other conclusions on economic questions generally or any other enterprises in Manchuria were signed by the members of the council at Port Arthur, and matters of an economic nature were not looked into.

It is evident, from the facts above set forth, that the statement in which M. Roslavleff charges the members of the council with signing minutes of proceedings that gave the Bezobrazoff adventure a place among useful Imperial enterprises is fiction. Upon what it was based we do not know. The duty of immediately carrying into effect the conclusions of the council—to put an end immediately to the military-political activity of the timber enterprise on the Ya-lu—rested upon Admiral Alexeieff, by virtue of the authority given to him. The thing that he had to do, first of all, and that he was fully empowered to do, was to recall our force from Feng-huang-cheng, and the mounted rifles from the Ya-lu. Why this was not done I do not know. Personally, I did not allow Lieutenant-Colonel Madritoff, of the General Staff, to continue his connection with the Timber Company, and I may add that he and other officers who had associated themselves with the enterprise did so without my knowledge. But no matter how effective might be the measures taken by Admiral Alexeieff to give the Ya-lu enterprise a purely commercial character, I still feared that this undertaking, which had obtained world-wide notoriety, would continue to have important political significance. In my report of August 6, 1903, which was presented to the Emperor upon my return from Japan, I therefore expressed the opinion that an immediate end must be put to the operations of the Timber Company, and that the whole business should be sold to foreigners. The thought that our interests in Korea, which were of trifling importance, might bring us into conflict with Japan caused me incessant anxiety during my stay in the latter country. On June 26, 1903, when I was passing through the Sea of Japan on my way to Nagasaki, I made the following note in my diary:

"If I were asked to express an opinion, from a military point of view, upon the comparative importance of Russian interests in different parts of the Empire, and on different frontiers, I should put my judgment into the form of a pyramidal diagram, placing the least important of our interests at the top and the most important at the bottom, as follows:

```
            ┌─────────────────┐
            │ Our interests in │
            │     Korea.       │
         ┌──┴─────────────────┴──┐
         │ Our interests in Man-  │
         │       churia.          │
      ┌──┴───────────────────────┴──┐
      │ Military District of the Pri- │
      │ Amur. Safe-guarding of this   │
      │ territory for Russia. Defence │
      │ against China and Japan.      │
   ┌──┴──────────────────────────────┴──┐
   │ Securing the safety of Russia against│
   │ Turkey, Persia, Afghanistan, Great Britain, │
   │ and China. Military Districts of the │
   │ Caucasus, Turkestan, and Siberia.    │
 ┌─┴────────────────────────────────────┴─┐
 │ Maintenance of domestic peace and order by │
 │ the forces of all Military Districts.      │
┌┴──────────────────────────────────────────┴┐
│ Maintenance of the territorial integrity of Russia │
│ against the Powers of the Triple Alliance. The foun- │
│ dation of Russia's safety in her western boundary.   │
└─────────────────────────────────────────────┘
```

"This diagram shows clearly where the principal energies of the Ministry of War should hereafter be concentrated, and in what direction in future Russia's main powers and resources should be turned. The interests that lie at the foundation of our position as a nation are: (1) The defence of the territorial integrity of the Empire against the Powers of the Triple Alliance; and (2) the employment of the forces of all our military districts for the preservation of internal peace and order. In comparison with these tasks all the others have secondary importance. The diagram shows, furthermore, that our interests in the Pri-Amur region must be regarded as more important than our interests in Manchuria, and that the latter must take precedence of our interests in Korea. I am afraid, however, that, for a time at least, our national activity will be based on affairs in the Far East, and, if so, the pyramid will then be turned bottom upwards, and made to stand on its narrow Korean top. But such a structure on such a foundation will fall. Columbus solved the problem of making an egg stand on its end by breaking the egg. Must we, in order to make our pyramid stand on its narrow Korean end, break the Russian Empire?"

Upon my return from Japan I showed the above diagram to M. de Witte, who agreed that it was correct. Notwithstanding the disastrous conclusion to the recent war, we did not adopt Columbus's method. Russia is not yet broken; but undoubtedly, now that the war is over, the above diagram must be considerably altered.

The establishment of the Viceroyalty in the Far East was for me a complete surprise. On August 15, 1903, I asked the Emperor to relieve me of my duty as Minister of War, and after the great manœuvres I was granted long leave of absence, of which I availed myself, expecting that my place would be filled by the appointment of some other person. In September, 1903, the state of affairs in the Far East began to be alarming, and Admiral Alexeieff was definitely ordered to take all necessary measures to avoid war. The Emperor expressed his wish to this effect with firmness, and did not, in any way, limit or restrict the concessions that should be made in order to avoid a rupture with Japan. All that had to be done was to find a method of making these concessions as little injurious as possible to Russian interests. During my stay in Japan, I became satisfied that the Japanese Government was disposed to consider Japanese and Korean affairs calmly, with a view to arriving at an agreement upon the basis of mutual concessions. The Emperor's definitely expressed desire that war should not be allowed to take place had, for a short time, a tranquillizing effect on Far Eastern affairs. In view of the disturbing situation in the Far East, I cut short my leave of absence, and, in reporting to the Emperor for duty, I gave this threatening state of affairs as my reason for returning. On October 23, 1903, the Emperor made the following marginal note upon my letter: "The alarm in the Far East is apparently beginning to subside." In October I recommended that the garrison at Vladivostok should be strengthened, but permission to reinforce it was not given. Meanwhile there was really no re-establishment of tranquillity in the Far East, and our relations with Japan and China were becoming more and more involved. On October 28, 1903, I presented to the Emperor a special report on the Manchurian question, in which I showed that, in order to avoid complications with China and a rupture with Japan, we must put an end to our military occupation of Southern Manchuria, and confine our activity and our administrative supervision to the northern part of that territory.

At the time when this report was presented, and later—in November—the negotiations that Admiral Alexeieff was carrying on with Japan not only made no progress, but became more critical, the Admiral still believing that to show a yielding disposition would only make matters worse.

Bearing in mind the clearly expressed will of the Emperor that all necessary measures should be taken to avoid war, and not expecting favourable results from Alexeieff's negotiations, I submitted to His Majesty, on December 6, 1903, a second memorandum on the Manchurian question, in which I proposed that we should restore Port Arthur and the province of Kuan-tung to China, and sell the southern branch of the Eastern Chinese Railway, securing, in lieu thereof, certain special rights in the northern part of Manchuria. In substance, this proposition was that we should admit the untimeliness of our attempt to get an outlet on the Pacific, and abandon it altogether. The sacrifice might seem a heavy one to make, but I showed the necessity for it by emphasizing two important considerations. In the first place, by surrendering Port Arthur (which had been taken away from the Japanese), and by giving up Southern Manchuria (with the Ya-lu enterprise), we should escape the danger of a rupture with Japan and China; in the second place, we should avoid the possibility of internal disturbances in European Russia. A war with Japan would be extremely unpopular, and would increase the feeling of dissatisfaction with the ruling authorities.

At the end of this memorandum occurred the following passage:

"The economic interests of Russia in the Far East are negligible. We have as yet, thank God, no overproduction in manufactures, because our domestic markets are not yet glutted. There may be some export of articles from our factories and foundries, but it is largely bounty-fed, and will cease—or nearly cease—when such artificial encouragement is withheld. Russia, therefore, has not yet arrived at the pitiable necessity of waging war in order to obtain markets for her products. As for our other interests in that quarter, the success or failure of a few coal or timber enterprises in Manchuria and Korea is not a matter of sufficient importance to justify the risk of war. The railway-lines built through Manchuria cannot change the situation quickly, and the hope that these lines will have world-wide importance as arteries of international commerce is not likely to be soon realized. Travellers, mails, tea and possibly some other merchandise will go over them, but the great masses of heavy international freight, which alone can give such importance to a railway, must still go by sea, on account of the heavy railway rates. Such is not the case, however, with local freight to supply local needs. This the railroad—and especially the southern branch—will carry in increasing amount, thus deriving most of its revenue, and, at the same time, stimulating the growth of the country, and, in Southern Manchuria particularly, benefiting the Chinese population. But if we do not take special measures to direct even local freight to Dalny, that port is likely to suffer from the competition of Newchuang. Port Arthur has no value for Russia as the defence and terminus of a railway, unless that railway is part of an international transit route. The southern branch of the Eastern Chinese road has commercially only—or chiefly—local importance, and Russia does not need to protect it by means so costly as the fortifications of Port Arthur, a fleet of warships, and a garrison of 30,000 men. It thus appears that the retention of a forward position in Kuan-tung is no more supported by economic than it is by political and military considerations. What, then, are the interests that may involve us in war with Japan and China? Are such interests important enough to justify the great sacrifices that war will demand?

*   *   *   *   *

"The Russian people are powerful, and their faith in Divine Providence, as well as their devotion to their Tsar and country, is unshaken. We may trust, therefore, that if Russia is destined to undergo the trial of war at the beginning of the twentieth century, she will come out of it with victory and glory. But she will have to make terrible sacrifices—sacrifices that may long retard the natural growth of the Empire. In the wars that we waged in the early years of the seventeenth, eighteenth, and nineteenth centuries, the enemy invaded our territory, and we fought for our very existence— marched forth in defence of our country and died for faith, Tsar, and Fatherland. If, in the early years of the twentieth century, war breaks out as the result of Far Eastern complications, the Russian people and the Russian army will execute the will of their monarch with as much devotion and self-sacrifice as ever, and will give up their lives and property for the sake of attaining complete victory; but they will have no intelligent comprehension of the objects for which the war is waged. For that reason there will be no such exaltation of spirit, no such outburst of patriotism, as that which accompanied the wars that we fought either in self-defence or for objects dear to the hearts of the people.

"We are now passing through a critical period. Internal enemies, aiming at the destruction of the dearest and most sacred foundations of life, are invading even the ranks of our army. Large groups of the population have become dissatisfied, or mentally unsettled, and disorders of various sorts—mostly created by revolutionary propaganda—are increasing in frequency. Cases in which troops have to be called out to deal with such disorders are much more common than they were even a short time ago. Secret revolutionary publications directed against the Government are being more frequently found, even in the barracks. ... We must hope, however, that this evil has not yet taken deep root in Russian soil, and that by strict and wise measures it may be eradicated. If Russia were attacked from without, the people, with patriotic fervour, would undoubtedly repudiate the false teaching of the revolutionary propaganda, and show themselves as ready to answer the call of their revered monarch, and to defend their Tsar and country, as they were in the early years of the eighteenth and particularly in the nineteenth century. If, however, they are asked to make great sacrifices in order to carry on a war whose objects are not clearly understood by them, the leaders of the anti-Government party will take advantage of the opportunity to spread sedition. Thus there will be introduced a new factor which, if we decide on war in the Far East, we must take into account. The sacrifices and dangers that we have experienced, or that we anticipate, as results of the position we have taken in the Far East, ought to be a warning to us when we dream of getting an outlet on the warm waters of the Indian Ocean at Chahbar.[65] It is already evident that the British are preparing to meet us there. The building of a railroad across Persia, the construction of a defended port and the maintenance of a fleet, etc., will simply be a repetition of our experience with the Eastern Chinese Railway and Port Arthur. In the place of Port Arthur we shall have Chahbar, and instead of war with Japan, we shall have a still more unnecessary and still more terrible war with Great Britain.

"In view of the considerations above set forth, the questions arise: Ought we not to avoid the present danger at Port Arthur, as well as the future danger in Persia? Ought we not to restore Kuan-tung, Port Arthur, and Dalny to China, give up the southern branch of the Eastern Chinese Railway, and get from China, in place of it, certain rights in Northern Manchuria and a sum of, say, £25,000,000 as compensation for expenses incurred by us in connection with the railway and Port Arthur?"

Copies of this report were sent to the Minister of Foreign Affairs, the Minister of Finance, and Admiral Alexeieff. Unfortunately, my views were not approved, and meanwhile the negotiations with Japan had been dragging along and becoming more and more involved. The future historian, who will have access to all the documents, may be able, from a study of them, to determine why the will of the Russian monarch to avoid war with Japan was not carried into effect by his principal subordinates. At present it is only possible to state definitely that, although neither the Emperor nor Russia desired war, we did not succeed in escaping it. The reason for the failure of the negotiations is evidently to be found in our ignorance of Japan's readiness for war, and her determination to support her contentions with armed force. We ourselves were not ready to fight, and resolved that it should not come to fighting. We made demands, but we had no intention of using weapons to enforce them—and, it may be added, they were not worth going to war about. We always thought, moreover, that the question whether there should be war or peace depended upon us, and we wholly overlooked Japan's stubborn determination to enforce demands that had for her such vital importance, and also her reliance upon our military unreadiness. Thus the negotiations were not carried on by the respective parties under equal conditions.

Again, our position at this period was made worse by the form that Admiral Alexeieff gave to the negotiations entrusted to him. Japanese pride was offended, and the whole correspondence became strained and difficult as a result of the Admiral's unfamiliarity with diplomatic procedure and his lack of competent staff assistance. He proceeded, moreover, upon the mistaken assumption that it was necessary to display inflexibility and tenacity. His idea was that one concession would inevitably lead to another, and that a yielding policy would be more likely to bring about a rupture in the end than a policy of firmness.

The paper *Nasha Jizn*, on July 4, 1905, published an article entitled "The Viceroy Alexeieff's Firm Policy," which was circulated all over the world. It ran as follows:

"Now, when the disasters which have befallen our operations by land and sea, together with all the terrible, incredible sufferings of our soldiers and sailors, are turning our thoughts to the persons responsible for the wretched war, we must remember, in deciding the extent to which different departments and persons were responsible for the 'preliminary events,' that Russian interests in the Far East were represented by the Viceroy, who was intimately acquainted with all the political circumstances, and who must be considered an authority on Far Eastern affairs.

"Admiral Alexeieff's policy was 'firm,' and all his endeavours were directed to prevent Russia's political position in those regions being weakened, and it was on this account that he did not feel able to recommend the evacuation of Manchuria after it had been occupied for three years. Notwithstanding the absolute necessity for making concessions, he reported in September, 1903, that the Japanese proposal was 'quite an impossible pretension,' that it must be definitely laid down as a preliminary to any negotiations with Japan that we should continue in occupation of Manchuria, and that he 'was firmly convinced' that this was the only settlement in accordance with our position in the Far East.

"The opinion of the late Viceroy, 'based' on the general political situation, was such that a successful issue to the negotiations could only be 'expected' if the Japanese Government were clearly given to understand that Russia was determined to support her rights and interests in Manchuria by force of arms. With this idea, and owing to the 'provocative action of the Japanese,' Alexeieff proposed a whole series of measures, amongst which was one that we should at once attack them on the sea in the event of a landing at Chemulpo, Chinampo, or the mouth of the Ya-lu. He was 'deeply convinced' that, in order to arrive at an agreement with Japan, the most important thing was 'an inflexible resolution and timely action, which alone can prevent Japan realizing her extraordinarily ambitious intentions.'

"When, in December, 1903, the Japanese Government presented their proposals in reply to the draft agreement drawn up by Alexeieff, and described by him as 'an honourable retreat for her from a position which she has herself created by her arrogant behaviour,' he characterized these as being 'equivalent to a demand that the Russian Government should formally acknowledge Japan's protectorate over Korea.' Indeed, he considered the requests made by her 'so presumptuous that we should at once reject them.' In presenting such requests, he said, 'Japan exceeds the limit of all reason,' and he consequently felt that no concession was possible, and that it would be better to break off negotiations, after clearly explaining that in her proposals Russia 'had reached the extreme limit of concession.' Then, when the Japanese began to occupy Korea at the end of December, 1903, Alexeieff represented most strongly that 'for self-defence corresponding steps should be taken to maintain the balance of power upset by the occupation of Korea'—*i.e.*, that the lower reaches of the Ya-lu should be occupied, and the mobilization of the Far Eastern districts and the province of Siberia should be carried out. He was of opinion that Japan's final proposals, received in the middle of January, 1904, were 'in tone and substance still more pretentious and bold than before,' and he insisted on the negotiations being broken off, asserting that their continuation 'could not lead to a settlement of mutual interests,' and that 'any display of yielding on our part would lead to a great loss of dignity to Russia and to a corresponding augmentation of the prestige of Japan in the eyes of the whole East.'

"This was three weeks before the diplomatic negotiations were broken off. Has Russia's dignity not yet suffered in full measure?

"Finally, our last answer to Japan—despatched only a few days before the declaration of war—which contained a refusal to consider a neutral zone, and admitted Japan's right to predominate in Korea, was stated to be 'an exhibition of generosity beyond which Russia could scarcely go.'

"After three or four days—*i.e.*, on February 6, 1904—diplomatic relations were broken off by Japan, and so began that awful war which might have been prevented without loss of dignity to us if the Viceroy's policy had been a little less 'firm,' and—it must be added—a little less eccentric."

My opinions with regard to the relative importance of the tasks which confronted our War Department made me a convinced opponent of an active Asiatic policy.

Realizing our military unreadiness on our western frontier, and taking into account the urgent need of devoting our resources to the work of internal reorganization and reform, I thought that a rupture with Japan would be a national calamity, and did everything in my power to prevent it. Throughout my long service in Asia I had not only been an advocate of an agreement with Great Britain on that continent, but I was also certain that a peaceable delimitation of spheres of influence between us and Japan was possible.

In my opinion, the carrying of the main line of the Trans-Siberian Railway through Manchuria was a mistake. I had nothing to do with the adoption of that route, as I was then Commander of the Trans-Caspian Military District; it was also contrary to the opinion of General Dukhovski, representative of the War Department in the Far East.

CHAPTER VII

WHY THE JAPANESE WERE SUCCESSFUL

The army we put in the field was unable to defeat the Japanese in the time allotted to it. Many historians will probably essay to solve the riddle of how a Power, which we regarded as belonging to the second class, and one which not long ago possessed no army, was able to crush us absolutely on the sea, and to defeat a strong force on land, and doubtless we shall eventually be furnished with the reasons in full. For the present I propose to mention only some general causes which contributed to Japan's success. Broadly speaking, we underestimated her power, particularly her moral strength, and entered upon the war far too lightly.

The Japanese first became our neighbours when we occupied Kamchatka in the reign of Peter the Great. In 1860, after the peaceful occupation of the extensive Ussuri region—by virtue of the Treaty of Peking—we moved down to the frontier of Korea and the Sea of Japan. This sea, which is almost completely enclosed by Korea and the Japanese Islands, is of immense importance to the whole of the adjacent coasts, and as the outlets from it into the ocean were in her hands, Japan might have easily prevented our obtaining free access to the Pacific. But, by our acquisition of Saghalien, we gained an outlet through Tartar Strait.[66] This, however, was frequently and for long periods icebound, and for about forty years the only spot developed on the Ussuri coast was Vladivostok. Our new neighbour did not attract any attention from us for a long time—so long, in fact, as her life did not come into contact with ours—and we remained confident of her military weakness. We knew the Japanese as skilful and patient artisans; we were fond of their productions, of which the delicate workmanship and brilliant colouring charmed us; our sailors spoke with appreciation of the country and its inhabitants, and were full of pleasant reminiscences of their visits, especially of Nagasaki, where they appeared to be popular with the inhabitants; but as a military factor Japan did not exist. Our sailors, travellers, and diplomats, had entirely overlooked the awakening of an energetic, independent people.

H.I.M. THE EMPEROR OF JAPAN.

In 1867 the armed forces of Japan consisted of 10,000 men, organized in nine battalions, two squadrons, and eight batteries. This force, which constituted the cadre of the standing army, was trained by French instructors, from whom, also, the troops obtained the pattern of their uniform. In 1872, as a result of the Franco-German War, Japan was subjected to the law of universal service; the French instructors were replaced by Germans, who organized the army according to German ideas, and officers were sent every year to Europe to study their profession. At the time of the Chino-Japanese War the army consisted of seven infantry divisions; but, being prevented from enjoying the fruits of her victories in this war by reason of her weakness both on land and sea, the nation strained every nerve to create an army and navy capable of protecting its interests. On April 1, 1896, the Mikado issued a decree for the reorganization of the military forces, by which the strength of the army would be doubled in seven years. In 1903 this reorganization was completed. Statistically the creation and growth of this great naval and military force were not overlooked by us; the construction of every warship and the formation of every new division of infantry was mentioned in the reports of our Navy and War Departments. But we did not properly appreciate the meaning of these beginnings, and were unable to gauge the fighting value of the mere numbers by any European standard. Detailed information as to the organization and strength of the army, with an appreciation of its technical preparedness and capability of mobilization, was compiled in a handbook by the Headquarter Staff and revised annually. This book contained the following figures as to the strength of the Japanese troops which took part in the Chinese War of 1894–95, and in the expedition in 1900 to the province of Pei-chih-li:

1. *War with China, 1894–95.*—In this war Japan was forced to put forward the whole of her military strength. Each of the seven divisions which then existed were mobilized and despatched from Hiroshima to the theatre of war as operations developed. Half of the 5th Division was sent to Korea in the middle of June before war had actually been declared, followed in August, after hostilities had commenced, by the other half and the whole of the 3rd Division. These two divisions constituted the 1st Army, which defeated the Chinese forces at Pingyang in September, forced the passage of the Ya-lu in October, and moved on Mukden through South-East Manchuria. After a naval engagement at the mouth of the River Ya-lu, the 2nd Army, consisting of the 1st Division and half of the 6th, was, by September 30, concentrated at Hiroshima. This army landed north of Pi-tzu-wo, and fought its way into Port Arthur. Towards the end of 1894, three and a half divisions, of a total strength of 52,600 men, were in Southern Manchuria. In the beginning of 1895, the 2nd Division and the other half of the 6th Division were landed on the Shan-tung Peninsula; these troops composed the 3rd Army, numbering about 24,000 men. Thus, by the beginning of 1895, more than 75,000 men had been landed in China. Thirty vessels of a steamship company, subsidized by the Japanese Government, were chartered for the conveyance of these troops. On account of the roughness of the country in the theatre of war the land transport consisted mostly of carriers organized into corps, the majority of whom were recruited in Japan; the remainder were coolies collected in Korea and Manchuria. For the preliminary expenses of the war the Japanese Treasury allotted £4,500,000; later, an internal loan of £15,000,000 was raised. When the whole of the extraordinary expenditure was totalled, it was estimated that the war cost Japan about £20,000,000, of which £16,420,000 was chargeable to the War Department and £3,580,000 to the Navy Department.

2. *The Expedition to China in 1900.*—At first, a force of three battalions, one squadron, and one company of sappers—total 3,000 men—of the 5th and 11th Divisions was mobilized in July, followed about a month later by the mobilization of the 5th Division. The troops were conveyed to Ta-ku in twenty-one transports, chartered from the Nippon-Yusen-Kaisha.[67] Excluding the first force, 19,000 men in all were taken (the whole of the

5th Division, the Zopoleff batteries, part of the railway battalion from Tokio, and 6,000 to 7,000 hired coolies wearing uniform). Altogether, 22,000 men were transported—the 5th Division with its units and coolies—and all the supplies were sent from Japan. During the whole time, about 6,000 sick and wounded were returned to the base, while one-half of the cavalry and artillery and three-quarters of the transport horses died. The cost of the expedition, estimated at £3,800,000 to £4,000,000, was taken from the fund of some £5,000,000 set aside for the construction of warships and emergency expenditure. Within seven years of the war of 1894–95 Japan had almost doubled her armed forces, and was very largely enabled to do this by the war indemnity received from China, the payment of which was made through our mediation.

The strength of the Japanese army, before the war with us, was calculated by our Headquarter Staff to be as follows:

The peace strength of the standing army (excluding the garrison of Formosa) was estimated at 8,116 officers and 133,457 men. For economy, however, only 6,822 officers and 110,000 men were actually with the colours in peace, and of these, about 13,500 were continually on furlough. The war strength was fixed at 10,735 officers (without depôt troops) and 348,074 men. Thus, to bring the peace numbers up to the war establishment, about 3,900 officers and 240,000 more men were required. On January 1, 1901, there were in the standing army, reserve, and territorial forces a total of 2,098 staff and general officers, 8,755 regimental and warrant officers, 35,248 non-commissioned officers, 6,964 second-lieutenants and *yunkers*, and 273,476 men, a total of 10,853 officers and 315,688 men.[68] Taking the peace establishment of the standing army at 8,116 officers and about 110,000 men, it is evident that on January 1, 1901, there were 2,737 officers and about 205,000 men in the reserve and territorial forces. Comparing these numbers with those required to bring the peace establishment up to war strength, we find that on January 1, 1901, the numbers could not have been obtained; that there was a shortage of officers equal to those required for the reserve troops,[69] and a shortage of some 35,000 men. Taking into consideration the probable yearly contingent of recruits (45,000 men), and also the periods of service in the different classes of troops, it may be said that by January 1, 1903, the number of men in the reserve and territorial forces was approximately 265,000.[70] Finally, to complete the army in an emergency, some 50,000 men were obtainable from the reserve of recruits, the majority of whom were quite untrained. No mention has been yet made of reserve troops, but preparations were made for their formation, and, according to the number of battalions, they must have increased the standing army by two-thirds of its establishment. The latest information prior to the war which we had of the strength, organization, and training of the Japanese army was based on the reports of our military attaché in Japan, Colonel Vannovski, of the General Staff. Colonel Adabash, who visited Japan in 1903, forwarded to General Jilinski, of the Headquarter Staff, very important information as to the reserve units, towards whose formation steps were then being taken; but as this information differed completely from that sent by Colonel Vannovski, Major-General Jilinski unfortunately did not consider it reliable. Some months later, Captain Rusin, our naval attaché in that country, an extremely able officer, forwarded to the Headquarter Staff of the navy very much the same information as that furnished by Adabash. His report was transmitted by the Navy Department to General Sakharoff, Chief of the Headquarter Staff. It was ascertained later that both these reports were quite accurate, but that they had been pigeon-holed because neither General Jilinski nor General Sakharoff believed them. Consequently, the information in the printed handbooks as to the Japanese armed forces in 1903–04 did not include a single word as to reserves. Similarly, we did not attach a proper value to their numerous depôt troops. According to our calculations, based on information sent in by our military attachés in Japan, the available supply of men for the permanent and territorial armies and for the depôt troops amounted only to a little over 400,000.

The official figures as to the Japanese War casualties have now been published by the principal medical officer of the Japanese army, Surgeon-General Kipke. From these it appears that their losses amounted to: killed, 47,387; wounded, 172,425—total, 219,812. The total killed, wounded, and sick amounted to 554,885 [a considerably greater number than the total we thought they could put in the field against us], and 320,000 sick and wounded were sent back to Japan. From other sources we now know that they buried 60,624 killed in the Cemetery of Honour in Tokio, and that 74,545 besides died from wounds and sickness. They must admit, therefore, to 135,000 killed and dead. As Surgeon-General Kipke states that the killed and wounded amounted to 14·58 per cent. of their total strength, it would appear that the total number of troops put in the field against us was over 1,500,000, or was more than three times the number anticipated by our Headquarter Staff. In view of these facts, it is evident that our information as to their fighting strength was incorrect. As an instance of the neglect, referred to in the preceding paragraph, to take any account of the formation of reserve units, a scheme drawn up in Port Arthur in November, 1903, for the strategical distribution of our troops in the Far East in the event of complications, estimated the numbers that Japan could place against us as follows:

"At the beginning of hostilities, when her territorial army is not completely organized, out of her 13 field divisions, she will only be able to put 9 divisions of a strength of 120 infantry battalions, 46 squadrons of cavalry, 10 engineer battalions, and 1 siege battalion— a total of 125,000 combatants—in the field."

This calculation agrees with the reports furnished in 1903 by our military attaché in Japan, Lieutenant-Colonel Samoiloff, of the General Staff, who informed me, when I was in Japan, that they could only put in the field 10 divisions out of 13; of the reserve troops he knew nothing. Again, in a memorandum written in the Operations Branch of the Headquarter Staff, and submitted to me by the Chief of the General Staff on February 12, 1904, it was stated that, according to available information, the Japanese could put 11 of their 13 divisions in the field, leaving 2 in Japan. In this memorandum, again, no mention was made of the reserve units.

The readiness of their army for mobilization, owing to their adoption of a territorial system, and the consequent short distances the depôt troops had to travel, was known to be very complete. We knew that the troops could complete their mobilization in three or four days, while the supply and other departments would require seven to ten. Information as to transports available showed that even in 1902 they could have collected in seven days 86 ships with an aggregate displacement of 224,000 tons, and in fourteen days 97 ships with a displacement of 268,000. For a mobilized division about 40,000 tons are required for a journey of more than forty-eight hours, while 20,000 tons would suffice for a journey of less than forty-eight hours. Thus the tonnage available was sufficient to allow embarkation to be commenced at once on completion of mobilization of six divisions for a journey of not more than forty-eight hours, or of almost the whole army for a lesser distance.

As regards the tactical readiness of the Japanese before the war, our people in Manchuria did receive certain information. The operations of large bodies of their troops of all arms had been commented upon by our Headquarter Staff as follows:

"The most noticeable points in the operations of bodies consisting of all three arms as seen at the manœuvres were—

"1. The inclination to take up too extended defensive positions.

"2. A hard-and-fast, inelastic form of attack independent of local conditions.

"3. The absence of proper flank protection both on the march and in action.

"4. The tendency, when on the move, to keep the main body too far from the advance guard, which would in consequence have to fight unsupported for a long time.

"5. The absence of a definite objective in the attack.

"6. The tendency to use up reserves too quickly. As a result, there are frequently no troops with which to meet turning and enveloping movements.

"7. The disbelief in cold steel.

"8. The inclination to avoid enclosed and, in particular, hilly ground.

"9. The inclination to use direct frontal attacks without turning movements.

"10. The neglect of field fortifications in the defence; infantry fire trenches, gun-pits and epaulements alone are made.

"11. The complete absence of any idea of pursuit.

"12. The tendency to retire too rapidly: the infantry of the main body withdraws first; this is followed by the whole of the guns, and then the remaining infantry.

"13. The disinclination for night operations.

"14. The absence of contact between divisions: each division operates independently without keeping in touch with others; this is due to the lack of general control by the officer in chief command.

"In reviewing their own operations against China in 1900, the Japanese Press expressed the opinion that the operations of small bodies were excellently carried out, but that the troops, if operating in force, would probably be considerably inferior to Europeans. In the last grand autumn manœuvres in 1903 it was noticed that the troops were well trained. Considerable initiative was observed amongst the junior officers, which was more than could be said of the seniors; great interest was taken in the work, and everything was very thoroughly done. The technical services were excellent. The artillery and infantry manœuvred well; the cavalry were learning to ride, and appeared keen, but the generals did not know how to use cavalry, and employed it little; the instruction, however, was good. The thing which most attracted attention was the rapidity with which the mountain artillery came into action. On being ordered out from column of route, they got into action and opened fire in three and a half minutes."

From the above remarks it may be gathered how badly the officers, to whom was entrusted the duty of studying the Japanese troops on the spot, carried out this duty; particularly faulty was their deduction regarding the inability of the senior officers to command in war.

After the war with China, which ended in the expulsion of the Japanese from the Liao-tung Peninsula and our occupation of Kuan-tung, they began to prepare in haste for war with us. From a little more than £2,000,000 in 1893, 1894, and 1895, their military Budget rose in 1896 to £7,300,000, in 1897 to £10,300,000, and in 1900 to £13,300,000. In 1902 all her preparations were apparently complete, and the Budget again fell to £7,500,000. Of the expenses incurred from 1896 to 1902 on increases to the forces, the War Department spent £4,800,000, and the Navy Department spent in nine years £13,800,000 [in building ships for the fleet]. It should be added that, while developing her forces, Japan was in other ways preparing for hostilities. A number of officers were sent to study their profession in Europe, including our own country, and the probable theatre of operations was investigated with great care, reconnaissances being organized in every direction. At great self-sacrifice also many officers were performing the most menial duties in our employ in the Far East in order to study our ways at a time when our military representatives in Japan were looking upon their nation with immense condescension!

As regards the organization of their forces, our information was sufficiently complete regarding everything which concerned the standing army; we also knew the number of depôt troops and the supposed dispositions of the territorial forces. But, while ourselves preparing to fight the Japanese with an army half composed of reserve troops, we never suspected that they, too, were organizing a great formation of reserve units, and that, owing to our slow concentration, they would be able to complete this formation. Amongst their reserve troops were men of all classes, and while our "second category" men constituted, according to our generals in the field, an element of particular weakness, their reserve soldiers, thanks to the patriotism and the martial spirit which permeated all ranks, fought not only no worse than their regulars, but in some cases better.[71] The appearance of their reserve units in the first battles was indeed a complete surprise for us. Nor did we properly appreciate the organization of their strong depôt units, which enabled every regiment of the standing army to have its depôt battalion, from which its wastage was uninterruptedly and quickly made good. Later, many of these battalions received extra companies, which brought them up to a strength of over 1,500 men, and some were moved into Manchuria and stationed close to the field troops. I fancy, also, that they were occasionally even used in the field—for instance, in protecting portions of positions which had been vacated by the field army—but their main function, that of repairing the wastage of men, was very successfully performed. The army possessed fewer battalions than we had, but they were kept up to strength even during a series of battles, and were usually superior in numbers to ours. Generally speaking, each Japanese battalion, taking the number of rifles, was equal to one and a half, and sometimes two and three, of ours. With us, on the contrary, the replacement of casualties was very fitful and unsatisfactory.

Though our information as to the material points of the enemy's strength can hardly be described as good, we very much underestimated—if we did not entirely overlook—its moral side. We paid no attention to the fact that for many years the education of the Japanese people had been carried out in a martial spirit and on patriotic lines. We saw nothing in the educational methods of a country where the children in the elementary schools are taught to love their nation and to be heroes. The nation's belief in and deep respect for the army, the individual's willingness and pride in serving, the iron discipline maintained among all ranks, and the influence of the *samurai* spirit, escaped our notice, while we attached no importance to the intense feeling of resentment that we aroused when we deprived the Japanese of the fruits of their victories in China. We never recognized how vital the Korean question was to them, and that the "Young Japanese" party had long ago determined to fight us, and was only restrained by the wise action of their Government. True, when hostilities began we did see all these things, but it was too late. And at that time, when the war was neither popular with, nor understood by, our nation, the whole manhood of Japan was responding with unanimous enthusiasm to the call to arms. There were instances of mothers committing suicide when their sons were rejected for the army on medical grounds. A call for volunteers for a forlorn hope produced hundreds ready to face certain death. While many officers and men had their funeral rites performed before leaving for the front, to show their intention of dying for their country, those who were taken prisoners at the commencement of operations committed suicide. The one idea of the youth of Japan was to serve in the army, and all the great families tried to do something for their country either by giving their children to it or by providing money. This spirit produced regiments which hurled themselves upon our obstacles with a shout of "Banzai!" broke through them, and throwing the corpses of their comrades into the *trous de loup*,[72] climbed over them on to our works. The nation as well as the soldiers felt the vital importance of the war, appreciated the reasons for which it was being fought, and spared no sacrifices to obtain victory. In this and in the co-operation of the nation with the army and the Government lay the strength which brought Japan victory. And it was with an army weakened by the feeling of opposition in its own country that we had to face the armed might of such a nation!

While they had hundreds of secret as well as avowed agents studying our military and naval forces in the Far East, we entrusted the collection of information to one officer of the General Staff, and unfortunately our selection was bad. One of the so-called "Japanese experts" declared in Vladivostok before the war that we might count one Russian soldier as being as good as three Japanese. After the first few fights he modified his tone, and acknowledged that one Japanese soldier was as good as one Russian. A month later he affirmed that if we meant to win, we must put three men into the field for every Japanese! In May, 1904, one of our late military attachés at Tokio predicted, as an expert, that Port Arthur would very soon fall, and Vladivostok immediately after it. I reprimanded this cowardly babbler, and threatened to send him away from the front if he could not restrain his ill-timed and mischievous remarks.

After the Chino-Japanese War, which I had studied with great care, I, personally, was inspired with great respect for the Japanese army, and I watched its growth with considerable alarm. The behaviour of their troops which fought alongside ours in the Pei-chih-li province in 1900 only confirmed my opinion as to their value. In the short time I spent in Japan itself I was unable to get to know the country and its troops, but what I saw was sufficient to show me how astounding were the results attained by the Japanese in the previous twenty-five to thirty years. I saw a beautiful country filled with a numerous and industrious people. Great activity was visible on all sides, and underlying everything could be felt the national happy nature, love of country, and belief in the future. The system of education I witnessed in the Military School was of a Spartan nature, the physical exercises of the future officers being like nothing I had ever seen in Europe; it was really fighting of the fiercest kind. At the end of a bout with weapons the competitors got to hand grips, and fought till the winner had got his opponent down and could tear off his mask. The exercises themselves were performed with the greatest possible keenness and determination, the men hitting one another with wild shouts; but the moment the combat was over or the signal to stop was given, the usual wooden, impassive expression again came over the faces of the combatants. In all the schools military exercises were very conspicuous, and the children and boys were greatly interested in them. Even their walks out were always enlivened by tactical tasks adapted to the localities; turning movements as well as surprise attacks were practised and performed at the double. The study of Japanese history in all the schools had strengthened the people's love for their native land, and filled them with a deep-rooted conviction that it was invincible. Their successes in war were everywhere sung, the heroes of those campaigns continually extolled, and the children were taught that not one of Japan's military enterprises had ever failed. In the small-arm factories I saw large quantities of rifles being turned out, and the work was carried on with rapidity, accuracy, and economy. In

Kobe and Nagasaki I inspected the shipbuilding yards, in which the construction not only of ocean-going destroyers, but of armoured cruisers, was proceeding; everything was being done by Japanese workmen under their own foremen and engineers. The trade of the whole country was most splendidly and instructively represented at the Great Exhibition of Osaka, where there was a large collection of manufactured articles of every sort, including textiles and complicated instruments, such as grand-pianos, engines, and heavy ordnance. These were all made in Japan with Japanese labour, and mainly from Japanese materials, except in the case of raw cotton and iron, which were imported from China and Europe. Not less impressive than their progress in manufacture was the orderly and dignified demeanour of the Japanese who thronged the Exhibition. Agriculture was still carried on in a primitive manner, but it was very close. Though the soil was most carefully cultivated, the keen competition for every plot of ground, the struggle to make even the hills productive, and the general scarcity of food-stuffs in the country (despite the intensive culture), showed how crowded the population was becoming, and how vital the Korean question was for the whole nation. After ten days spent among the fisher class, I got an idea of the reverse side of Japan's rapid development according to European ideals, and many were the complaints made to me of the heavy taxes, which had increased so rapidly of late, and of the great cost of all the necessaries of life.

I saw some of their troops on parade (Guards Division, two regiments of the 1st Division, several batteries, and two cavalry regiments). Nearly everything was excellent, and the men marched well, and looked like our *yunkers* but the poor quality of the horses was very noticeable. Even after such short acquaintance, many of the officers and men gave the impression of being fitted by training and knowledge of their profession to fill honourable posts in any army. Besides the War Minister (General Terauchi), whom I had known in 1896, when we were both attached to the 17th Army Corps at the great French manœuvres, I met Generals Yamagata, Oyama, Kodama, Fukushima, Nodzu, Hasegawa, Murata, Princes Fushima, Kanin, and others. I also met numerous leaders in other spheres of life, among whom were Ito, Katsura, and Kamimura, and, in spite of the sad war which has placed a barrier between two nations that seem created to be friends and allies, I still feel affectionately towards my Tokio acquaintances. I especially remember the intense love of country and devotion to the Sovereign which permeated all, and showed itself in their daily life. In the report made after my visit, I stated my opinion that the Japanese army was fully equal to the armies of Europe; that while one of our battalions on the defensive could hold two Japanese battalions, we would require to be twice as strong as they when attacking. The test of war has shown that I was correct. There were, of course, regrettable instances when the Japanese, with fewer battalions than were opposed to them, drove our troops from their positions; but this was due to bad leadership on our side, and to the inferior war-strength of our battalions. In the latter phases of the Battle of Mukden, for instance, some of our brigades[73] could muster little more than 1,000 rifles. To be superior to such a brigade the Japanese only needed two to three battalions.

Everything that I saw and studied concerning the country—its armed forces, and its work in the Far East—convinced me how necessary it was to come to a peaceful agreement with Japan, even at the expense of concessions which might at first sight appear to be derogatory to our national self-esteem. As already stated (in Chapter V.), I did not hesitate to recommend even the restoration of Kuan-tung and Port Arthur to China, and the sale of the southern branch of the Eastern Chinese Railway. I foresaw that a Japanese war would be most unpopular in Russia, and that, as the reasons for it would not be understood by the nation, it would find no support in national feeling, and I showed that the anti-Government party would take advantage of it to increase the disturbance in the interior. But even I did not give our enemy credit for the activity, bravery, and intense patriotism which they exhibited, and was, therefore, mistaken in the time I thought that such a struggle would last. We ought to have allowed three years for the land operations, owing to our very inferior railway communication, instead of the one and a half years estimated by me. We did less than the world expected of us, and the Japanese did more.

Major Emmanuel, of the German army, a lecturer at the Military Academy at Berlin, gives the following appreciation of the Japanese military forces in his work on the Russo-Japanese War:

> "At the beginning of the war the Japanese possessed an army, organized and trained according to the German ideal, but carefully adapted to the national peculiarities. It was excellently armed, in a high state of efficiency, and was commanded by a splendidly trained corps of officers, worthy of the deepest respect. The fleet is, however, the vital necessity of the country, and every Japanese is a born sailor, and, thanks to his intelligence and the practice he gets, handles the most modern ships admirably. Having adapted modern methods to her national idiosyncrasies, Japan has put in the field an army without nerves, and one that thoroughly understands the conditions of modern war. To great natural intelligence and aptitude for learning the Japanese soldier adds dash, a contempt for death, and a preference for the attack."

The British General, Sir Ian Hamilton, who was attached to the Japanese during the war, states his opinion that a Japanese battalion has no equal in European armies. Of their characteristics generally, he says:

"... and upon the patriotism which they have absorbed with their mother's milk, the Government has been careful to graft initiative, quickness, and intelligence. This is accomplished in the schools, which keep the soldierly virtues in the forefront of their curriculum."[74]

*   *   *   *   *

With all their strong points, however, the Japanese had weaknesses which I need not enumerate here. There is a saying that "a conqueror cannot be judged," and we must bow to the victor. I will only add that the issue of the fighting was often in doubt and nearly in our favour, while in some cases we only escaped serious defeat owing to the mistakes of their commanders.

It will be seen from the above that before the war we underestimated Japan's material, and particularly her moral strength. But I will add some further reasons for her success. Without doubt the main rôle in the war should have been played by our fleet. The Headquarter Staffs of the navy and army did keep a detailed account of all Japanese warships, but our naval representatives in the Far East made their calculations in tons, and in the number and calibre of guns. Having thus arrived at a statistical total, satisfactory to us in comparison with the same figures for our Pacific Ocean squadron, they came to the conclusion in 1903 that

"Our plan of operations should be based on the assumption that it is impossible for our fleet to be beaten, taking into consideration the present relationship of the two fleets, and that a Japanese landing at Newchuang, and in the Gulf of Korea, is impracticable."

The number of men we would require on land depended on three things:

(*a*) The strength in which the Japanese might be able to move into Manchuria and into our territory;

(*b*) The strength of our own fleet, and—

(*c*) The carrying capacity of our railway communication.

Of course, had our fleet gained an initial victory, land operations would have been unnecessary. But, putting this aside, it was only by actually gaining command of the sea that the Japanese were able to denude their own coast of defenders, and, what is still more important, risk a landing in the Liao-tung Peninsula. Had they been compelled to move through Korea, we should have had time to concentrate. Having gained a local superiority in armoured ships by their desperate attack [before a declaration of war] on the fleet in Port Arthur, they obtained the temporary command of the sea, and took advantage of it to the full; while at this, the most crucial period of the war, our fleet did nothing to prevent their concentration. This was especially the case after the death of Admiral Makharoff, when even their operations close to Port Arthur were not hindered at all. The consequences of this inaction were most serious, for instead of being unable to land in the Gulf of Korea, as had been assumed by our Navy Department, the enemy were in a position to threaten the whole coast of the Liao-tung Peninsula.

As our troops were so few in number, Admiral Alexeieff decided to disperse, so as to be in a position to oppose landings at Newchuang, at Kuan-tung, and on the Ya-lu. He also permitted a dispersion of the fleet, with the result that we were scattered everywhere, and too weak in any one spot. The Japanese transport facilities enabled them to land three armies on the Liao-tung Peninsula and only one in Korea. Sending one army to Port Arthur, they commenced with the other three their advance against our Manchurian army, which was slowly concentrating in the Hai-cheng, Liao-yang area. Having taken the initiative at sea, they also seized it on land, and by their quick concentration and advance, were enabled from the very first to place superior numbers against us. Their consequent success in the first engagements also elevated their spirits as much as it depressed our own. They possessed immense advantages in communication, and the transport of supplies, which took us months, was carried out by them quickly and easily. And, what was not less important, a continuous stream of war materials and supplies poured into their ports and arsenals from Europe and America, thanks to the absolute inaction of our fleet. Owing to our inferior railway communication, also, Japan was able to form a large number of new units whilst we were slowly concentrating our army.

The theatre of operations in Manchuria had been known to the Japanese since their war with China. They were perfectly acquainted with its climate, its rains, its mud, its hills, and the peculiarities of *kao-liang*.[75] In the hills, in which we were almost helpless, they felt at home. Having been preparing for war for ten years, they had not only studied the country, but had sown it with agents, who were of immense service to them. In spite of their severe, almost cruel attitude, the Chinese population assisted them greatly in their operations; and, notwithstanding our superiority in cavalry, they generally had good information as to our strength and dispositions. We, on the contrary, often operated in the dark. They were greatly superior to us in their high explosive artillery projectiles, their numerous mountain and machine guns, and their abundance of explosives and technical material, both for attack and defence, such as wire, mines, and hand-grenades; while their organization, equipment, and transport were better adapted to the local conditions than ours. They also had a greater proportion of sapper troops than we had. Their educational system was calculated to develop their initiative and intelligence, and the battle instructions with which they commenced the war were very materially altered as it proceeded. For instance, their original regulations did not recommend night attacks; but they soon became convinced of the advantages of this form of fighting, and frequently resorted to it. Owing to the more advanced education of their poorer classes, their non-commissioned officers were better than ours, many being quite fitted to take the place of officers, and their corps of officers exhibited the most determined bravery, foresight, and knowledge, and wielded great authority. Even those in the highest ranks lived simple and strict lives at the front. But the principal thing which gave success to the Japanese was their high moral tone. It made victory seem worth any sacrifice, and led directly to that determination to win which characterized all ranks from Commander-in-Chief to private soldier. In many cases their forces found themselves in so desperate a plight that either to hold their ground or to advance required the most extraordinary effort of will. The officers possessed the strength to ask for this almost impossible effort; did not hesitate to shoot men who tried to retire; the private soldier, in response, made the effort, and thereby often robbed us of victory. One thing is certain: that if the whole army had not been saturated with patriotism, if it had not felt the friendly support of the nation behind it, if it had not realized the supreme importance of the struggle, the endeavours of its leaders would have been in vain. The order to advance might have been given, but the soldiers, unsupported by the feeling that the country was with them, would not have had the strength to perform feats of heroism almost superhuman.

CHAPTER VIII

REASONS FOR OUR REVERSES

The minor part played by the fleet—The small carrying capacity of the Siberian and Eastern Chinese Railways—Absence of any diplomatic arrangements to permit of the unhampered despatch and distribution of our forces—Delay in mobilization of reinforcements—Disadvantages of "partial mobilization"—Transfer during the war of regulars from military districts in European Russia into the reserve—Delay in the arrival at the front of drafts—Weakening of the disciplinary powers of commanders as to the punishment awarded to private soldiers—Delay in promoting those who distinguished themselves on service—Technical shortcomings.

After a succession of great battles,[76] our army retired fighting on to the so-called Hsi-ping-kai positions in March, 1905, and remained there, increasing in strength, till the conclusion of peace. This peace, which was as unexpected as it was undesired by the troops, found them putting the finishing touches to their preparation for a forward movement. Later on, in its proper place, will be described the high state of readiness to which we had arrived in August, 1905—a pitch of efficiency never before known in the history of the Russian army.

General Linievitch was awaiting the arrival of the 13th Army Corps—the last to be despatched—before commencing decisive operations. The leading units of this corps had arrived at Harbin and its rear had passed through Cheliabinsk, and the army, now 1,000,000 strong, well organized, with war experience to its credit, and with established reputation, was making ready to continue the bloody struggle; while the enemy, so we learned from reliable reports, was beginning to weaken both in strength and spirit. The resources of Japan appeared to be exhausted. Amongst the prisoners we began to find old men and mere youths; more were taken than formerly, and they no longer showed the patriotic fanaticism so conspicuous among those captured in 1904. We, on the other hand, were able to free our ranks to a great extent of elderly reservists by sending them to the rear and to perform non-combatant duties; for we had received some 100,000 young soldiers, a great portion of whom had volunteered for the front. For the first time since the commencement of hostilities the army was up to its full strength. Some units—the 7th Siberian Corps, for instance—were over strength, so that companies could put more than 200 rifles into the firing-line after providing for all duties. We had received machine-guns, howitzer batteries, and a stock of field railway material which made it possible to transport to the army the supplies which had been collecting for some months. We possessed telegraphs, telephones, wire and cable, tools—everything. A wireless installation had been put up, and was in working order; the transport units were up to strength, and the medical arrangements were magnificent. The force was in occupation of the strongly fortified Hsi-ping-kai positions, between which and the Sungari River there were two more fortified defensive lines—Kung-chu-ling and Kuang-cheng-tzu. There is little doubt that we could have repulsed any advance of the enemy, and, according to our calculations, could have assumed the offensive in superior force. Never in the whole of her military history has Russia put such a mighty army in the field as that formed by the concentration of the 1st, 2nd, and 3rd Manchurian Armies in August, 1905.

PRINCE KHILKOFF.

Such were the favourable conditions existing when we suddenly received the fatal news that an agreement had been come to with Japan at Portsmouth.

It is clear, therefore, that the war ended too soon for Russia, and before Japan had beaten the army which was opposed to her. After defending every yard, we had retired to Hsi-ping-kai, and were, after a year's fighting, still in Southern Manchuria. The whole of Northern Manchuria, including Harbin and part of Southern Manchuria, with Kirin and Kuang-cheng-tzu, was still in our hands, and the enemy had nowhere touched Russian territory, except in Saghalien. Yet we laid down our arms, and besides ceding half the Island of Saghalien to the enemy, literally presented them—what was strategically far more important—with the Hsi-ping-kai and Kung-chu-ling defensive lines, together with the fertile districts which had fed our hosts, and it was with mixed feelings of shame and bewilderment that we withdrew in

October, 1905, into winter quarters on the Sungari River. None of the many misfortunes which had befallen us had such an evil effect on our troops as this premature peace. Upon assuming command, I had assured the army that not a man would be allowed to return to Russia until we were victorious, that without victory we would all be ashamed to show our faces at home, and the men had really become imbued with the idea that the war must be continued till we won. This was even recognized by the reservists, many of whom said to me: "If we return home beaten, the women will laugh at us." Such a sentiment is, of course, not as valuable as a wave of patriotism and a display of martial spirit before hostilities; but under the conditions in which this war had to be conducted, the mere acknowledgment by the whole army that without victory a return to Russia was impossible augured well for any future fighting. Such, then, being the conditions, the future historian must admit that, although unsuccessful in the first campaign, our land forces had grown in numbers, had gained experience, and had acquired such strength at last that victory was certain, and that peace was concluded before they had been really defeated. Our army was never fully tested; it had been able to concentrate but slowly, and, consequently, suffered in detail from the blows of a more ready enemy. When, after enormous sacrifices, it was eventually able to mass in strength, and was furnished with everything requisite for a determined campaign, peace was concluded.

It cannot be truly said that the Japanese land forces had defeated ours. At Liao-yang, on the Sha Ho, and at Mukden, a comparatively small portion of our army was opposed to the whole armed might of Japan. Even in August and September, 1905, when almost all our reinforcements had been collected in the Manchurian theatre of operations, we had only put about one-third of all our armed forces in the field. Our navy was almost entirely destroyed at Port Arthur and in the battle of Tsushima, but our army in the Far East was not only not destroyed, but had been gradually strengthened by the reinforcements received, and, after the battle of Mukden, by the expansion of the three-battalion East Siberian Rifle Regiments to four-battalion regiments, and the formation of the 10th East Siberian Rifle Division. These measures alone added seventy-six battalions of infantry to its strength. We must, therefore, look further afield than to our numerical strength for the causes of our disasters. Why was it that right up to March, 1905, our troops were unable to win a battle? It is difficult to reply to this, because we do not yet know the strength of the enemy in the principal battles. We know approximately the numbers of battalions of the peace army which were in the field, but not the number of reserve battalions at the front, and, consequently, the actual number of rifles. In war the issue is not decided by the number of men present, but by the number of rifles actually brought into the firing-line.

It is quite possible that when a trustworthy history of the war compiled from Japanese sources is published, our self-esteem will receive a severe blow. We already know that in many instances we were in superior strength to the enemy, and yet were unable to defeat them. The explanation of this phenomenon is simple. Though they were weaker materially than we were, the Japanese were morally stronger, and the teaching of all history shows that it is the moral factor which really counts in the long-run. There are exceptions, of course, as when the side whose *moral* is the weaker can place an absolutely overwhelming force in the field, and so wear out its opponents. This was the case of the Federals as compared with the Confederates in America, and of the British against the Boers. It is indeed a lucky army which, starting a campaign with the weakest *moral*, is able to improve in both spirit and numbers at the same time.

This was the case with us. Between the battle of Mukden and the end of the war our army almost doubled in numbers, had taken up a strong position, and was quite ready to advance. The strength of the Japanese, on the other hand, was exhausted (they were reduced to filling up their ranks with their 1906 recruits), and many things pointed to a weakening of their spirit. As Japan was pre-eminently a naval Power, our principal operations should have been on the sea; and had we destroyed the enemy's fleet, there would have been no fighting on Chinese territory. As I have already pointed out, our fleet scarcely assisted the army at all; for while taking shelter in Port Arthur, it did not attempt to prevent the enemy's disembarkation. Three Japanese armies—those of Oku, Nodzu, and Nogi—landed unhindered on the Liao-tung Peninsula; the forces of Oku and Nogi actually landed close to where our squadron was lying. Though we possessed an excellent base at Vladivostok, our main fleet was collected at Port Arthur—in a naval sense a very inferior place, for it possessed no docks nor workshops, and no protection for the inner basin.

As regards our naval strength, I am unable to refer to official figures, for I write from the country,[77] but I quote from an article published in the *Ruski Viestnik* in 1905 by M. Burun, as much of what he says agrees with what I had previously known. Our fleet began to increase after the Chino-Japanese War, the naval estimates reaching £11,200,000 in 1904. At the outbreak of hostilities it consisted of 28 sea-going and 14 coast-defence battleships, 15 sea-going gunboats, 39 cruisers, 9 ocean-going destroyers, 133 smaller destroyers, and 132 auxiliary vessels of less importance. Between 1881 and 1904 we had spent £130,000,000 in the creation of this fleet. The naval estimates of the two nations for the years preceding the war were, in millions of pounds:

1899. 1900. 1901. 1902. 1903.

| Russia | 9 | 9·6 | 10·8 | 11·2 | 12·0 |
| Japan | 6 | 4·5 | 4·1 | 3·2 | 3·2 |

The Japanese fleet consisted of:

Sea-going battleships	6
Coast-defence battleships	2
Armoured cruisers	11
Unarmoured cruisers	14
Destroyers	50
Gunboats	17

At the commencement of war our Pacific Ocean Squadron consisted of:

Sea-going battleships	7
Large cruisers (of which only four were armoured)	9
Small cruisers and minor ships	4
Destroyers	42

Our fleet was neither ready nor concentrated. Four cruisers were at Vladivostok, one at Chemulpo, and the greater part of the Port Arthur Squadron lay in the inner roads. A few days before the attack of February 9 it moved out into the outer roads to carry out steam trials, but proper precautions were not observed, even though diplomatic relations had already been broken off.

As far back as 1901 our Headquarter Staff had estimated that in the event of war our Pacific Ocean Fleet would be weaker than Japan's, but within two years of that date Admiral Alexeieff, the Viceroy, stated in the scheme for the strategical distribution of our troops in the Far East[78] that the defeat of our fleet was impossible under existing conditions.

In their night attack of February 9 the Japanese put several of our best ships out of action; but, serious as the damage was, it could have been speedily repaired had we possessed proper facilities in Port Arthur. Though we had expended many millions in constructing docks and quays at Dalny, Port Arthur was without a dock, and repairs could only be executed slowly. Still, our Pacific Ocean Squadron revived when Admiral Makharoff arrived, and for a short time its chances of success were much increased. After Makharoff's death the command passed to Admiral Witgeft, who, upon receiving instructions to force his way through to Vladivostok, put to sea and engaged Togo's squadron. Witgeft was killed, and the fleet inflicted some damage on Togo's squadron, and returned to Port Arthur without the loss of a single ship. The battle of August 10 was indecisive, though our blue-jackets fought gallantly the whole day against a numerically superior enemy, and beat off numerous attacks by destroyers. After returning to Port Arthur the fleet finally assumed its passive rôle, and was gradually disarmed—as in the Siege of Sevastopol—in order to strengthen the land defence of the fortress, where our sailors did most excellent work. What it might have accomplished on its own element can be gauged from the performances of the gallant little cruiser squadron under Admiral Essen, which made a daring sally from Vladivostok to the coasts of Japan. Not only did Essen's success cause considerable consternation in Japan, but it resulted in action of practical value to the army, for one vessel sunk by the squadron was conveying siege material for use against Port Arthur. On October 14, 1904, Admiral Rozhdestvenski's fleet, consisting of 7 battleships, 5 first-class cruisers, 3 second-class cruisers, and 12 destroyers, with a complement of 519 officers and 7,900 men, left Libau for the Pacific Ocean, and Admiral Nebogatoff's squadron left to join it on February 16, 1905. The latter consisted of 1 sea-going battleship, 3 coast-defence battleships, and 1 first-class cruiser, with a complement of 120 officers and more than 2,100 men. Rozhdestvenski's squadron had to steam 16,400 miles to reach Vladivostok. In spite of the lack of coaling stations *en route*, and in the face of extraordinary difficulties, it eventually succeeded in reaching the Sea of Japan, where it was utterly destroyed on May 27 and 28, 1905, off Tsushima. In twenty-four hours we lost 30 pennants sunk or captured out of 47, and 137,000 from a total tonnage of 157,000. The light cruiser *Almaz* and 2 destroyers—the *Grozni* and *Bravi*—alone reached Vladivostok. According to Admiral Togo's reports, he lost only 3 destroyers, while his casualties amounted to 7 officers and 108 men killed, 40 officers and 620 men wounded. Many gallant exploits were performed by our sailors in the fight: the battleship *Suvaroff* continued firing until she sank, and of the *Navarin's* complement only two men were saved; while the small ironclad *Ushakoff* replied to the Japanese summons to surrender with a broadside, and foundered with the whole of her crew. M. Burun closes his remarkable article in the following words:

"Undoubtedly many tactical mistakes were among the contributory causes of the Tsushima catastrophe: our initial error in allowing transports to be with the fleet, the unseaworthiness and the conspicuous colour of our ships, and many such details; but the real cause was the unreadiness of our fleet for war, and the criminal short-sightedness of our Administration. Such a contingency as war was never contemplated, and the fleet was kept up entirely for show.

"Our crews were of the best material in the world; they were brave and capable of learning, but besides being unversed in the use of modern implements of war (such as automatic gun-sights, etc.), they were not accustomed to life at sea. Our officers were possessed of a strong sense of duty, and thoroughly appreciated the immense importance of the task before them; but they were new to the crews and to the ships, which they had suddenly to command against a fleet trained in the stern school of war. Born sailors, the Japanese seamen never left their ships, while our vessels had neither permanent nor full crews. Even in the last eight months of the cruise of our fleet our captains were unable, owing to the shortage of ammunition, to put their crews through a course of gunnery, or to test their training. The ships only carried enough ammunition for one battle. Yes, we lost our fleet because the most important element—the *personnel*—was unprepared. We lost the war, and lost our predominance on the Pacific Ocean, because, even while preparing to celebrate the anniversary of the gallant defence of Sevastopol, we quite forgot that the strength of a navy is only created by the spirit of every individual member belonging to it.

"But can it be that there is no one left of all those gallant sailors who so proudly sailed under the Cross of St. Andrew who possesses the secret of training men? If so, then our Navy Department will never succeed in creating a fleet. However many the milliards spent, it will only succeed in constructing a collection of ships such as now rest at the bottom of the Sea of Japan. Mere ships do not make a fleet, nor do they form the strong right arm of an empire, for the strength of a nation does not lie in armour, guns, or torpedoes, but in the souls of the men behind these things."

Far from assisting our army, Rozhdestvenski brought it irreparable harm. It was the defeat of his squadron at Tsushima that brought about negotiations and peace at a time when our army was ready to advance—a million strong. As at Sevastopol in 1855, the only assistance given by our fleet to Port Arthur, except at Chin-chou, was to land blue-jackets and guns.

Next to the absence of a Russian fleet, the most important factor to assist the Japanese in their offensive strategy and to impede us was the condition of the Siberian and Eastern Chinese Railways. If these lines had been more efficient, we could have brought up our troops more rapidly, and, as things turned out, 150,000 men concentrated at first would have been of far more value to us than the 300,000 who were gradually assembled during nine months, only to be sacrificed in detail. In my report upon the War Ministry in 1900 (before Japan had completed her armaments), I wrote that she could mobilize 380,000 men and 1,090 guns, about half of which could be transported across the sea; that there were immediately ready only seven divisions, with a war strength of 126,000 rifles, 5,000 sabres, and 494 guns. In March, 1903, before visiting Japan, I calculated that if the views then held by our naval authorities as to the comparative strength of the two fleets were correct, we ought to be ready, in the event of war, to throw an army of 300,000 into Manchuria. In the battles of Liao-yang and the Sha Ho we only had from 150,000 to 180,000. If we had had a better railway, and had been able to mass at Liao-yang the number specified, we should undoubtedly have won the day, in spite of our mistakes.

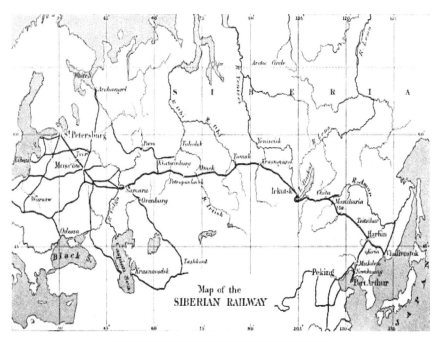

MAP OF THE SIBERIAN RAILWAY.

THE SIBERIAN RAILWAY: WESTERN LINE.

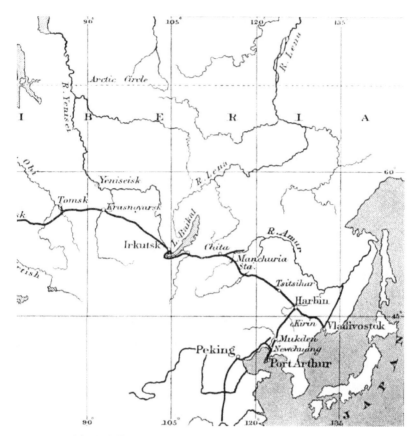

THE SIBERIAN RAILWAY: EASTERN LINE.

As regards the railway problem, we counted, in August, 1901, on having for military transport purposes on the Eastern Chinese Railway 20 waggons running in the twenty-four hours, while in the summer of 1903 we calculated we should have 75. We were promised from January 1, 1904, five pairs[79] of military trains of 35 waggons each, or 175 waggons each way; and it was supposed at the same time that the Siberian Railway would be in a condition to run seven pairs of military trains in the twenty-four hours, but these hopes were not realized. Let us see what actually did happen.

In 1903 we were only able to reckon on four through military trains on the Siberian line, and on three short trains on the Eastern Chinese. Towards the end of that year relations with Japan became strained; it seemed as if, having made all her preparations, she was seeking a pretext for war, and was therefore meeting all the concessions we made by fresh and quite impossible demands. Our unreadiness was only too plain, but it seemed at that time that we should be able, with two or three years' steady work, so to strengthen our position in the Far East and improve the railway, the fleet, the land forces, and the fortresses of Port Arthur and Vladivostok, that Japan would have small chance of success against us. It was proposed, in the event of trouble, to send out, to begin with [in addition to the troops already in the Far East], reinforcements consisting of four army corps (two regular and two reserve) from European Russia. Owing to the unreadiness of the railways, and the uncertainty as to the time it would take to improve them, it was impossible to draw up concentration time-tables with any accuracy. According to these tables, 500 troop trains and a large number of goods trains would be necessary to transport from European Russia the drafts for the Far East, the 3rd Battalions of the East Siberian Rifle Regiments, several batteries, local units and ammunition parks for the East Siberian Rifle Divisions, the 4th Siberian Corps, and the two army corps from Russia (10th and 17th). Moreover, upon mobilization, the Siberian Military District would require local transport for a very considerable distance. This would add about three weeks to the time required for through transport of the above reinforcements.

As I have said, we expected that from January, 1904, the Siberian and Eastern Chinese lines would be able to give us daily five trains each way; but the concentration of one-half of the reinforcements to go to the Far East actually took five months from the declaration of war. One of the most important of the War Minister's tasks, therefore, was to get the Siberian and Eastern Chinese lines into a more efficient state as rapidly as possible. My scheme was to improve them at first up to a capacity of seven trains each way in the twenty-four hours, and on the southern branch of the Eastern Chinese (along which movements would have to take place through Harbin from both sides, from Pri-Amur and Trans-Baikal) to fourteen pairs of trains. My proposal was approved by the Tsar, who noted against the figure fourteen the words, "Or even up to twelve pairs of military trains." In the middle of January, 1904, he appointed a special committee to consider the questions of the money and time required for the immediate improvement of the railways as suggested. This committee, consisting of the Ministers of War, Ways and Communications, Finance, and the State Comptroller, was under the presidency of General Petroff, of the Engineers. It was instructed to ascertain what should be done to enable seven pairs of military trains to be run on the Siberian and Eastern Chinese lines, and twelve pairs on the southern branch (from Harbin to Port Arthur).

On January 29, 1904, the Viceroy wrote of the state of the Eastern Chinese Railway as follows:

"According to my information, there is reason to doubt the official figures as to the carrying capacity and the ability to cope with increased traffic of the Eastern Chinese Railway. Rolling-stock is deficient, and many engines are out of order. The water-supply is so uncertain that the officials have recently been forced to refuse to accept goods for transport. The soldiers are the only reliable portion of the subordinate railway staff, and on this account some alarm is already felt by the higher officials. But the most serious want is that of a sufficient fuel reserve. The bulk of the coal is stocked at Dalny, whence 1,000 tons have to be distributed over the line daily, of which amount only half goes to increasing the reserve, the other half being required for current consumption. To transport the whole of the reserve by rail from Dalny would take about twenty-five days, but the railway would even then be able to cope with the increased traffic for a period of three months only. In war we can scarcely count on the large railway demands being met, as the coal is sea-borne."

An official statement, prepared to show the then position of the railway, was laid before the special committee at a sitting held four days before the commencement of hostilities. According to the Minister of Ways and Communications (Prince Khilkoff), the Siberian line could only run six pairs of through trains, of which four were military, one was passenger, and one service (for the railway); owing to the scarcity of rolling-stock, only three of the four military trains could carry troops, the fourth being given up to goods (trucks). But the War Department representative in charge of Transport, who was at the meeting, pointed out that on the portion of the Trans-Baikal line, between Karim and Manchuria station, only three trains altogether, whether of troops or goods, could be run. The official information furnished by the Ministry of Ways and Communications thus differed from that of the military railway representative. The representative of the Eastern Chinese Railway stated that it would soon be possible to run a total of five pairs of trains on that line, while he calculated on working up by April to a running capacity of six pairs along the main line and seven pairs on the southern branch. On going into details as to the work that would be necessary before this could be done, it was discovered that, owing to the very inferior equipment of the different branches of the Siberian and Eastern Chinese lines, the necessary additions to rolling-stock and the construction of sidings, crossings, and water-supply would absorb a very large sum. The workshops on the Eastern Chinese line were poorly equipped, and there were not nearly enough engine depôts, while the large amount of rails, fish-plates, sleepers and ballast necessary would have to be conveyed while the transport of troops was going on. On March 9 I wrote to General Sakharoff, then in charge of the

War Department, and pointed out that, owing to what I had heard as to the deficiency of engine depôts in the Viceroyalty, and in order to facilitate concentration, I considered it essential that, up to Manchuria station, not more than one train a day should be taken up for goods, the remainder being reserved for troops.

Lake Baikal was the great obstacle on the Siberian Railway. The ice-breaker did not work regularly, and progress on the construction of the Circum-Baikal line was slow. Prince Khilkoff conceived and carried out the idea of laying a temporary line across the ice of the lake, and so passing the waggons over. He also proposed to dismantle the locomotives, take the parts across by horse traction, and reassemble them on the eastern side. On February 16 I received the following letter from him:

RUSSIAN TRANSPORT CARS BEING DRAGGED ACROSS
LAKE BAIKAL ON THE ICE BY HORSES.

"I have returned from inspecting the Trans-Baikal line. The line will be able immediately to run six pairs of trains of all kinds. I have started work building sidings for nine pairs, but this number will not run until the warm weather sets in and we get rolling-stock. Almost all the rivers now are frozen solid. Thirteen temporary water-supplies are now under construction. I will write again about the warm weather and the increase up to twelve pairs of trains. Khorvat, whom I saw in Manchuria, tells me that the following numbers of military trains can be run on that line[80]: three pairs on the western portion, five on the southern. The further traffic acceleration depends almost exclusively on the receipt of rolling-stock. Heavy snowstorms have somewhat delayed the laying of the line across

Lake Baikal; but I have hopes of success. Arrangements are being made at Manchuria station for the temporary accommodation of 4,000 to 6,000 men in hut barracks."

It is clear from this letter that when we entered upon hostilities we had for mobilization, concentration, and the carriage of supplies only three military trains in the twenty-four hours, for the carrying power of the western branch of the Eastern Chinese line from Manchuria station to Harbin fixed the capacity of the line throughout its whole length from Europe to Harbin. Thus, in the first period of the war, Lake Baikal was not the only obstacle to rapid transit. The freezing of the rivers in Trans-Baikalia was also a serious difficulty, and necessitated the improvisation of water-supply at numerous stations. But what was most wanted was an early delivery of rolling-stock for the Trans-Baikal and Eastern Chinese lines, where the running capacity was considerable, but the carrying capacity was limited—owing to the shortage of rolling-stock—to three military trains in the twenty-four hours. Under normal conditions we should have been compelled to wait for the opening of Lake Baikal in the spring before commencing the transport of rolling-stock eastwards from it, which would have meant that we should have had to be content with three pairs of trains till the middle of March. The ability and immense energy of Prince Khilkoff, however, rescued us from this serious plight. Though in very bad health, he took the matter in hand personally, regardless of the climate and all other difficulties. On March 6 I received the following message from him:

"On the 17th [February] we began to send rolling-stock across the ice [Lake Baikal]. More than 150 waggons have been sent across, and about 100 are now on their way over. If the weather is favourable, I shall start sending engines over."

On March 9 I received another message, recounting the difficulties that were caused by the frequent great changes of temperature, for the ice on the lake cracked badly, and it was often necessary to relay the line just put down. He asked me to help him with fatigue-parties from the army, which I gave him.

What had to be done in order to improve, to some extent, the Manchurian line, is recorded in the report of the special committee submitted to me on March 9, 1904. The officials of the Eastern Chinese Railway calculated that to increase the carrying capacity of its main line up to seven, and of the southern branch to twelve, pairs of military trains, would entail an expenditure of £4,424,000. With this sum the following improvements in actual traffic might be made: On the main line, up to 7 pairs of troop trains, 1 pair of passenger, 1 pair service; total, 9 pairs; running capacity, 10 pairs;

water-supply for 10 pairs. On the southern line, up to 12 pairs troop trains, 1 passenger train, and 2 service; total, 15; running capacity, 16; water-supply for 16. Among the chief items were the laying of eighty odd miles of sidings, which necessitated the delivery and distribution along the line of between 9,000 and 10,000 tons of rails, sleepers, and fish-plates, and the construction of 224 engine-sheds, 373,400 square feet of workshops, and 265,600 square feet of platforms. For the construction of dwelling-houses £400,000 was necessary. The water-supply of the southern branch was to be increased by 60 per cent., and rolling-stock, of the value of £2,300,000, including 335 engines, 2,350 covered waggons, 810 trucks, and 113 passenger coaches, were to be supplied. This increase in traffic to seven pairs of military trains on the Siberian and Eastern Chinese lines and twelve on the southern branch was, of course, only a first instalment of what was required. Orders were issued in June, 1904, when I was in Manchuria, for the respective lines to be brought up to the above capacity.

Before my departure to take over command of the army in the Far East, I submitted a statement to the Tsar on March 7, showing what was most urgently required to enable us to fight Japan successfully. This was endorsed by the Tsar himself, and sent to the War Minister, General Sakharoff. The following is an extract from it:

"I have the honour to report that the following are the measures which, in my opinion, are most urgently required:

"1. Improvement of the Siberian and Eastern Chinese lines so as gradually to work up to fourteen pairs of military trains in the twenty-four hours over the whole length, and eighteen pairs on the southern branch. Every additional pair of trains will not only shorten the time for concentration, but will at the same time help the supply services. Great difficulties will be encountered in carrying out what I recommend, especially in increasing the running capacity on the Central Siberian and Trans-Baikal lines. Once these difficulties are overcome, the necessary increase of traffic can easily be attained by means of a loan of rolling-stock from other lines. I venture to assert that of all urgently pressing questions, that of improving the railway communication between Russia and Siberia is the most important. It must therefore be taken up at once in spite of the enormous cost. The money expended will not be wasted; it will, on the contrary, be in the highest sense productive, inasmuch as it will shorten the duration of the war.

"2. ... Together with the carriage of troops and goods by rail, a transport service must be organized on the old Siberian road and on that alongside the Eastern Chinese Railway. For a successful concentration and the rapid transit of supplies, we ought to have thirty troop trains in the twenty-four hours. Even when the measures I suggest are carried out, we shall only have a total of fourteen pairs—less than half of what are really required. Our present precarious position, therefore, can be realized, as the total number of military trains we are able to count upon between Baikal and Harbin is four pairs!"

When I travelled over the Siberian and Manchurian lines in March, 1904, I was accompanied by M. Pavlovski, who was in charge of the Siberian line. He told me that if he were given rolling-stock on loan, he would be able that year to increase the number of military trains to ten, and later on to fourteen, pairs, at a cost of £650,000. On receiving his report, I sent on March 19 the following message to General Sakharoff:

"With this I am telegraphing to Secret Councillor Miasiedoff Ivanoff as follows:

" 'I earnestly request you to arrange for the early improvement of the running and carrying capacity of the Siberian Railway. Engineer Pavlovski, in charge of the Siberian line, informs me that he has already represented that, in order to work up the number of trains on the western portion to thirteen, in the central to fourteen, and in the hilly portion fifteen (of which nine, ten, and eleven will be military) during the summer, an expenditure of £650,000 is absolutely necessary. Please arrange as soon as possible to credit him with this amount and an equal sum for the Trans-Baikal line. I have informed the Tsar as to my opinion of the necessity of eventually working up the whole line from the Volga to Harbin to fourteen trains, though it be only twelve at first. Pavlovski considers it desirable and possible to get seventeen pairs of through trains. I cannot hope to act energetically unless the railway to Harbin is improved to the extent I recommend. From Harbin onwards it is absolutely necessary eventually to have eighteen, and temporarily fourteen, pairs of trains. I earnestly beg you to support this request.' "

By the middle of March Prince Khilkoff succeeded in sending across the ice-line on Lake Baikal sixty-five dismantled locomotives and 1,600 waggons. [When I met him he was very ill, but had succeeded in accomplishing a tremendous work, which it is to be hoped the country will appreciate.] Échelons[81] of troops marched twenty-nine miles over the ice in the day, every four men having a small sledge to carry their kit, etc. When I passed across the lake not more than four échelons were crossing in the twenty-four hours. The Trans-Baikal line was working very badly, and together with the lake was a great cause of delay.

In order to expedite the troop moves in Southern Manchuria, I telegraphed to the Viceroy on March 16, emphasizing the necessity of improvising road transport on the many roads between Harbin and Mukden for the carriage of units and supplies from the former place, and of not taking up more than one train in the day on the southern branch for goods. At the same time I drew attention to the fact that the troops should not be allowed to take with them more than their field-service scale of baggage. I had noticed that the 3rd Battalion of the East Siberian Rifles, which I had inspected on the way to the front, were taking as much baggage as if moving in the course of ordinary relief. On March 27 I reached Liao-yang, where the weary wait for the arrival of reinforcements began. The first troops to arrive were the 3rd Battalions for the seven East Siberian Rifle Brigades, at first one and then two in the day. These were followed by the artillery units and drafts for the brigades of the 31st and 35th Divisions. Meanwhile the money required for the improvement of the Siberian and Eastern Chinese lines had not been allotted as quickly as it should have been. On May 19 I received from the Ministry of Finance a telegram forwarding a copy of another to the Viceroy, dated 15th. From this it appeared that the question of bringing the carrying capacity of the Eastern Chinese Railway up to seven pairs of trains, and that of the southern branch to twelve pairs, had been thoroughly gone into at numerous meetings of the special committee, and that the necessity for despatching the following to the line was recognized: 190 miles of rails with joints, 770 sets of crossings, 355 engines, 88 passenger coaches, 2,755 goods vans and trucks. In addition to these, Admiral Alexeieff asked for 30 miles of rails, 265 sets of crossings, and 1,628 vans. The Finance Minister stated that it would be necessary, in order to improve and develop the line, to provide it with 3,000 truck-loads of various stores. But as it had only been found possible to send 200 trucks in April and 201 in May, or a total of 401, he was of opinion that "the whole amount could not possibly be guaranteed earlier than the autumn." The extent to which the despatch of these was delayed is evident from the fact that out of 1,000 vans, only 60 had been sent off by May 18, and out of 355 engines, only 105. By July 30, 120 more engines had been sent, but it was not proposed to forward the remaining 130 till a good deal later.

Owing to three regiments of the 1st Siberian Division being detained in Harbin during the whole of April, the Manchurian army was not augmented by a single battalion. Meanwhile we had been defeated on May 1 at the Ya-lu, and on the 6th Oku's army had begun to disembark at Pi-tzu-wo.

Though the 2nd Siberian Division reached Liao-yang in the second half of May, we were still very weak. On May 23 General Jilinski brought me a letter from the Viceroy, in which Admiral Alexeieff wrote that the time had come for the Manchurian army to advance towards the Ya-lu or Port Arthur. In spite of my opinion as to our unreadiness for any forward movement, in spite of the fact that out of twelve divisions of reinforcements only one had arrived, in spite of the inefficiency of the railway, an advance with insufficient numbers was ordered and carried out. The result was the disaster on June 14 at Te-li-ssu. The leading units of the 10th Corps did not reach Liao-yang till June 17; thus it took more than three months from the beginning of hostilities for our troops in the Far East to receive reinforcements from European Russia. During this prolonged and particularly important period the burden and heat of the campaign was borne by five East Siberian Rifle Divisions, whose two-battalion regiments had been expanded into three-battalion regiments as late as March and April; the 4th Siberian Corps, which arrived in May, did not take part in any fighting. Taking advantage of our inferiority in numbers, and especially the inaction of our fleet during these three months, the enemy disembarked their three armies on the Liao-tung Peninsula and in Kuan-tung. The 1st Army, under Kuroki, moved from Korea into Southern Manchuria, and Japan won three battles on land—at the Ya-lu, Chin-chou, and at Te-li-ssu. Had the railway only been ready at the beginning of hostilities, even to run only six through military trains, we should have had three army corps at Te-li-ssu—namely, the 1st and 4th Siberians and the 10th Army Corps, instead of only the 1st Siberian Corps. The issue of this battle would have been different, and this would undoubtedly have affected the whole course of the campaign, for we should have secured the initiative.

The arrival of the first units of the 10th Army Corps was more than opportune, but events did not permit us to await the concentration of the whole of it. Kuroki's army was advancing, and the line Sai-ma-chi, An-ping, Liao-yang, on which he was moving in force, was only covered by our cavalry and one regiment of infantry. Consequently, as soon as the leading brigade of the 9th Division arrived at Liao-yang, it was sent off in that direction. Similarly, troops of the 17th Army and 5th Siberian Corps went straight into action from the train without waiting the concentration of their corps. It was only on September 2—*i.e.*, after seven months—that the three army corps (10th, 17th, and 5th Siberian), sent from Europe to reinforce the field army, were all concentrated in the Manchurian theatre. During the decisive fighting at Liao-yang, the 85th Regiment was the only unit of the 1st Army Corps which had arrived, and it went straight from the train into the battle. If, at the beginning of the war, we had had only one more military train a day, we would have had present at the battle of Liao-yang the 1st Army Corps and 6th Siberian Corps, and with these sixty extra battalions must certainly have defeated the enemy. But the railway fatally affected us in other ways, for while we were feeding our army with fresh units as reinforcements, we were unable at the same time to find carriage for the drafts for the advanced troops, which had suffered heavy losses in killed, wounded, and sick. For example, in the fighting of five long months, from May 14 to October 14, the Manchurian army lost in killed, wounded, and sick, over 100,000 men, to replace which, during that period, it only received 21,000. The enemy, on the other hand, were making good their casualties quickly and uninterruptedly.

By the beginning of October the 1st Army Corps and the 6th Siberian Corps had arrived. Taking advantage of these reinforcements, I ordered an advance. In the bloody battle on the Sha Ho, where we lost about 45,000 men, killed and wounded, neither side could claim a decisive victory. During the four months immediately preceding the February (1905) battles the army received drafts to replace wastage, and was reinforced by the 8th and 16th Corps, besides five brigades of Rifles, but in that month it was still short of its establishment by 50,000 men—*i.e.*, two whole army corps. In other words, as regards numbers, the 8th and 16th Corps might be said merely to have made up the wastage in the others. It is true these corps brought us additional artillery; but looking at it purely from the point of view of their fighting value, I should have preferred to have received them in the shape of drafts; I could then have incorporated them in the battle-tried corps, instead of having them as separate inexperienced units. Even with these considerable reinforcements our position in February, 1905, was worse than before, for the fall of Port Arthur enabled the Japanese to be augmented by Nogi's army. Immediately after the 16th Corps the field army was to have received two Rifle brigades, one Cossack infantry brigade, and the 4th Army Corps; but their despatch was delayed for more than a month, in order to allow a quantity of stores which had collected on the line to be railed up. It was only on March 5—*i.e.*, five weeks after the arrival of the last units of the 16th Army Corps—that the leading battalions of the 3rd Rifle Brigade (the 9th and 10th Regiments) reached Mukden, and they at once went into action. But for this break we should have had at the battle of Mukden a main reserve of more than sixty battalions, which, even allowing for our mistakes, might have turned the balance in our favour. In a full year, from the beginning of March, 1904, till the beginning of March, 1905, we railed up eight army corps, three Rifle brigades, and one reserve division to the front. Thus each corps on the average required, roughly, one and a half months to perform the journey. These figures indicate the peculiar disabilities under which we laboured in massing superior numbers. Owing to our far too slow concentration, our forces were bound to be destroyed in detail, as we were obliged to accept battle. With the transit of troops, the materials necessary for the work of improving the railways had to be railed up, and from August onwards the progress made in this work was remarkable. In October, 1904, I received a message from General Sakharoff to the effect that, according to the Minister of Ways and Communications, the Siberian main line would have a carrying capacity, after October 28, of twelve pairs of military trains. But this promise was not carried out for almost a year, though the traffic in October and November was heavy. Altogether, in one and a half months (forty-seven days), from October 28 to December 14, there arrived in Harbin 257 military, 147 goods (commissariat, artillery, red cross, and railway service), and 23 hospital trains (total, 427), which gives an average of nine pairs in the twenty-four hours, of which only five and a half carried troops. In ten months of war the railway had increased its traffic from three military trains to nine, so it took on an average more than one and a half months to add one pair of trains to the traffic. Finally, in the summer of 1905, after sixteen months of war, the railways worked, I believe, up to a rate of twelve pairs of military trains on the main line and eighteen on the southern branch—*i.e.*, on the main line we did not even then get so high as the number (fourteen pairs) which I had asked for on March 7, 1904, when leaving for the front.

From all I have said it must be amply clear what a decisive factor the railway was. Every extra daily train would have enabled us to have at our disposal one or two corps more in the decisive battles. Thus a very great responsibility—that of not losing a single day in improving the lines—lay with the Ministries of Ways and Communications, of Finance, and, to a certain extent, with the Ministry of War. Looking back to what was done by these departments, it must be confessed that the results attained were very great, and that the railway employés did magnificent service. By the end of the war we had within the limits of the Viceroyalty an army of 1,000,000 men, well supplied with everything necessary for existence and for fighting. As this army was conveyed while work was being simultaneously carried out on the railway-line, the result, though largely attained by forced labour, was, for a badly laid single line of railway, somewhat striking. By means of good lines of railway, mobilization and concentration are very quickly effected nowadays. Germany and Austria can throw about 2,000,000 soldiers on to our frontiers in from ten to fourteen days, and their rapid concentration will enable them to seize the initiative. Our forces reached the front, so to speak, by driblets, which resulted in paralysis of all initiative on our part.

Thinking that the information with regard to the railways, sent by the War Minister in October, 1904 [which reached me on November 8], meant the realization of my recommendations of February, 1904, I considered it time to submit to the Tsar my views as to the necessity for further work, for I considered it most necessary that the line should be at once doubled over its whole length. I expressed my opinion on this question in a letter to the Tsar, dated November 12, 1904. As there is nothing in this letter that can be regarded as secret, I will quote it literally:

"YOUR MAJESTY,

"Before leaving to join the army, I was permitted to give my opinion as to our principal requirements to insure success in the war. My opinion was submitted in a memorandum dated 7th March, and was marginally annotated by Your Majesty. Eight months ago I expressed in this memorandum the opinion that, for a successful concentration and rapid transport of all the supplies necessary to an army in the field, the running of 30 pairs of military trains in the 24 hours was essential. As a first step I considered the improvement of the Siberian and Eastern Chinese lines should be taken in hand, so as to bring up the number of trains to 14 pairs in the 24 hours along the main line, and 18 pairs along the southern branch. Against the words 'up to 14 pairs in 24 hours' Your Majesty was pleased to note, 'Very necessary.' In a message reaching me on the 8th November the War Minister has informed me that from the 28th October the Siberian and Trans-Baikal lines will have a carrying capacity of 12 pairs of trains in the day, and that it is proposed further to work up the Siberian main line to 14 pairs, and that the Minister of Finance[82] has been approached with regard to the urgency for improving the Eastern Chinese lines so as to correspond with the Siberian. Thus, we have not, in eight months, reached the number indicated as necessary in my former memorandum. I now earnestly request that as a first step the whole Siberian main line and the Eastern Chinese line as far as Harbin should be worked up to a carrying capacity of 14 pairs, and on the southern branch to 18 pairs. I know that this is no easy matter, but it is absolutely essential, and admits of no delay. These 14 pairs will by no means supply all our requirements. The larger number of men in the field has increased the demand for transport. It is calculated that, to supply the army with everything necessary, and to carry back what is not required, not 30 pairs of trains, but 48, are essential. This is not exaggerated; it is the minimum under normal conditions. Each Manchurian army should have its own line (like the Bologoe-Siedlce)[83] giving 48 pairs of trains in 24 hours. We must bow, of course, to the impossible, but we shall have to pay in human life and in money for a prolonged war. The urgency of every extra train can easily be seen. If we had had one more pair of trains available at the beginning of the war, we should have had 2 extra army corps—the 1st and 6th Siberian Corps—in the August fights at Liao-yang, and our success would practically have been assured. This one extra train could have brought in drafts during September and October an extra 50,000 men, of which we are now in such urgent need.

"In the future, every month will increase the necessity of strengthening the line still more. When the field army was small, we drew our supplies almost entirely from local sources (wheat, barley, hay, straw, fuel, and cattle), but these will soon be exhausted, and the provisioning the army will depend on supplies from Europe. When we move forward our position will become worse, for we shall be moving into a part of Manchuria already devastated by war, and into a hilly tract which was never rich in supplies. The daily transport of provisions (flour, groats, oats, hay, and meat) for our present establishment takes up 5 trains, and we soon shall have to provide carriage for live-stock. But the army cannot live from hand to mouth. A quantity of supplies must be collected, sufficient to form a reserve for the force for some months, besides satisfying current requirements, and this must be distributed in the advance and main depôts. It will take 5 additional trains a day for one month to collect one month's reserve. Only by having a large number of trains can we organize our advance depôts with necessary rapidity, and move them to fresh points. The demand for trains is greatest on those days when fighting is in progress. A number of urgent demands— amounting sometimes to hundreds during two or three days—are made, not only for supplies, but for the carriage of military and engineer stores, troops, parks, and the transport of drafts and of wounded. The needs of an army in war are so varied and so vast that it is considered necessary in Europe to have for each army corps a special line of rails (single track), capable of running 14 to 20 pairs of trains in the 24 hours. For our 9 army corps we have only one single line of rails running (in the last few weeks) from 8 to 10 pairs of trains. The inability of the line to cope with the necessities of the war is the main reason for the slow and indecisive nature of the campaign. Our reinforcements arrive in driblets. Supplies despatched from Russia in the spring are still on the Siberian line. Waterproofs sent for the summer will arrive when we want fur coats; fur coats will be received when waterproofs are wanted. But so far, during all these months that we have been in contact with the enemy, have fought and have retired, we have not been hungry, because we have been living on the country. The situation is now altogether changed, for local resources will last only for a short time longer. Our horses will soon have to be fed on hay and straw, and if we do not make extraordinary efforts to improve the railway and concentrate a large quantity of supplies at the advanced base, our men, who are concentrated in great numbers on small areas, will, after the horses, begin to suffer hardship and hunger, and will fall sick. Any accidental damage to the railway will be sorely felt.

"I am expressing my firm conviction with complete frankness as the officer in command of three armies, that, for their successful operations, we must at once start laying a second track throughout the whole Siberian trunk line and on the Eastern Chinese Railway. Our army must be connected with Russia by a line capable of running 48 pairs of trains in the day.

"I have some experience of my profession, and was for eight years in charge of the management of the Trans-Caspian Railway, and I am convinced that all these difficulties can be overcome if Your Majesty is pleased to order it. Possibly the war will be finished before we shall have laid the second line of rails over more than a fraction of the whole distance; on the other hand, it may continue so long that only a double track will save the situation. Only with a double line also shall we be able at the end of the war to send back rapidly all the troops which came from Russia and to demobilize. We are living in the midst of events of immense importance on which depends the future, not only of the Far East, but, to a certain extent, that of Russia. We must not shirk sacrifices that will insure victory and subsequent peace in the Far East. Neither a conquered Japan nor a sleeping China will permit such peace unless Russia possesses the power to despatch army corps to the Far East more rapidly than she can at present. A double line alone will enable this to be done. While keeping this as our main ultimate object, we should make every effort now to work the railways up to a traffic capacity of 14 pairs of trains as far as Harbin, and 18 beyond.

"Having set to work to double the line, we must try to arrange that one section will give us 18 pairs of military trains a day (perhaps it will be best to begin from the hilly portions). As the second line is laid, we shall be able to work up to a running and carrying capacity along the whole line to Harbin and southwards of at first 24 pairs of trains, then 36, and eventually 48."

Upon receipt of this letter from me, the first thing that the St. Petersburg authorities did was to work out the details of the preliminary arrangements for doubling the line. They tried to formulate some scheme whereby the necessary construction material could be carried on the railway without cutting down the number of troop trains. It was suggested that the rails should be sent via the Arctic Ocean, and apparently some attempt to do this was carried out, but later all idea of doubling the line during the war was abandoned. It was a pity, for the earth-work might have been carried out without interfering with the traffic. Had we carried out this important measure, we should have made our position in the Far East far stronger than it is now.

While they were making ready for war with us, the Japanese concluded a treaty with Great Britain, by which they were assured of the non-interference of any other Power. We, on the contrary, had not only made no preparations for war in the east, but did not even consider it possible to weaken to any great extent our frontiers on the west, in the Caucasus, or in Central Asia. Our diplomats neither steered clear of war with Japan, nor insured against interference in the west. The result was that, while Japan advanced against us in her full strength, we could only spare an inconsiderable portion of our army in European Russia to reinforce the Far East. We had to fight with one eye on the west. The army corps stationed in Western Russia were in a much higher state of preparation than those in the interior as regards the number of men in the ranks and the number of guns, horses, etc., and they were armed with quick-firing guns. We, however, took corps that were on the lower peace footing (the 17th and 1st), and gave them artillery from the frontier corps; while the efficiency of some of the units we took, which had companies from 160 to 100 strong in peace-time, varied a great deal. It was due to this quite natural fear for our western frontier that of five army corps sent to the Far East, three were composed of reserve divisions. We had to keep troops back for the maintenance of internal order; Japan did not have to do this. Our picked troops—the Guards and Grenadiers—were not sent to the front; on the other hand, the Japanese Guards Division was the first to attack us at the Ya-lu. Thus, though we had a standing army of 1,000,000 men, we sent reserve units and army corps on the lower establishment to the front, and entrusted the hardest work in the field, not to our regular standing army, but to men called up from the reserve. In a national war, when the populace is fired with patriotism, and everything is quiet in the interior of the country, such a course might be sound; but in the war with Japan, which was not understood, and was disliked by the nation, it was a great mistake to throw the principal work on to the reserves. In the summer of 1905 we corrected this mistake, and filled up the army with young soldiers, with recruits of 1905, and drafts from the regular army. These young soldiers arrived at the front cheerful and full of hope, and in a very different frame of mind to that of the reservists. It was a pleasure to see the drafts of regulars proceeding by train to the front—they were singing and full of spirit. The majority of them were volunteers, and they would undoubtedly have done magnificently if they had had a chance, but more than 300,000 of them saw no service owing to the hasty peace.

In her war with France in 1870, Prussia, assured of our neutrality, had nothing to fear from us, and was able to leave only an inconsiderable number of men on our frontier and to enter upon the struggle with all her strength.

Similarly, Japan was able to throw her full strength into the struggle from the very commencement. We, on the other hand, considered it advisable to keep our main forces in readiness in case of a European war, and only a small part of the army stationed in European Russia was sent to the Far East. Not a single army corps was taken from the troops in the Warsaw Military District, our strongest garrison. Even my request to send the 3rd Guards Division to the front from there was not granted, while our numerous dragoon regiments were represented by a single brigade. We kept our dragoons on the western frontier, and sent to the war the 3rd Category regiments of the Trans-Baikal and Siberian Cossacks, consisting of old men mounted on small horses. They reminded one more of infantry soldiers on horseback[84] than of cavalry. In my report to the Tsar on March 7, 1904, I requested that the reinforcements from Russia might be mobilized simultaneously and immediately after the Easter holidays, and I gave the following reasons:

> "By this measure the units, especially the reserve ones, will get time to settle down. It will also be possible to put them through a course of musketry and some military training, and it will give time to organize the transport, parks, and hospitals."

I considered it important that units detailed for the Far East should have as long as possible to shake down, and to receive some training before starting for the front.

The above memorandum, with the Tsar's remarks on it, was sent to the War Minister for his guidance; but General Sakharoff either did not carry out some of the important recommendations I had emphasized most, or altered them, and carried them out too late. As regards the date of mobilizing the reinforcements, he did not share my view (1) as to the necessity for a simultaneous mobilization, and (2) as to the necessity for mobilizing immediately after Easter. In a memorandum drawn up by him, dated March 18, 1904, he asked permission to mobilize the reinforcements in three lots instead of at once. Six Cossack regiments were first of all detailed for mobilization in the end of April, then the 10th Army Corps on May 1, the 17th Army Corps on May 1 or a little later, and four reserve divisions of the Kazan Military District at the end of June. In a second memorandum (July 31) the question was again raised whether all the reinforcements should be mobilized simultaneously or at different times. The Headquarter Staff preferred the latter alternative. Besides the poor carrying capacity of the Siberian Railway, the reason given was that—

"... The political horizon might become so clouded as to make the simultaneous mobilization of all the troops mentioned in the statement inadvisable."

Against this part of the memorandum I wrote the words, "It would be better to do it simultaneously." On my way to the front I received a telegram from General Sakharoff, dated March 21, in which he said that my request for the troops guarding the line to Harbin to be supplied from one of the divisions of the Kazan Military District, and for this division to be mobilized together with the other reinforcing troops directly after the Easter holidays, could not be acceded to, owing to the inconvenience to which the people of that district would be put by so early a mobilization. He suggested that guards for the railway might be found from one of the divisions of the 4th Siberian Corps— in other words, that this corps should be broken up. The result of the reinforcements being mobilized at different dates, contrary to my wishes, was that when the leading units reached the front, they had not settled down properly; the men did not know their officers, and *vice versâ*. Few corps had been able to do a musketry course, the 2nd Category reservists did not know the rifle, and hardly any had been tactically exercised, or if they had, it had been only for a few days. Divisions and corps had not been practised with the three arms. The 6th Siberian Corps was mobilized under fairly favourable circumstances, the 55th and 72nd Infantry Divisions being sent into camp in 1904, but these divisions were trained without artillery or cavalry.[85]

In former days troops had to make long marches in full field-service order before they reached the battle-field. If properly conducted, these marches hardened the men, and enabled units to settle down; all superfluous baggage was discarded, the weaker men were left behind, and officers and men got to know one another. But nowadays, with railway transport, the results are very different. Going to the Far East, our men were crowded up in railway carriages for as long as forty days at a time, out of the control of their officers, who were in different compartments. In the old and well-disciplined units no particular harm resulted, but in the case of newly formed units, whose reservists—particularly those of the 2nd Category, just summoned from their homes—consisting of peasants and town-bred men, were all in carriages together, instead of with regulars, it was most harmful. If to this fact be added their original unwillingness to go to the front, their lack of military spirit, and the frame of mind induced by the seditious proclamations with which they were lavishly supplied, the small fighting value of these reinforcements can be easily imagined. Many commanding officers of such regiments told me that not only did they not know the men under them, but that, in spite of a journey of from forty to fifty days, even the company commanders had not got to know their companies.

The command of the various units of the field army was in a bad enough way, for, owing to the numerous changes in the staff, there were many newly appointed commanding officers; but among the reserve troops the case was worse, for almost all the commanders were fresh men. The value of even the regular units was still further diminished by the proportion and class of the reservists joining. For instance, in some companies of the 10th Army Corps there were only sixty regulars, of whom thirty were young soldiers who had hardly finished their recruits' course; when 150 reservists from the Poltava province were added to this nucleus—all of them old men—a company lost almost all semblance of a regular one. The spirit of the Poltava reservists was at first specially bad, for a number of these men had taken part in the agrarian disturbances. Can it be wondered at that, in such circumstances, reinforcements which arrived from European Russia, and went into action straight from the train, were not so useful as they would have been had proper pains been taken with them?

What, then, were the motives which induced the War Minister (General Sakharoff) to act in this important matter contrary to the recommendations I had made, both as War Minister in 1903 and as Officer Commanding the Manchurian Army in 1904? In a memorandum written by him on March 18, after explaining his views as to the number of days which he considered the 10th and 17th Corps would take on their journey to the front, he stated that if the reserve units were mobilized in the middle of April, at the same time as the ordinary units, as I had asked, they would have to wait an unnecessarily long time before being despatched, and that it would be sufficient if reserve units,

"... having finished their mobilization, had two or three weeks for field exercises.... The units mobilized at the beginning of April would have to wait some three and a half months before being despatched. This, besides taking the men away prematurely from their spring work in the fields, would put the War Department to great and unnecessary expense in maintaining some 60,000 men. Mobilized units, of course, do not require so long to settle down."

Thus, in spite of the importance of the matter, and of the fact that we could have trained well the men going to the Far East, my request was refused for financial reasons, and in order that men who were to be soldiers should not be taken away at sowing-time! The grounds for General Sakharoff's opinion that newly raised reserve units only required two or three weeks to shake down instead of three and a half months are not obvious. Did he not know that the three-line[86] rifle now in the possession of the army was quite new to the 2nd Category reservists?

The Easter holidays were early in 1904, coming on April 10. I had asked that the general mobilization of all reinforcements should be ordered immediately after the holidays—*i.e.*, in the middle of April—but General Sakharoff fixed the date for a month later; thus the reservists of the 10th and 17th Corps received a month's less training before their departure for the front than I had stipulated for. The actual dates of mobilization were: 10th and 17th Army Corps, May 1, 1904; 5th Siberians, June 14. The leading échelons[87] entrained as follows: 10th Army Corps, May 18, 1904; 17th Army Corps, June 14; 5th Siberians, July 12. Thus those of the 10th Corps only had ten days to complete mobilization and get ready. If from this number be deducted the days on which reviews were held, it can be seen that the leading units of this corps could neither have gone through the shortest musketry course, nor have carried out any tactical exercises, while the rest of the corps had only about two weeks for this important work. The leading échelons of the 17th Corps were in a similar plight. The first units of the 5th Siberians, which was formed of reserve divisions, had one month from the day mobilization was ordered till it entrained. If review days and the time taken to mobilize be deducted, only a fortnight was available for instruction and shaking down, and the whole experience of the war has shown that this is insufficient, especially for 2nd Category reservists. Had the troops of the 5th Siberians only been mobilized at the same time as the 10th and 17th Corps, its leading units would have had about two and a half months for this process of preparation. In these circumstances the efficiency of its regiments would have been higher in the first fights than they were in General Orloff's column at Liao-yang. Another result of the postponed mobilization was that the first échelon of the 10th Army Corps (9th Division), which arrived at the front on June 30, was much below strength, especially as regards officers. Not only had the Poltava reservists not settled down with the regulars, but in some companies they almost came to blows with them after the first fights. The regulars reproached the reservists for leaving the ranks in action, to which the latter replied: "You are soldiers; it's your job; we're peasants." Feeling between the two classes of men ran so high that they were with difficulty restrained from actually fighting. I should in justice add that these peasants, under the command of the able and gallant General Hershelman, became hardened soldiers, and in later battles fought most gallantly, especially at Mukden. Units of the 5th Siberian Corps reached the front with their men in much the same state, and in the first battles some regiments of this corps did not display the steadiness they should have done, but later on, especially at Mukden, the 51st and 54th Divisions fought splendidly.

Although we had a large number of reservists at our disposal, instead of mobilizing the youngest, in some districts we took men of all ages, while in others we did not discard the elderly men. Directly they arrived at the front it was noticed that the older reserve men were both physically and morally less reliable than the others. Indeed, according to their officers, they were an actual source of weakness instead of strength to the units they joined. Nearly all the men who left the ranks in action were 2nd Category reservists. Of course, there were splendid exceptions, but the one idea of the majority of these men was to get put on non-combatant duties on the line of communication, on transport work, or appointed as hospital orderlies, and after the first fights they were given their desire. Our peasants generally put on fat, grow beards, and lose their soldierly appearance when they get over thirty-five. Naturally, also, they find the discomforts of campaigning harder to bear than younger men. The "Little Russian" 2nd Category reservists of the Poltava province were too heavy to scramble over steep slopes, and found the Manchurian hills very difficult to negotiate after the plains of their native country. The small active hillmen of Japan had indeed a great advantage over our soldiers in the July and August battles. It must also be remembered that villagers of over thirty-five are generally married men with large families. Our reservists were continually thinking of the homes and families they had left behind, which was not exactly conducive to the cheerful mind so necessary to the soldier. Added to all this, they did not understand the reason for the war, and far from being urged on by their country to deeds of gallantry, were fed with seditious proclamations, advising them to kill their officers instead of fighting. During the retreat from Mukden several units retired in disorder, and many men were met who had thrown away their rifles. One of these was heard by my staff to ask: "Where is the road to Russia?" On being told he was a cowardly cur, he answered: "Why should I have to fight? I have got six children to support."

The partial mobilization proved unsatisfactory, but it was not merely an accident of the war. Owing to the enormous extent of our frontiers, we might have been drawn just as easily into a European struggle that would have necessitated a general mobilization as into a war which required only a partial one. Thus, in addition to having a plan for general call to arms, we had to work out different schemes for partial mobilization to meet certain contingencies. It was laid down as a basis for these schemes that their application should not interfere with a general mobilization if that also proved necessary, so certain areas had to be selected for the calling out of reserves which would not interfere with the general and more important scheme. The number of these areas could only be kept down by taking from them the maximum of reserve men—*i.e.*, those of all categories irrespective of age. The first scheme for partial mobilization on these lines was drawn up and approved in 1896, when General Vannovski was War Minister, and when it was found necessary, in 1903, to work out fresh plans in case of complications with Japan, they were naturally based upon the old scheme. Having at that time complete faith in the reliability of the 2nd Category reservists, I (then War Minister) concurred in the general lines adopted, and submitted the new plan to the Tsar for approval, but only as regards the first reinforcements to be sent to the Far East. After I had seen the first consignment which actually reached the front, I asked that no more 2nd Category reservists or men with large families should be sent. When the second partial mobilization (54th, 61st, and 71st Divisions) took place, a half-hearted attempt was made to reject men with large families; but it was not till the fifth and sixth mobilizations that 2nd Category reservists and family men were, by the Emperor's wish, left behind. Neither the people nor the reservists could understand why 2nd Category reservists with families were taken from one district or one set of villages, and bachelors who had only just passed into the reserve from the colours were rejected in others. Future schemes for partial mobilization must be drawn up on entirely different lines from those of 1896 and 1903. Although 2nd Category reservists were being sent to the front, we continued to allow men to pass as usual from the regular army into the reserve, even letting them go before they had completed their five years with the colours. This state of affairs was extremely harmful to the army, but can be partly explained as follows:—In the spring of 1904, just after the commencement of the war, the recruits of that year should have begun to join all units in European Russia. In peace, infantry soldiers are usually passed from the colours to the reserve at the end of the manœuvres when they have done only three years and a few months' service out of five (four manœuvres and three winters). It did not occur to the Headquarter Staff to make use of these men for the army in the field, though there were more than 200,000 of them—young soldiers, splendidly trained—who might have been enrolled in reserve units and then sent as drafts to the front. In this matter Headquarters were guided by considerations quite unconnected with the war. The advisability of retaining in their regular units the men about to pass to the reserve was indeed considered, but it was put down as having many disadvantages. The political side of the matter was what carried most weight at Headquarters; moreover, questions of finance were involved, for the men so retained with the colours would, upon arrival of the recruits, have been supernumerary to the establishment. But, owing to the shortage caused by the formation of new corps, it was found difficult to carry out guard and other duties, and in some units the men due to leave were retained with the colours till the young soldiers had joined the ranks. General officers in command of districts gave various replies when asked for their opinions on this matter; some were for retaining the men, others for letting them go. In the summer of 1904 the War Minister asked the Tsar's permission to authorize commanding officers to pass men of the infantry, field artillery, and engineers into the reserve if they thought fit, provided that men were not kept with the colours longer than March 31, 1905. The transfer in other arms of the Service was to be as usual. Thus the retention in the ranks of these time-expired soldiers was the exception, and was not dependent on the war. Always fearful of a European war, we replaced the troops sent from Russia to the front by forming a large number of new divisions from the reservists. This course was also necessary for the maintenance of internal order. On August 23, 1904, officers commanding districts were authorized to transfer men retained with the colours into the newly formed infantry and artillery units, and thus to get rid of the same number of 2nd Category reservists. Thus the reserve divisions formed for service in the interior of Russia began to be filled by good men and rid of 2nd Category men before the divisions at the front were. In the autumn of 1904, at the request of the authorities in the field, authority was given to transfer men retained with the colours up to March 31, 1905, into the units mobilized and expanded by the seven partial mobilizations, and to discharge from these units the 2nd Category reservists and men of large families. It was only on December 27, 1904, when the young soldiers joined the ranks, that arrangements were made to transfer the men retained with the colours into the units that were not mobilized or expanded. These men were available for despatch to the front as drafts in the summer and autumn of 1904, but they only arrived a year later, after the Mukden battles, when they were too late. These splendid men saw no fighting at all.

I have endeavoured to explain (Chapter VII.) on what a large scale the Japanese made use of their reserve troops, and how rapidly they replaced casualties. The organization of the reserve units in the Russian army, on the other hand, was not fully completed before the war, for we had only been able to go ahead as funds permitted. The number of reserve troops in the Far East corresponded to the small number of units stationed there in the first instance, but while we increased our numbers out there it was not considered convenient to increase the reserve units, the number of reservists living there and in Siberia being insufficient to fill them. But if we had had the cadres of a large number of reserve units there, it would have been easy to send the reservists to them from European Russia. The six reserve battalions stationed in Pri-Amur had lost most of their permanent cadres in the first fights. The army generally had to operate with a constantly decreasing establishment, due to a variety of causes:

1. Units arriving as reinforcements sometimes came with a shortage of 15 to 20 per cent. among the men, and 25 per cent. among the officers. The 10th Army Corps in particular arrived very short—a fact which I immediately reported to the War Minister.

2. Owing to the shortage of men in the administrative services and of the auxiliary troops, many duties had to be carried out by the regiments in the field—i.e., duties in rear, at camps, on the line of communication, at hospitals, in the commissariat and transport, as well as guards for the different store

depôts. Advantage was taken of these duties to get rid of the 2nd Category reservists.

3. A large number of men had to be told off to guard property left in the staff quarters of the Viceroyalty, and the stores, supplies, and droves of cattle collected for the troops at work on the railways, bridges, and for other odd duties.

4. On the days of heavy engagements the shortage increased by tens of thousands, and even in periods of comparative quiet the number of killed and wounded in some units was very high.

5. Sickness.

All these reasons combined necessitated a continual stream of reinforcements to the front. But owing to the state of the railway there were intervals, and fairly long ones, when the army received no drafts—as, for instance, in July, August, and September, 1904, when, as I have already mentioned, we lost 100,000 men, and only received 21,000.

The advance at the beginning of October, 1904, was made when the army was much below strength, some regiments having only half, and even less, of their proper complement. And this shortage of men was increased on the eve of a battle by the large numbers left with the transport, at the staff quarters and as officers' servants—men who were in reality combatants. Curiously enough, many commanding officers showed no particular anxiety to take their units into action as strong as possible. But what was most serious was the speed with which some units melted away as soon as they came under fire; directly casualties happened this dissolution commenced. Men were told off, with the knowledge of their commanding officers, to assist company and divisional stretcher-bearers in carrying the wounded out of action. If the number of wounded were large, an enormous number of unwounded men went to the rear. The cowardly and the skulkers did their best to get detailed for this duty, or went off with wounded men without orders, or left the ranks without any excuse. I have seen stretchers with wounded men accompanied by as many as ten unwounded soldiers. In some regiments the numbers thus voluntarily retiring from the field amounted to hundreds; in one regiment[88] more than 1,000 men left the ranks in the first fight in which it took part. These were generally reservists, and chiefly those of the 2nd Category. The men with the colours, as a rule, did most of the fighting, and fought magnificently; sometimes even when companies were reduced to a handful of men they continued fighting. Of course, there were some gallant men amongst reservists, but, as a rule, any brave deeds that were performed were done by the men with the colours and 1st Category reservists. Even for the drafts, the men sent to the front were not selected with adequate care, and many were quite unfit for active service. In 1905, of some 76,000 who arrived for the 1st Army, 4,100 were sick or otherwise unfit. The following statement by the Adjutant-General of that Army is interesting:

> "The drafts sent to the Army before the battle of Mukden were composed of 2nd Category reservists who left the colours about 1887. They were quite ignorant of the present rifle, and their training was in other ways far below the level of the men forming the permanent cadres of their units. Many of them were physically quite unfitted to endure the hardships of a campaign or of any military service, being chronic sufferers from diseases such as rheumatism. But those who arrived after the battle of Mukden were splendid. Reservists were sometimes drafted to an Arm of the service in which they had not served before passing to the reserve; for instance, men were put into the artillery who had done all their colour service in cavalry or infantry, while to engineer units were sent men who had served in the infantry. This, of course, caused considerable complication as regards training, and could not but militate against our field operations, especially in the case of the technical troops."

The above is an accurate representation of the facts. Until the battle of Mukden the drafts sent to the front were much less reliable than those arriving afterwards, when they were too late to see any fighting. Those which were composed of 2nd Category men were often so bad that if a fight were imminent, commanding officers asked to be relieved of them, as their steadiness could not be relied on. These officers felt that their more or less veteran units would do better in the field, even if weak in numbers, than if filled up just before a fight with these men. Such a request was made to me by the officer commanding the 1st Army Corps and many others.

The shortage of officers was also a bad feature of our arrangements. In spite of the stream sent out to replace casualties, many units went short of their proper complement of officers all through the war. Both the troops actually in the Far East and the reinforcements sent out were at their peace strength when hostilities commenced. Indeed, there were instances in the beginning of the war of companies going into action for the first time commanded by junior lieutenants. As things went on, this deficiency in leaders was found to exist even in those units whose muster rolls showed an excess above their proper complement, and after the first fights, owing to the specially heavy casualties among the officers, cases were quite common of battalions and companies in action which were commanded by captains and second lieutenants. This dearth at the front was increased by the number of officers absorbed in departmental and other duties in the rear, and, in the case of the reinforcements, by so many—both medical and combatant officers—being left at the different bases; the latter were, of course, intended, in case of a general mobilization, to be available for general or regimental duties with the newly formed units. These remarks apply more particularly to the infantry. In the cavalry and artillery the numbers, though less than the establishment, were generally sufficient to carry on with. This was due to the fewer casualties in those arms. There is no doubt that the question of providing officers for an army in the field is a very serious one, which is complicated by many extraneous circumstances. We found that when the period of great battles and consequent heavy losses amongst the officers commenced, the discrepancy between the number of them shown on paper and of those actually present with a regiment rapidly increased. The names of a large number of wounded and sick were kept on the rolls for a long time. Some of the wounded and sick who stayed in the theatre of war gradually drifted back to their regiments, but the great number who had gone to Russia remained there, and did not rejoin even after they had quite recovered. There were instances where commanders of regiments, who had gone to Russia convalescent and had not returned, were still shown as commanding, and were still drawing command pay. Several who went home sick or wounded loafed about the streets of our cities or large towns for months, and the curious thing is that no one seemed to question such behaviour. In spite of what was done to obviate this, the medical officers and the medical board were far too lenient to those who wished to return home, and gave them every facility. On the other hand, many who were considered incompetent for field service, and sent back to Russia on this account, appeared again as fit, and returned to their corps, thus squeezing out from the command of companies and battalions those who had honourably borne all the hardships of the campaign, had acquired war experience, and had earned accelerated promotion. An excellent article on this subject by M. Glinski, called "The Resurrected Dead," was published in the *Razviedchik* in 1906. It should be stated, in fairness to our officers, however, that if many remained absent who could have returned to the front, there were a very large number who, though they had been wounded, made every effort to rejoin, often, indeed, doing so before they had quite recovered. Several officers rejoined after having been wounded two and three times, and these gallant gentlemen would have been a credit to any army in the world. In the 1st Army Corps, over 837 officers who had been wounded rejoined. For all these reasons my requests that fresh officers might be sent to the army were frequent and persistent, but the War Ministry were not always able to comply. They had to collect officers stationed in European Russia, the Caucasus, and Turkestan—wherever they could be obtained, and were not always able to pick and choose. Some of them were quite useless owing to alcoholism, others to the irregular lives they had led, while several got drunk and became violent even on the way out.

Such men stayed at Harbin as long as they could, did nothing but harm on joining the corps to which they were appointed, and were eventually removed. Our most reliable officers were the regulars, particularly those who volunteered for the front, many of whom greatly distinguished themselves. The least reliable were the reserve officers, who had been removed from the service, and had managed to squeeze into the reserve owing to our mistaken kindness.

When I was War Minister I had directed General Narbut, a member of the Military Council, to work out a scheme whereby a reserve of officers might be obtained in war. The essence of this scheme was that our cadet schools should, on mobilization, pass out a larger number of cadets as officers, and should then set to work to train as soon as possible those officers of the 1st and 2nd Categories who volunteered, and also the men of the regulars who were possessed of an intermediate standard of education, thousands of whom were good enough to be given the rank and duties of lieutenant. Why this scheme was not carried out during the war I do not know, but unless steps are taken to do something of this kind in future we shall be in difficulties. We did not take advantage of the possibility when war was declared, or even immediately afterwards, of passing out a greater number of the senior classes of the military and cadet schools. In 1902 these colleges supplied the army with 2,642 officers; we might, therefore, have received at the beginning of 1904 and 1905 more than 5,000 young officers wherewith to fill vacancies in the field. This is precisely what the Japanese did. Foreseeing how we should be placed, on March 19, 1904, I asked the War Minister that officers might be commissioned from the military and *yunker* schools, before the manœuvres, at the rate of 2 per battalion, 1 per battery, 4 per Cossack regiment, and 100 to the reserve. This was not done. On my repeated representations as to the urgent necessity for increasing the supply, I received in 1904 a curt reply to the effect that the maintenance of the number of officers up to establishment was the duty of the War Minister, not that of the officer commanding the army in the field. When the output was eventually increased, we received only a comparatively small number of those who had just got their commissions. These formed a most desirable element in the army, and in the majority of cases behaved splendidly in action.

On the whole, our troops were, for the reasons explained, very short of officers in the greater number of actions. Although the War Department accomplished a great work in sending out the large number of officers that did go to the front, very little discrimination was shown in their selection. It must be acknowledged, also, that we made little use either of our non-commissioned officers in the way of preparing them to take the places of officers, or of the splendid material to our hand in the cadets of the military and cadet schools.

The behaviour of our troops in the field was, on the whole, excellent, but the further from the advanced positions they were the worse did their discipline become. Even at the actual front it varied with the different classes of men, as I have explained. Of course, had good discipline prevailed in the units in which the 2nd Category reservists served, they would never have been able to leave the field in action as they sometimes did. But men, even of the best regiments, when they saw looting all round them, and acts of violence being committed with impunity, were themselves liable to become tainted with the spirit of lawlessness, and to get out of hand. This especially applied to the lines of communications, for strict and uncompromising discipline was maintained in the advanced positions. In the time of Frederick the Great the saying went that the soldier should fear the corporal's cane more than the enemy's bullet, but nowadays, though of course the liability of all to serve has improved and raised the average moral condition of the rank and file, it is not easy to make our uneducated peasantry appreciate what discipline is. Belief in God, devotion to the Tsar, love of the Fatherland, are the factors which have, up till now, welded the mass of soldiers in each unit into one family, and have made them fearless and obedient; but these principles have latterly been much shaken amongst the people, and the result was, of course, felt in the recent war. It was chiefly noticeable in an increase in the number of men who were slack and insubordinate, who criticized their seniors, and generally exercised a bad influence on their comrades. Such men could only be controlled by severity, for fear is the only thing which appeals to them. But while this deterioration in the discipline of the whole nation has been going on, our defence against it has been weakened, for in the summer of 1904 corporal punishment had been abolished in the army even on active service. I supported its abolition in peace myself—indeed, conducted the measure for this through the Military Council; but many of us thought it unwise to alter the existing law which authorized its infliction in war, for the fear of it kept many bad characters from crime, and prevented the cowards leaving the ranks in action. However, our officers were deprived of this deterrent, and no substitute was given.

In war such minor punishments as confinement to barracks or in cells and extra duty are out of the question. We therefore had no summary and effective punishment for many offences, such as insubordination, etc. A certain number of crimes are punishable with death, but what is lacking is some adequate punishment between the capital award and nothing at all. To make the position worse in our case, men who had been sentenced to a term of service in the disciplinary battalions remained on in the ranks, and at the slightest show of gallantry on their part our kind-hearted officers asked that their sentence might be remitted or modified. As if this were not enough, insubordinate sailors used to be sent to the army for punishment! The action of the military courts was unsatisfactory, their procedure complicated and slow. The usual result of the withdrawal from commanding officers of the power to award a flogging was that they let a man off altogether or else took the law into their own hands. As a matter of fact, corporal punishment continued to be given in certain cases, sometimes on the verdict of the men and at their own suggestion; but the culprits were beaten with cleaning-rods instead of canes. Taking into consideration the peculiar conditions under which this war was conducted, owing to the want of national sympathy in the struggle, and to the anti-Government propaganda which permeated all ranks of the army, this weakening of the disciplinary powers of officers was on the whole very ill-advised, and was carried out without reference to the officers actually in command of troops.

The reasons for the unpopularity of the war also affected the steadiness of the troops in action. Amongst many instances of real gallantry, cases of cowardice in detachments, and particularly in individuals, were noticeable. Occasions when soldiers, and even officers, surrendered when still unwounded were only too frequent, and they were, unfortunately, not visited with the full severity of the law. Many officers, on returning after release from capture, were not tried by court-martial at once, but were straightway placed in command of units going to the front, and then took command of companies and battalions as soon as they rejoined. This attitude towards those of our people who had surrendered could not but cause bad feeling amongst the best elements in the army who had been doing good work all along. This feeling of disgust was particularly aggravated when it became known that various persons removed from the army for incompetence— even for cowardice—had received high appointments in Russia. Such action destroyed all discipline. For instance, the conveyance of General Grippenberg by special train after he had just thrown up his command was in itself sufficient to encourage insubordination on the eve of decisive battles; it certainly undermined the authority of the Commander-in-Chief. The wholesale criticism pronounced on all ranks by the Press, the abuse of the officers, particularly of those in high command, together with the underhand efforts made to tempt the men not to fight, but to mutiny and kill their superiors, undermined their faith in their commanders, destroyed discipline, and made the troops cowardly in action. Such a state of affairs was enough to discount all the efforts of the very best officers, and had the most evil effect on those who were already inclined to show the white feather.

War is terrible; therefore the methods of maintaining discipline amongst troops, to be effective, must be as terrible. We certainly desired success, yet how often did we not act so as to make success improbable, if not impossible? The very causes which were undermining authority in the army were those which kept victory from us. Peace reputations are no criterion of ability in war, and many commanders who had been noted throughout their career as "brilliant," "above the average," proved in physical strength and force of character of very little use. On the other hand, those who had remained unnoticed in the piping times of peace showed great strength of character and brilliant military qualities amid the stress of war. Amongst the latter was General Kondratenko, the hero of Port Arthur.

After the first engagements it was found necessary to remove from the army as rapidly as possible those officers who had shown themselves unfit for their duties, and, without attaching undue weight to mere seniority, to promote others who had proved themselves capable soldiers in the field. On June 3, I reported to the War Minister the unfitness of two generals commanding army corps then proceeding to the front, but no notice was taken. Every obstacle was put in the way of my efforts to get rid of incapable commanders of army corps and divisions, and amongst other things I was informed from St. Petersburg that I asked for commanders of corps to be changed far too often. My orders removing from duty a General Officer commanding an East Siberian Rifle Division, who was liable to attacks of nerves in action, and left his division before a certain great battle, drew a series of questions as to my reasons. As I have mentioned, persons who had left the army owing to incompetence, sickness, or even cowardice, sometimes received high appointments in Russia, and all my recommendations that gentlemen of this spirit should be removed from duty as speedily as possible were pigeon-holed. To turn to another point, some regiments were commanded for twelve months and more, by temporary commanders. A characteristic example of this kind is the story of the removal from duty of the officer commanding one of the Caspian Regiments, Colonel F—. This officer, who was slightly wounded (contusion) in the first fight in which his regiment took part, went in the beginning of October, 1904, to Russia to recover, and only rejoined after he had been absent nearly a year, during a considerable portion of which time he was quite well. In his absence the regiment was commanded by an excellent officer, a certain colonel, who was awarded the Cross of St. George for gallant behaviour when with the regiment at the battle of Mukden. During those twelve months I sent in ten recommendations asking that Colonel F— might be gazetted out of the command, and that it might be given to the colonel acting for him. When Linievitch was Commander-in-Chief he supported my request, adding his own recommendation to mine, and sending it on to the War Minister and the Chief of the Headquarter Staff. The latter, however, did not agree, and asked why Colonel F— [who had then rejoined] was not commanding the Caspian Regiment. I again sent in my recommendation, and again received a refusal. These absolute refusals of my request were the more inexplicable as I had already received information that the officer commanding the troops in the St. Petersburg Military District was not opposed to the appointment of my nominee. In the end the long-waited-for appointment was made, but the Chief of the Headquarter Staff informed me that it was made at the request of General Baron Meyendorf, lately commanding the 1st Army Corps! Several colonels commanding regiments specially distinguished themselves in the early engagements, and showed fine military qualities, and owing to the lack of brigade commanders I frequently asked that some of them then in command of regiments—for instance, Lesha, Riedko, Stelnitski, and Dushkevitch among others—might be promoted to Major-Generals, and I called attention to brigades in the army that were vacant. The Headquarter Staff delayed for a long time, continually asking for further information, and the end of the matter was that Colonel Ostolopoff, commanding the Omsk Regiment, a worthy officer, but one who had in no way distinguished himself in the field, and whose name came up in the ordinary way, was promoted before the above-mentioned colonels.

My recommendations as to giving accelerated promotion to the best officers of the General Staff with me were negatived, because these gentlemen would then have passed over the heads of their contemporaries polishing office-stools in Russia. For example, Captain Kruimoff was an exceedingly capable officer of the General Staff on the staff of the 4th Siberian Corps. General Zarubaeff, his corps commander, and I several times recommended him for promotion to Lieutenant-Colonel[89] for distinguished service in the field. We were unsuccessful in our effort, but, to the amazement of myself and of the officers of the General Staff who were at the front, I ascertained that a contemporary of Zarubaeff, who was not at the war, and who was not qualified for the promotion, had been promoted to Lieutenant-Colonel. And this was only one instance of many. As regards the promotion of captains of infantry of the Line to Lieutenant-Colonel, the Headquarter Staff, I am glad to say, made no difficulty, and by this course we obtained a large number of energetic young staff officers. Some of them possessed, indeed, such brilliant military qualities that they might well have been put at once in command of regiments. I tried, in the interests of the public service, to get some officers who were personally known to me as good men appointed to the field army. Some were sent to me, others were not, the reason being given that the strength of the army was sufficient to satisfy all official needs.

To organize intelligence work successfully special experience is required. I was dissatisfied with the way this important duty was being performed, and I asked that a certain officer of the General Staff, particularly well qualified for it, should be appointed, but I received a refusal on quite insufficient grounds. Again, the Headquarter Staff paid very little attention to what they allowed to be published from the reports from the theatre of war, and gave out information containing the names of localities, units, etc., which must have made it easier for the enemy to fix the position of our troops. At the same time, though Headquarters knew the totals of our losses and the numbers of guns we had abandoned in the fights at Mukden, they for a long time did not contradict the Press reports which stated we had lost several hundreds of guns. The long absences from the army of officers commanding units compelled me frequently to ask that a time-limit should be fixed, after which, if they did not rejoin, the absentees should forfeit their appointments. This recommendation was eventually approved, and numerous general and other officers who had been for long merely officiating in command of brigades and regiments were, on the authority of the Commander-in-Chief, confirmed in their appointments. But soon afterwards demobilization began, and an order was then issued from St. Petersburg to the effect that the Commander-in-Chief was, to the prejudice of his own authority, to issue an order cancelling his previous ones making the appointments, because the "resurrected dead" thought of returning to the army, and wished to command the units from which they had so long absented themselves. It is essential that such harmful interference from Headquarters with an army in the field should be put a stop to, and that full power should be given to those in actual command on the spot.

I have not alluded to our marked inferiority to the enemy in technical troops and material. This chiefly applies to the proportion of sapper units. With each Japanese division of all arms was a strong battalion of sappers, while we had only one to each army corps. But, owing to the demand for work at one and the same time on the line of communications, and in constructing bridges and railways, only two sapper companies of the battalion were as a rule actually with our corps. In other words, each division had one company, a proportion which proved to be quite insufficient. The Japanese telegraph and telephone troops were also far more numerous than ours, and their material was better, and it was only after the Mukden battles that we were able to remedy these defects. Owing to their sea transport, the enemy were of course able to deliver with far greater ease light-railway material in the theatre of operations, as well as technical material for construction of fortifications and for the attack. It was only after Mukden that we received an adequate stock of field railways, wire, cables, explosives, and tools.

In spite of the superiority of our guns, we made a mistake in having only one type of shrapnel. We hoped, of course, that it would give good results when burst on contact[90]; but it turned out to be ineffective when used in this way, and for this we paid heavily, as we were unable properly to prepare by artillery the attack of even hastily fortified positions. When the Japanese prepared by artillery for an attack on a village held by us, they destroyed it in the most thorough manner. The instructions issued to Kuroki's army (in October, 1904) contained the following remarks regarding our artillery:

"The enemy has apparently no common shell; his shrapnel is ineffective, and the splinters do little damage, as the walls of the shell are too thin."

For a long time we possessed no mountain-guns, though we very often had to move by roads impassable by field-guns when operating in the hills. The enemy were greatly superior to us in this point. It was only for the Mukden battles that we were able to provide a few of these batteries to some of our army corps operating in the hills on the east, but even then the force under General Rennenkampf was insufficiently supplied.

The Japanese began the war with no machine-guns. We had a few machine-gun companies attached to some of the East Siberian Rifle Divisions, and in the very first fight—at the Ya-lu—one of these companies attached to the 3rd East Siberian Rifle Division was most valuable. The Japanese were quick to profit by this experience, and, after the September fighting at Liao-yang, put in the field a great number of these guns of a light, portable type. These were of great service to them, particularly in strengthening the defence of hastily prepared positions held by small numbers of men. The supply of these guns to our army was carried out very slowly, and was, in fact, only finished by the time peace was concluded. The proportion also was too small—only eight per division.

Our four-wheeled transport carts were unsuitable both for hill-work and for the Manchurian mud; but my request that two-wheeled carts should be substituted with the troops to come from Russia was not heeded. The quantity of ammunition with the guns was found to be insufficient for continued fighting. In spite of the reserves provided, the quick-firing artillery expended nearly all its ammunition at the fights of Liao-yang, the Sha Ho, and Mukden, and replenishment after each of these great battles was a slow process. We also found the need for howitzers firing high explosive shell. One battery for the army arrived as peace was concluded. Hand grenades, which were an innovation, were locally improvised, but were not sufficiently powerful in their action.

In my memorandum, from which I have already given extracts, submitted before my departure for the front,[91] detailing what was most urgently required in order to insure success, I emphasized—

1. The necessity of ordering ninety-six mountain-guns in addition to the forty-eight already ordered on my former recommendation. This was approved, and the order placed, but it was not carried out quickly enough.

2. The necessity of despatching without delay to the Far East eight machine-guns per division already there and going out.

According to official figures, the following were ordered and delivered in 1904:

	Ordered.	Completed.
Pack machine-guns	246	16
Machine-guns on wheels	411	56
Mélinite shells	25,600	0
Shells for 6-inch field-mortars	18,000	0
Quick-firing howitzers	48	0
Mountain-guns	240	128

In 1905 a large number of machine-guns were ordered, amongst them being some Danish ones of inferior design; but during the period the operations lasted—up to March, 1905—we had to do as best we could with a very few machine-guns, without high explosive shell, without sufficient mountain artillery, and without howitzers. All these had been supplied, or had begun to be supplied, in 1905; but it was too late.

FOOTNOTES

[1] "The War in the Far East, 1904–1905," by the Military Correspondent of the *Times*. John Murray.

[2] P. 68, Volume II., of this book.

[3] With a small portion of the third volume in Chapter XIII.

[4] As adopted in the "Official History of the Russo-Japanese War," now being published by the Historical Section of the Committee of Imperial Defence.

[5] [Of these only portions of the Introduction and Conclusion of Volume III. have been translated.—ED.]

[6] The motives of those who started writing upon their return to Russia, also, were not entirely above suspicion.

[7] The money put aside by the Treasury for the War Department is not allotted annually, but for quinquennia periods.

[8] [Chapters I. to XII. in the following translation.—ED.]

[9] On the north-west, from Varanger Fiord to Pskoff (about 1,350 miles), we marched with our powerful neighbour Sweden, who possessed an army of 100,000 men. At this disturbed period she was mistress of the country round the Baltic coasts and of the present province of St. Petersburg, and possessed in the fortresses of Finland and in the Baltic littoral an enveloping base for a gradual movement on our Pskoff and Novgorod provinces. On the west, from Pskoff to Tchigrin (about 1,000 miles), we marched with Poland, the frontier re-entering like a wedge near Smolensk to a distance of 300 miles from Moscow. Poland, the ally of Sweden and Turkey, was Russia's natural enemy, for she was in occupation of our soil in White and Little Russia. On the south, from Tchigrin to Azov (about 400 miles), the boundary ran practically undefined, shared with the Tartar hordes subject to Turkey, who then possessed an army of some 500,000 men, and a strong fleet on the Black Sea. From Azov to the Caspian (about 400 miles) our neighbours were Tartars and nomadic Caucasian mountaineers, who were continually raiding our borders. Lastly, in Asia our frontier, which was here also only vaguely defined, marched with that of the Kirghiz tribes and races subordinate to China.

[10] [In 1792.—ED.]

[11] In the year 1800 the weakest portions of our frontiers, which had increased since 1700 to a total length of 11,333 miles, were: On the side of Finland (Swedish), from Neyshlot to the mouth of the Kumen (about 200

miles), owing to the proximity of this boundary to St. Petersburg; from Grodno to Khotin (about 130 miles), due to the absence of natural obstacles and strong fortresses, and to the propinquity of Prussia and Austria; on the Caucasian side only a portion lay within our sphere of influence, and after the annexation of Georgia conflicts became frequent with the Caucasians; on the Central Asian side, because the annexation of the Kirghiz tribes, in the time of Anne Ivanovna, had brought Russia into immediate contact with the Khanates of Khiva, Bokhara, and Khokand, whose inhabitants looked upon our approach with no friendly eye.

[12] The troops of Suvoroff, Rimskov-Korsakoff, Herman, and those afloat in the fleet of Admiral Ushakoff.

[13] The armies of Lassa (about 65,000; headquarters, Grodno) and of Gudovitch (about 65,000 to 70,000; headquarters, Kamenetz-Podolsk).

[14] "Memoirs of a Sevastopol Man" (N. S. Maloshevitch, 1904), chaps. ix., x.

[15] In this fight our weapons had a range of 300 to 450 yards, as compared with the enemy's (Minié) rifle, which had a range of 1,200 yards. Our Rifle battalions, of which we had one per army corps, were alone armed with rifles.

[16] [? Tchernaya.—ED.]

[17] Only fourteen men were left of the company in whose advanced trench the standard was. The officer commanding the battalion, the company commander, and company subaltern, were all killed.

[18] [An affair of outposts on the Afghan frontier, which caused a considerable stir at the time —ED.]

[19] [In the eighteenth century, 1,500,000; in the nineteenth century, 1,700,000.—ED.]

[20] [This is apparently extracted from General Kuropatkin's report of 1900.—ED.]

[21] The frontiers with Norway and Sweden were settled by the Treaty of Friederichsham in 1809, and the St. Petersburg Convention of 1826.

[22] [Written before the partition.—ED.]

[23] In Trans-Caucasia the frontier along the Rivers Araks and Astara was fixed by the Treaty of Turkmanchai in 1828, and in Trans-Caspia along the Artek and the Kopet Dagh ridge by the Agreement at Teheran in 1881.

[24] The Trans-Caucasian frontier has held good for seventy years.

[25] [The line to Nushki is evidently referred to.—ED.]

[26] [Sic.—ED.]

[27] [This view is interesting in the light of more recent events.—ED.]

[28] In 1897 the chief exports were: Cotton-stuffs, £344,100; naphtha and its products, £100,800; and wool, £40,400. The chief imports were: Tea, £3,210,900; cotton goods, £170,200; woven materials, £165,800; live stock, £78,700; and leather, £72,300. Total exports, £640,000; total imports, £3,920,000.

The central and largest section of the Chinese frontier was fixed by the Nerchinsk Treaty of 1687, and the Burinsk and Kiakhta Treaties of 1727; the most western by the Treaties of Chuguchag in 1864, and St. Petersburg in 1881 (after the pacification of Kuldja); the most eastern, along the Rivers Amur and Sungari, by the Treaties of Aigun in 1858, and Peking in 1860; and our last acquirement of territory in China—the southern part of the Kuan-tung Peninsula—was ceded to us in 1898.

[29] The route through Manchuria shortens the line of the Great Siberian Railway, and is therefore of great commercial value, but is dangerous for military reasons. The route along the Amur would be better, for it traverses Russian territory only, and is covered by that river.

[30] To enable us to provide sufficient units in Kuan-tung, the War Department was obliged to weaken the establishment of troops in the Odessa and Kieff Military Districts by 6,000 men.

[31] The recent arrivals are composed chiefly of Japanese, with a few Chinese. Their number is always greater in the warm weather, when they come to Korea on business (fishing, timber-cutting, etc.).

[32] [Sic. General Kuropatkin seems to have written this by an oversight.—ED.]

[33] [The Pri-Amur is the Russian Amur Province situated on the north side of the Amur River.—ED.]

[34] [This evidently refers to the Orenburg-Tashkent Railway, completed in 1904.—ED.]

[35] Our troops on that occasion numbered 2,000. It was an insignificant affair, in which we only had forty-three casualties.

[36] Seventy-three miles from Kushk fortified post.

[37] [Sic. ? Pan-Islamic.—ED.]

[38] [Galicia.—ED.]

[39] [So-called Chinese Turkestan.—ED.]

[40] Not far from Lake Lob Nor (discovered by Prejevalski), into which the River Tarin flows.

[41] [This is not the generally accepted view.—ED.]

[42] We had three rifles—the Berdan, the Krink, and the Karl; most of them were Krink, converted from the "six-line rifle." The Turks' Peabody was a far more perfect weapon.

[43] [As chief of the Headquarter Staff.—ED.]

[44] [Russia is divided into thirteen military districts.—ED.]

[45] Besides the allotments for artillery re-armament and house allowance.

[46] 96 battalions, 57 squadrons, and 236 guns.

[47] [Of the thirty-six East Siberian Rifle Regiments in the Far East when war broke out, all had two battalions except those of one brigade, which had three.—ED.]

[48] [*Sic.*—ED.]

[49] The proposals as to Kronstadt were approved before I became War Minister.

[50] Of this number, 8 East Siberian Rifle Divisions, 96 battalions; 1st, 2nd, and 3rd Siberian Reserve Divisions, 48 battalions; independent reserve battalions, 12; 2 brigades, 31st and 35th Divisions, 16 battalions—total, 172 battalions. All these troops were in April, 1904, in Siberia, in the Pri-Amur district, and in Manchuria. Of them, 27 battalions constituted the garrison of Port Arthur; 21 battalions the garrison of Vladivostok and the South Ussuri district; the 1st Siberian Division was kept in rear, while the independent reserve battalions guarded the railway. In April, 1904, of these 172 battalions, there were only 108 in the Manchurian army, distributed from the Ya-lu to Newchuang, and from Ta-shih-chiao along the railway to Omsk, as the 4th Siberian Corps was still on the way out.

[51] [See p. 121.—ED.]

[52] [In addition to the ordinary Quinquennial Budget.—ED.]

[53] [M. Sergius de Witte.—ED.]

[54] [Literally, "A man's own shirt is nearest his own skin."—ED.]

[55] [August, 1900.—ED.]

[56] [The German Field-Marshal commanding the Allied Forces of the Peking Relief Expedition.—ED.]

[57] Which the occupation of Port Arthur had made of considerable military importance to us.

[58] [The Maritime Province.—ED.]

[59] Ying-kou.

[60] [This ratio hardly seems correct.—ED.]

[61] [The Royal Timber Company. For fuller details of this undertaking and Bezobrazoff's connection with it, see Appendix I., p. 615.—ED.]

[62] [The Russian Minister in China.—ED.]

[63] [The Russian Minister in Korea.—ED.]

[64] "Decisions of the Council on the Manchurian Question," No. 10, July 11, 1903 (Port Arthur).

[65] [On the Mekran Coast of Persia.—ED.]

[66] [? Straits of La Pérouse.—ED.]

[67] [A Japanese steamship line.—ED.]

[68] In addition to these there were 2,716 departmental officers—*i.e.*, medical, veterinary, and supply, etc.

[69] By January 1, 1901, in the reserve and territorial army there were 2,737 officers, and it was necessary to add in war-time, without the reserve troops, 2,619 officers; thus the establishment of officers of the standing army and territorial forces could be fully completed, and 138 officers were left for reserve units. This was insufficient—*i.e.*, there were about 1,000 officers short.

[70] 145,000 in the reserve, and 120,000 in the territorial army.

[71] Some of the regulars were undersized recruits.

[72] [An obstacle formed of rows of conical pits, with a sharpened stake in the centre, and usually a wire entanglement across the top.—ED.]

[73] [A Russian brigade usually consists of eight battalions. Those of the E. S. Rifle Divisions had six.—ED.]

[74] ["A Staff Officer's Scrap-Book," vol. i., p. 11.—ED.]

[75] [A species of millet, which grows very high.—ED.]

[76] [On March 10, 1905, the battle of Mukden, which had lasted for several days, ended with the retreat of the Russians and the occupation of Mukden by the Japanese. On the 16th the Japanese entered Tieh-ling, and on the 21st

Chang-tu Fu. The latter represents the furthest point reached in the northerly advance of their main armies.—ED.]

[77] [General Kuropatkin's country estate in Russia.—ED.]

[78] "Scheme for the Strategical Distribution of Troops in the Far East in the Event of War with Japan," November 18, 1900 (Port Arthur).

[79] [Being a single-line railway, the number of trains in one direction depended on those travelling in the opposite direction; they are, therefore, alluded to in pairs. A pair of trains implies two trains, one each way.—ED.]

[80] [? Eastern Chinese Railway.—ED.]

[81] [An échelon of troops consisted of the troops from a certain number of trains. See Footnote 87.—ED.]

[82] [The Eastern Chinese line was under the Minister of Finance.—ED.]

[83] [A strategic line of railway in European Russia, some 700 miles long.—ED.]

[84] [General Kuropatkin does not refer to mounted infantry.—ED.]

[85] In his report to the War Minister, dated October 19, 1906, General Soboloff, the late commander of the 6th Siberian Corps, said: "The general concentration in July, 1904, of the 55th and 72nd Divisions, which composed my corps, was by no means instructive, as the War Minister refused to let us have any artillery or cavalry. In Tamboff and Morshansk masses of infantry, 16,000 strong, manœuvred about without a single gun or squadron."

[86] ["Three line" indicates the calibre of the rifle, a "line" being a Russian measure equal to 1/10 of an inch. Three lines = ·299 inches.—ED.]

[87] [An échelon is a collection of trains containing a unit or units despatched together. In South Africa these collections of trains were sometimes called "coveys."—ED.]

[88] [A Russian regiment generally contains four battalions, and equals a British brigade.—ED.]

[89] [There is no rank of Major in the Russian Army.—ED.]

[90] [Presumably with a percussion-fuse.—ED.]

[91] [March 7, 1904.—ED.]

END OF VOL. I.

Milton Keynes UK
Ingram Content Group UK Ltd.
UKHW041159040324
438885UK00007B/506